The Hungarian Economy
in the 1980s:
Reforming the System and
Adjusting to External Shocks

**INDUSTRIAL DEVELOPMENT AND
THE SOCIAL FABRIC, VOLUME 9**

Editor: John P. McKay, *Department of History, University of Illinois*

INDUSTRIAL DEVELOPMENT AND THE SOCIAL FABRIC

An International Series of Historical Monographs

Edited by **John P. McKay**

Department of History
University of Illinois

The Hungarian Economy
in the 1980s:
Reforming the System and
Adjusting to External Shocks

Edited by JOSEF C. BRADA
Department of Economics
Arizona State University

ISTVAN DOBOZI
Research Institute for
World Economy
Hungarian Academy
of Sciences

 JAI PRESS INC.

Greenwich, Connecticut *London, England*

LIBRARY OF CONGRESS
Library of Congress Cataloging-in-Publication Data

The Hungarian economy in the 1980s : reforming the system and
adjusting to external shocks / by Josef C. Brada, István Dobozi.—
(Industrial development and the social fabric : v. 9.
  Includes bibliographies and index.
  Papers originally presented at the Ninth Hungarian-American
Economists' Roundtable at Berkeley, Calif., June 10–12, 1985.
    1. Hungary—Economic conditions—1968–
Congresses.   2. Hungary—Economic policy—1968–   —
Congresses.   3. Central planning—Hungary—Congresses.
4. Hungary—Foreign economic relations—Congresses.   I. Brada,
Josef C., 1942–   .   II. Dobozi, István.   III. Hungarian-American
Economists' Roundtable (9th : 1985 : Berkeley, Calif.)   IV. Series.
HC300.28.H85 1988   ISBN: 0-89232-936-X   88-2943
338.9439—dc19   CIP

CONTENTS

LIST OF CONTRIBUTORS

Bela Balassa

Department of Political Economy
The Johns Hopkins University
Baltimore

Josef C. Brada

Department of Economics
Arizona State University
Tempe

István Dobozi

Research Institute for World Economy
Hungarian Academy of Sciences
Budapest

Béla Kádár

Research Institute for World Economy
Hungarian Academy of Sciences
Budapest

Péter Lórincze

Hungarian Chamber of Commerce
Budapest

José A. Méndez

Department of Economics
Arizona State University
Tempe

Resző Nyers

Institute of Economics
Hungarian Academy of Sciences
Budapest

Steven W. Popper

The Rand Corporation
Santa Monica

Mihály Simai

Research Institute for World Economy
Hungarian Academy of Sciences
Budapest

György Varga

Department of Economics
Karl Marx University of Economics
Budapest

Leyla Woods

Office of Trade and Investment Analysis
U.S. Department of Commerce
Washington, D.C.

Ernó Zalai

Department of Economics
Karl Marx University of Economics
Budapest

INTRODUCTION

In 1968 Hungary introduced the New Economic Mechanism (NEM) and abandoned detailed central planning. The results of this, the only significant economic reform in East Europe to last more than a few years, were paradoxical. Many elements of shortage on consumer markets were gradually eliminated, but other elements, both on consumer markets and for producers goods, remained. Firms were given new responsibilities and objectives as well as wider scope for decision-making, yet their relationship with central authorities retained many of the elements of dirigisme found in unreformed centrally planned economies. The government favored indirect instruments for the guidance of the economy, price flexibility and a responsiveness to the workings of the international economy. Yet these measures were introduced a few years before the international economy lapsed into chaos and market economies adopted direct controls over prices and international trade flows in an attempt to insulate themselves from international developments.

It is quite clear that the lessons of the Hungarian economic experiment have not been fully understood, either in Hungary or in the West. In part this is due to the evolutionary nature of NEM, in part to the inability in turbulent times to distinguish between the effects of the environment, of system change and of economic policies. This volume represents an effort to examine the performance of the Hungarian economy at a time when new reform measures are afoot as well as at a critical juncture in Hungary's economic fortunes. The papers collected in this volume were originally presented at the Ninth Hungarian-American Economists' Roundtable at Berkeley, California during June 10–12, 1985. As at previous Roundtables, the discussion of issues was candid and wide ranging. Based on these discussions, the papers have been revised and updated for publication here. They serve as a report on the status and future of economic reform, and, more important, of economic progress in Hungary.

* * *

The difficult task of distangling the effects of economic reform and economic policy on Hungarian economic performance is ably handled by Bela Balassa in the first chapter. While Balassa's analysis argues that poor policy choices and poor design of certain reforms both served to undermine Hungary's external and domestic economic performance, the bulk of the blame must fall on policymakers rather than on reformers. In the following chapter, Resző Nyers takes a more favorable view of the achievements of Hungarian policy in the late 1970s and early 1980s. In the light of Nyer's cautious and sober view of the world, one that reflects a bent toward monetarist orthodoxy and stresses the need for deflation as a short term cure for external disequilibrium, the reader can understand how risky and even inconceivable Balassa's call for stimulating the economy toward more rapid, export-led growth must seem to Hungarian policymakers. Despite this gulf between the two authors' views on macroeconomic policy, they do agree that further reform is both necessary and beneficial. Thus, paradoxically, after twenty years of reform, the future of the reform movement in Hungary appears more secure than does Hungary's ability to establish external balance and domestic economic growth.

The third chapter in this section, by Ernó Zalai, tackles the question of why the abolition of the plan did not sweep away many of the institutions whose presumed purpose had been to act as part of the planning and control mechanism, and why these institutions were able to continue functioning despite the non-existence of the detailed central plan that was their raison d'etre. Zalai shows that the abolition of the plan was insufficient to alter the behavior of these institutions, possibly because their existence had less to do with the process of planning than it did with other, unchanged, characteristics of the Hungarian economy. At the same time, these institutions may have filled an institutional vacuum that developed because plan-abolition did not bring with it either a strong market or the kind of institutions necessary for the market mechanism to function properly. Against this analytical framework Zalai then goes on to examine the current reforms.

* * *

A key objective of the Hungarian reforms is to increase productivity, efficiency, and technical progress. Viewed in this way, the reform then is about the way in which productive activities are carried out. Thus the front line of the reform battle is fought on the floor of Hungarian enterprises and workplaces, and Part II of the book consists of four reports from the battlefield. The most optimistic of these is by György Varga who examines in detail the recent privatization measures that have greatly increased the scope for private initiative both outside and within the socialist sector. While not undervaluing the initiatives that these new measures can engender, Varga does caution that they form a very small part of the economy and that both anticipated and unforseen difficulties can arise. Among those anticipated are the need to revise taxes to deal with incomes generated by private activity and the creation of appropriate regulations for private business activity. Beyond the issues raised by Varga looms an even more important question. Will the private sector be more a means of creating more and better products and services or more a means for exploiting price distortions and for re-distributing incomes from one group of citizens to another? It may well be that Hungarian reformers have overestimated the possibilities for the former, and that the privatization measures will exacerbate conflicts over income distribution without creating offsetting gains in the supply of goods.

While the private sector may be the most novel and interesting aspect of Hungarian industry, Hungarian industry is clearly dominated by a few large firms. This concentration of industry has given rise to a number of hypotheses about the negative and positive consequences of firm size for profitability, efficiency and foreign trade effectiveness. The contribution by Leyla Woods discusses these hypotheses and uses data on a sample of firms to test whether there is any relationship between firm size and economic performance. While a number of hypotheses are verified by the data, a surprising number, given wide currency in the literature, cannot withstand Woods' scrutiny.

Certainly a key element in the effort to increase productivity in Hungarian industry is the exploitation of technology imported from the west. Popper's study of the diffusion of numerically controlled machine tools in Hungarian industry reveals serious problems with the diffusion and effective utilization of this important technology. The problems stem from faulty incentives and the poor design of institutions responsible for the acquisition and dissemination of technology. While the following Chapter, by Simai, outlines steps being taken to remedy the problems disclosed by Popper's work, it too ends with the all too familiar call for reform. Thus as with the discussion of macro-economic policy in Part I, the analysis of the Hungarian micro-economy raises the disturbing feeling that economic problems in Hungary are not being accorded the urgency and attention they clearly deserve and that the appeal to reform is a means of avoiding often painful and unpopular, though necessary, courses of action.

* * *

In a country as small and trade dependent as Hungary there can be no distinction between domestic and international economic policy; the two are too interdependent for any such distinction. As a result, the viability of and the need for economic reform in Hungary depends to a great extent on the international environment. Because the bulk of Hungary's trade is with the CMEA, the effectiveness of CMEA in promoting inter-member exchanges and economic growth has a vital impact on Hungary's future prospects. In the first chapter of this section Brada and Méndez compare the static and dynamic consequences of economic integration in CMEA and in other customs unions. Their conclusions, which run counter to the conventional wisdom in both the East and the West, is that the CMEA has performed as well as, if not better than, western customs unions in stimulating inter-member trade and technological progress. Thus the CMEA environment can be viewed as being about as favorable as it can be, and little help for Hungary should be expected from CMEA reforms.

Although Hungary's trade with the West is quantitatively less than its trade with the CMEA, it is qualitatively as important because the West is an important source of new technology for Hungary and because Hungary's debt to the West is a critical constraint on Hungary's domestic and international policy options. Béla Kádár's contribution examines the importance of East-West trade for Hungary and places it in a global context. Kádár concludes that, to a large extent, Hungary's prospects for beneficial trade with the West depend on the state of Soviet-American relations and thus are largely beyond Hungary's control. Péter Lórincze follows up Kádár's broad overview with a narrow but interesting case study of Hungarian-United States commercial relations that nicely demonstrates the interplay of economic and political forces in East-West trade. The section on international trade ends with a study by István Dobozi of Hungary's responsiveness to the increase in world energy prices. Using a more sophisticated dynamic model than generally employed in such studies, Dobozi concludes that the Hungarian response to higher energy prices was more elastic than commonly believed.

* * *

These papers then serve as a synthesis of Hungarian and western views of economic and reform developments in Hungary. It is evident that both economic reform and the open discussion of reform measures and government policy enjoy widespread and deep support from Hungarian society. At the same time it is also evident that the economic policies pursued by Hungary have not been entirely successful in dealing with all of Hungary's problems. Whether more reform or better policymaking are needed can only be answered in the future.

Josef C. Brada
Volume Editor

PART I

MACROECONOMIC POLICY AND ECONOMIC REFORM

THE "NEW GROWTH PATH" IN HUNGARY

Bela Balassa

INTRODUCTION

This paper will analyze changes in economic policies in Hungary that began with the December 1978 resolution of the Central Committee of the Hungarian Socialist Workers' Party (for short, Party resolution). The impetus for policy change was provided by Hungary's growing indebtedness, with its deficit in convertible currency trade reaching $1.2 billion in 1978, equivalent to 6.7 percent of the gross domestic product.[1]

Changes in economic policies had the double objective of remedying the disequilibrium in Hungary's balance of payments and re-establishing the reform process that began in 1968 but was subverted in various respects after 1972. The new policies have been given the collective name 'the new growth path' that has been chosen as the title of this paper.

Section I of the paper will briefly review the policies that led to Hungary's rising indebtedness in the 1973–78 period and analyze the subsequent process of adjustment. Section II will examine the principal determinants of Hungary's export performance in recent years while Sections III and IV will consider possible reforms for accelerating the growth of exports and of national income in the future.

I. ADJUSTMENT POLICIES AND THE DEBT CRISIS

With its large exposure to foreign trade, the unfavorable balance-of-payments effects of external shocks through the deterioration of the terms of trade and the export shortfall associated with the slowdown of economic activity abroad averaged 10.5 percent of Hungary's gross domestic product in the 1973–78 period (Balassa-Tyson, 1983).[2] Over two-thirds of this loss occurred in trade with private market economies, which will be the subject of the following discussion. This occurred in part because Hungary's rising debt vis-à-vis private market economies was the principal factor motivating the stabilization measures taken following the December 1978 Party resolution and in part because of the constraint foreign exchange earnings in convertible currencies represent for economic expansion in Hungary.[3]

Hungary responded to the external shocks of the 1973–78 period by borrowing abroad. This was done in an effort to maintain earlier rates of growth of domestic consumption and investment, notwithstanding the deterioration of the external situation. Domestic investment rose particularly rapidly, doubling between 1973 and 1978, while consumption increased by one-fourth. Thus, Hungary did not make use of macroeconomic policies to reduce the imbalance in its external accounts that resulted from external shocks. And while some import substitution did occur, it was offset several times by losses in export market shares. These losses, representing an average decline of 18 percent in Hungary's share in the imports of private market economies,[4] amounted to $316 million in 1978. In the same year, import substitution associated with a slight decline in the income elasticity of import demand vis-à-vis the 1963–73 period was $63 million (Balassa-Tyson, 1983).

Losses in export market shares represented a reversal of trends observed in the previous period. In particular, Hungary's share in the imports of developed countries, accounting for three-fourths of its exports to private market economies, increased from 0.22 percent in 1965 to 0.28 percent in 1973, but declined again to 0.22 percent in 1979 (Lakos, 1981). While Hungary was adversely affected by restrictions imposed in 1974 on its cattle exports by the European Common Market[5], the principal reasons for this reversal can be found in changes in the policies applied.

The introduction of the new economic mechanism of January 1, 1968 represented a break with the centralized system of economic planning, under which production targets were set and materials allocated centrally and domestic prices were divorced from world market prices. The establishment of market relationships among firms and the adoption of a single commercial exchange rate (called foreign exchange conversion ratio at the time), supplemented by export subsidies, gave considerable impetus to exports to private market economies in the years following.

In turn, the measures of recentralization applied following the November 1972 Party resolution and, especially, the attempts made to isolate the Hungarian economy from external events after 1973, reduced the incentives to export. Profits derived from exporting were lowered through reductions in export subsidies and by ex post transfers to the state budget. These changes, together with the buoyancy of domestic markets, tended to discourage export expansion and the transformation of the export structure in response to the changing pattern of foreign demand (Balassa, 1983a).

The December 1978 Party resolution called for a return to the principles of the 1968 reforms, including the decentralization of the system of decision-making and the linking of domestic to world market prices. At the same time, recognizing the fact that Hungary could not continue indefinitely accumulating convertible-currency debt, which increased from $900 million at the end of 1973 to $4600 million at the end of 1978 in net terms (*Ibid*), the resolution called for re-equilibrating the balance of trade in convertible currencies.

Equilibrium in the balance of trade was restored by 1981, notwithstanding the adverse effects of increases in petroleum prices in 1979–80, the world economic slowdown, and the rise in interest rates on world financial markets. The adjustment, however, was not brought about by output-increasing policies in the form of export expansion and import substitution, but through the application of restrictive macroeconomic policy measures.

In fact, in its trade with private market economies, Hungary experienced little import substitution between 1978 and 1981, and this was increasingly offset by losses in export market shares. By 1981, Hungary's average market shares in the imports of these economies declined by 15 percent, giving rise to a foreign exchange loss of $511 million, whereas the balance-of-payments gain from import substitution was only $123 million (Balassa, 1985).[6]

During this period, Hungary suffered the adverse effects of the cessation of its cattle exports to the Common Market, but this was compensated by increases in meat exports. Furthermore, while exports of pig iron to the EEC halted, this was more than offset by higher exports of iron and steel products. At the same time, limitations on the exports of textile products to the Common Market apply to most socialist and developing countries and not only to Hungary. Finally, although individual EEC member countries impose quotas on certain manufactured goods imported from Hungary, these quotas reportedly affect only 3–4 percent of Hungary's manufactured exports to the Common Market (*Financial Times* May 1, 1984). It would thus appear that one can attribute no more than a fraction of the losses in Hungary's market shares to discrimination against its exports.

Restrictive macroeconomic policies, in turn, bore on investment rather than on consumption. Between 1978 and 1981, gross domestic investment fell by 21.3 percent in Hungary, with net investment declining by 40.7 percent. By contrast, domestic consumption increased by altogether 6.0 percent during the period. With the gross domestic product rising by a total of 4.5 percent between 1978 and 1981, the share of domestic consumption in GDP increased, partly offsetting the effects of reduced investment on Hungary's balance of payments.

The situation was aggravated in subsequent years as Hungary suffered the consequences of the events in Poland that brought into question the creditworthiness of the socialist countries for foreign private loans. There ensued the virtual cessation of commercial bank lending and the partial withdrawal of liquid funds, mostly by Middle Eastern countries, from the Hungarian National Bank.

In view of Hungary's debt payment obligations, the government's objective was changed from the re-equilibration of the balance of trade in convertible currencies to achieving a substantial surplus. This in fact occurred in 1984, when a $0.7 billion surplus in convertible currency trade was attained. The adjustment entailed the continued application of restrictive macroeconomic policies, again involving reductions in investment rather than consumption, supplemented by import restrictions while Hungary continued to lose export market shares. In turn, the expansionary measures taken contributed to the decline in this surplus to $0.3 billion in 1985.

Gross domestic investment fell by 15.7 percent between 1981 and

1985, with net investment declining by 47.4 percent whereas consumption increased by 4.7 percent. At the same time, increased import restrictions in convertible currency trade reduced the ratio of imports to the gross domestic product. Thus, a 6.1 percent rise in Hungary's GDP between 1981 and 1985 was accompanied by a 3.4 percent decline in its imports from private market economies. In this way, 'forced' import substitution occurred in Hungary.

Changes in Hungarian exports may be evaluated by making comparisons with the export performance of other countries at similar levels of economic development. This has been done in regard to the exports of newly-industrializing developing countries (NICs), including Argentina, Brazil, Chile, Israel, Korea, Mexico, Portugal, Singapore, Taiwan, Turkey, Uruguay, Hungary, and Yugoslavia, to the developed countries.

Using import data reported by the developed countries,[7] estimates have been made of hypothetical exports, defined as the exports that would have taken place had Hungary maintained its 1981 market share in the imports of each of the developed countries from the NICs. Under this hypothesis, the current dollar value of Hungary's exports to developed country markets would have increased from $2.4 billion in 1981 to $3.0 billion in 1985. In actual fact, exports were $2.5 billion, representing a decline in market shares of 14 percent and a loss of $0.5 billion in absolute terms.

The result for Hungary contrasts with that for the outward-oriented NICs, such as the Far Eastern countries, which gained export market shares during the period. This contrast represents a continuation of earlier trends, with the outward-oriented newly-industrializing countries gaining and Hungary as well as inward oriented NICs losing export market shares both in the 1973–78 and the 1979–81 periods (Balassa-Tyson, 1983; Balassa, 1985).

Comparison may further be made with Turkey that used to be considered an extreme case of an inward-oriented country. This comparison is of special interest, both because Turkey encountered debt servicing difficulties at about the same time as Hungary and because, in contradistinction with Hungary, the policies applied led to increases in Turkey's export market shares. While Turkish exports to the developed countries would have increased from $2.2 billion in 1981 to $2.7 billion in 1985 under the assumption of unchanged market shares, actual exports reached $3.8 billion, representing a gain of 41 percent or $1.1 billion.

The contrast is even greater if total exports to private market economies rather than only to the developed countries are considered, largely because of Turkey's success in entering Middle Eastern markets. Between 1981 and 1985, Turkey raised the dollar value of its exports to private market economies by 35 percent whereas a decline of 1 percent occurred in Hungary. In the same period, Turkey's imports from private market economies rose by 37 percent and those of Hungary declined by 13 percent.

The observed increases in Turkish imports point to the fact that the rapid growth of exports permitted limiting the use of deflationary measures. Correspondingly, Turkey's gross domestic product increased by 26.3 percent between 1981 and 1985, compared with 5.8 percent for Hungary. Economic growth in Turkey was also aided by the rapid rise of construction abroad whereas Hungary was largely unsuccessful with foreign construction (*Financial Times,* October 10, 1983).

The rapid growth of the exports of goods and services in Turkey can be attributed to the effects of the wide-ranging economic reform introduced in January 1980.[8] The reform included a substantial devaluation, the provision of export incentives, the liberalization of imports, as well as the freeing of the prices of a wide-range of products, followed by interest rate reform. From the point of view of export performance, the first three of these measures offer particular interest.

Changes in exchange rates have been evaluated by adjusting trade-weighted (effective) exchange rates for changes in domestic and in foreign wholesale prices.[9] The real effective exchange rate thus derived, calculated on a 1976–78 basis, appreciated by 9 percent in 1979, the year before the reforms were implemented. However, the rate depreciated by 32 percent in 1980, with further devaluations occurring after 1981. By 1985, Turkey's real effective exchange rate depreciated by 41 percent compared with its 1976–78 level.

Turkey has also provided export incentives in the form of preferential credits and tax rebates, with additional rebates granted to trading companies.[10] Furthermore, exporters have been given the right to import their inputs duty free even if a domestic substitute is available. Finally, imports have been liberalized, thereby reducing the protection of domestic markets and encouraging efficient production and exports.[11]

In turn, various influences have contributed to the poor performance of Hungarian exports. They include the appreciation of the exchange rate in real terms, the introduction of the so-called competitive pricing rules, relative risks and rewards for exporting to private market economies vis-à-vis domestic sales and exports to socialist countries, the system of wage determination, the taxation of profits, the remuneration of managers, access to funds for export-oriented investments, the availability of labor, and the imposition of import restrictions on inputs used directly or indirectly in exporting.

II. FACTORS AFFECTING HUNGARY'S EXPORT PERFORMANCE

After an initial depreciation, the Hungarian forint appreciated in real terms to a considerable extent. On a 1976–78 basis, the index of the real effective exchange rate rose to 109 in 1979, declining to 95 in 1980, 87 in 1981, and 85 in 1982, increasing slightly to 90 in 1984 and estimated at 89 in 1985. The figure for 1985 represents a 14 percent real appreciation of the forint compared to 1978, the year when policy changes were introduced, even though the external shocks suffered and the objective of turning the trade deficit into a surplus would have called for a devaluation.

The cited results may appear surprising in view of the frequent references made in Hungary to the devaluation of the forint. Thus, according to an official of Foreign Trade Ministry, "after the revaluations of the years 1980 and 1981, the forint was devalued by 27 percent, compared to the average of convertible currencies, between 1981 and 1984" (Dunai, 1984, p. 94). The explanation for this apparent discrepancy may be found in the inappropriate weighting of foreign currencies in Hungary's currency basket, with a much greater weight given to the U.S. dollar than warranted by its importance in Hungary's trade.[12] Yet, from the point of view of evaluating changes in the competitive position of Hungary, the country composition of its trade is relevant.

As the dollar was rising rapidly in recent years vis-à-vis other major currencies, its excessive weight in the currency basket limited the extent of devaluation of the forint. Thus, the trade-weighted nominal effective devaluation in Hungary was only 7 percent between 1981 and 1984, compared with the 27 percent figure cited above.[13] The extent of the devaluation was 6 percent if changes in foreign currency values are averaged by using Hungary's exports, rather than exports and imports, as weights (Table 1). At the same time, weighting by exports will be relevant for explaining changes in Hungary's export market shares.

Compared to 1978, Hungary's nominal effective exchange rate ap-

Table 1. Changes in Exchange Rates in Hungary

	1976–78	1978	1979	1980	1981	1982	1983	1984	1985
Trade Weighted Exchange Rates									
Nominal effective exchange rate									
(a) export and import weighted	100	101.1	99.7	89.6	76.7	73.3	78.1	78.6	78.6
(b) export weighted	100	101.3	100.5	89.9	76.1	72.3	76.0	75.8	75.3
Real effective exchange rate									
(a) export and import weighted	100	103.3	108.6	95.2	86.5	84.7	87.7	90.2	88.5
(b) export weighted	100	103.1	108.8	95.1	85.8	83.5	85.9	87.8	86.1
Nominal Exchange Rates									
Forint/US Dollar	100	94.4	88.6	81.0	85.5	91.2	106.3	119.7	124.8
Forint/Deutsche Mark	100	106.8	109.8	101.3	85.9	85.4	94.6	95.5	96.3
Forint/Austrian Schilling	100	105.7	107.8	101.8	87.3	87.0	96.2	97.3	98.1
Forint/Italian Lira	100	95.0	91.1	80.8	64.2	57.6	59.8	58.2	55.8
Wholesale Price Indexes									
Hungary	100	103.1	105.4	121.5	129.2	135.2	142.8	148.8	156.5
United States	100	107.1	120.5	137.5	150.1	153.1	155.0	158.7	157.9
Germany	100	101.6	106.5	114.6	123.5	130.8	132.7	136.6	139.6
Austria	100	101.6	105.9	115.0	124.3	128.2	129.0	133.8	137.3
Italy	100	110.6	127.7	153.3	178.8	203.6	223.4	246.5	264.7
Real Exchange Rates									
Forint/US Dollar	100	98.3	101.5	91.9	99.5	103.5	115.6	127.9	126.2
Forint/Deutsche Mark	100	105.3	111.0	95.5	82.2	82.6	87.9	87.7	86.0
Forint/Austrian Schilling	100	104.3	108.4	96.4	84.0	82.5	87.0	87.5	86.1
Forint/Italian Lira	100	102.4	110.9	102.5	89.3	87.2	94.0	96.9	94.9

Sources: IMF, *Direction of Trade* and *International Financial Statistics.*

Note: Nominal and real effective exchange rates have been calculated by weighting with Hungary's trade with the major partner countries in convertible currency trade. In order of their 1976–78 trade with Hungary, these were Germany, Austria, Italy, Yugoslavia, Switzerland, France, United Kingdom, United States, Brazil, Netherlands, Sweden, Belgium, Japan, Finland, Greece, and Denmark. Trade with Yugoslavia is regulated by intergovernmental agreements; its inclusion would make Hungary's exchange rate even more overvalued than indicated by the figures of the Table.

preciated by 22 or 26 percent by 1985, depending on whether export and import, or only export, weights are used in the calculations. The corresponding figure is 14 or 16 percent for the real effective exchange rate, depending on the choice of weights, reflecting the fact that wholesale prices (in effect, producer prices) rose less in Hungary than in its partner countries, on the average.

Table 1 also shows data on changes in the nominal and in the real value of the forint vis-à-vis Hungary's principal trading partners and, for comparison, the United States. As is apparent, the forint appreciated in real terms by 19 percent vis-à-vis the German mark, 17 percent vis-à-vis the Austrian schilling, and 7 percent vis-à-vis the Italian lira between 1978 and 1985. And while a 28 percent depreciation occurred vis-à-vis the U.S. dollar, Hungary's trade with the United States represented less than 5 percent of its trade with private market economies in the base period.

The revaluation of the exchange rate in real terms adversely affected Hungarian exports by reducing their profitability and by limiting the possibility of increasing their volume through price cutting. At the same time, the introduction of so-called competitive pricing in January 1980 tended to discourage industrial firms from increasing their convertible currency exports and even encouraged them to reduce such exports. This was the case because prices on domestic sales could be raised only if export prices increased *and* export profitability improved in convertible currency trade. In eliminating exports with below-average prices and/or profitability, then, the firm could raise domestic prices under the rules. Moreover, some firms endeavored to keep their convertible currency exports below 5 percent of their total sales, in which case the competitive pricing rules did not apply to them.

There is evidence that the introduction of competitive pricing rules unfavorably affected the volume of manufactured exports in 1980 (Balassa, 1983b). Nor did attempts made in subsequent years to remedy the situation by modifying the rules suffice to remove these adverse consequences. In fact, they were reinforced by the increased overvaluation of the exchange rate, which broadened the range of products that were unprofitable for the firm but profitable for the national economy.

While the application of competitive pricing rules adversely affected the profitability of exporting firms, under conditions of excess demand existing in the domestic market firms with less than 5 percent convertible currency exports had greater possibilities to improve their profitability by raising prices or by changing their product composition towards higher-priced products. This conclusion is supported by available empirical evidence.

To begin with, industrial firms that had less than nine-tenths of the average rate of profit, calculated on capital investment and wages combined, accounted for 49 percent of convertible currency exports in 1979, 53 percent in 1980, 57 percent in 1981, and 59 percent in 1982 (Kevevári, 1984, p. 486). In the latter year, in the iron and steel, machinery, chemical, and light industries, firms with profit rates of less than 5 percent on fixed capital exported 13, 24, 28, and 13 percent of their output for convertible currencies while export shares averaged 9, 11, 7, and 8 percent for firms with profit rates in excess of 20 percent (Petö, 1983, p. 3). It has further been reported that all firms showing losses were subject to competitive pricing rules (Juhász, 1983, p. 956) and that highly indebted firms had twice the average share of convertible currency exports in their output (Deák, 1983a, p. 36).

But, even if a firm could conceivably increase its profits by raising the prices, or expanding the volume, of exports to private market economies, these exports involved a considerable risk, which practically did not exist in the case of domestic sales and exports to socialist countries. There was a risk not only because of fluctuations in foreign demand and prices, but because of the possibility that the higher quality requirements of developed country markets led to the rejection of the merchandise.

Variations in profits obtained in exporting to private market economies had implications for wage setting. While in years of good profits increases in wages were limited by the highly progressive taxation of wage increments, in bad years firms could not raise wages, thus risking the departure of workers, in particular skilled workers and technicians. Nor could firms set up wage reserves with confidence, since such reserves were repeatedly confiscated by the state. Also, firms feared that fluctuations in profits would meet with adverse reception on the part of the supervising authority and that high profits may be taken away from them as it happened in several instances.

These considerations point to a tendency on the part of the firm to be risk averse. And, even apart from the risk involved, the prospects of profits derived from exporting might not have created sufficient encouragement for the firm to expand exports. Several reasons may be adduced in support of this conclusion.

To begin with, the firm producing for exports could not adequately remunerate its high-performing workers because of the progressivity of taxes on wage increments, with only about Ft. 4–5 of a profit increment of Ft. 100 allocable to such increases (Faluvégi, 1984, p. 1078). This fact created particular difficulties in manufacturing high-quality products, which are in demand in developed countries. These products require better work performance and/or higher quality labor, the remuneration of which would have necessitated raising average wages that was subject to very high taxes.

Furthermore, on the average, the profit tax and other taxes payable from the firm's profits amounted to about 80 percent of profits in recent years while government financial support accounted for 40–45 percent of profits.[14] As these ratios varied from firm to firm, the profits obtained after redistribution became to a large extent divorced from the pre-distribution profits.[15]

Nor could post-redistribution profits be freely utilized by management as they were divided between the profit-sharing and the investment funds. And, apart from confiscating the reserves for wage increases derived from the profit-sharing fund, limitations were repeatedly imposed on the use of the investment fund.

Finally, the sharing of the managers in increases in profits was limited. This was the case, first, because of the overall limitations imposed on the payment of bonuses after 1972; secondly, because of the importance given to considerations other than profits in the bonus scheme; and thirdly, because of the latitude of the supervising ministries to modify the bonus conditions.

In fact, according to one observer, "The incomes of the managers—within the strict limits on income differentiation—have little to do with their work, their performance, and their abilities" (Héthy, 1983, p. 66). At the same time, the deciding role played by supervising ministries in setting bonuses, and the subjective elements involved in these decisions, meant that the managers reportedly expressed more of an interest in pleasing the cadres of the ministries than improving the performance of the firm.[16]

At the same time, exports were adversely affected by the limited access financing. To begin with, the special fund of bank credits that had earlier been made available for investment in export activities was increasingly allocated to import-substituting projects. Yet, in the latter case, differences in quality and in specifications made it difficult to provide an objective appraisal of economic benefits, which may be measured in terms of net foreign exchange receipts in the case of exports.

Also, the time limits set for the repayment of loans for investments in export activities were reduced to a considerable extent. While three years had earlier been allotted for implementing the investment and five years for recouping the amount invested, in 1981 the total time limit for repayment was set at four years. This regulation benefited agriculture and food processing at the expense of manufacturing industries and favored capacity-increasing investments over the introduction of new products and technological change. Nor were the credits provided as a part of an investment program of the firm, aimed at structural change (Garamvölgyi, 1982, pp. 1, 11 and Draviczky, 1982, p. 11).

More generally, manufactured exports suffered from the reduction of investment funds that was more pronounced in the industrial sector than the average decline on the national economy level. Also, in the allocation of industrial investment funds preference was given to central investments in energy and heavy industry over enterprise investments in the light and machinery industries, which give promise for exports.

Thus, within the industrial total, the combined investment share of mining, electricity generation, and iron and steel increased from 32.9 percent in 1978 to 49.3 percent in 1984 whereas that of the light and machinery industries declined from 28.9 to 22.0 percent. Yet, the average age of machinery is 16 years in Hungary's manufacturing industries and product composition is far from up-to-date, with new products accounting for only 3–4 percent of output each year[17], which represents a deterioration compared to the situation existing earlier.

A further consideration is that export credits, and other export incentives, were provided to direct but not to indirect exporters. As a result, firms manufacturing intermediate products often undertook direct exports, even though from the point of view of the national economy exporting in processed form would have been desirable.

One-half of the firms exporting to private market economies indicated that the lack of manpower limited the possibilities for increasing exports. But import restrictions were considered to be a more important source of difficulties. Thus, it happened that by the time the import license was obtained higher prices had to be paid for the input or the would-be purchaser of the final product did not accept the delay that had occurred. More generally, the imposition of import restrictions discouraged exports by creating uncertainty for the firm.[18]

It was attempted to offset the inadequacies of the incentive system by the government reaching agreements with some large firms on export targets, providing certain advantages in return. The poor export results cited earlier indicate, however, that these attempts were far from being fully successful. At the same time, such a procedure tends to freeze the existing export pattern and does not ensure the efficient choice of export activities. Moreover, it increases the scope of ad hoc interventions.[19]

The last point leads to the general observation that while the December 1978 Party resolution simultaneously aimed at re-establishing external equilibrium and returning to the principles of the 1968 reform, in practice these objectives came into conflict. More often than not, the conflicts were resolved in favor of the former objective, so that there were increasing interventions in the firms' activities.

Such interventions originated with the Economic Committee, the Ministry of Finance, the Materials and Price Board, as well as the sectoral ministries. They involved ex ante actions, such as instructing the firm to undertake or not to undertake certain activities as well as ex post actions, such as the withdrawal of investment and wage funds from the firm. Apart from creating mistrust on the part of firms, these actions induced firm managers to curry favor with the supervising authorities that often appeared to be the easiest way to pursue the firm's objectives.

The adverse consequences of the increased scope of ad hoc interventions were well stated by János Hoós, the Vice-President of the Planning Office:

> The overall direction of economic activities has lost its transparency; its auto- maticity decreased to a considerable extent and there are adverse consequences in the price system and in the regulation of incomes. As a result, firms are not sensitive to costs and they do not have appropriate incentives. This is expressed in the fact that in practice every firm can obtain—if in no other way than through government support—the revenues it needs for continued opera- tion . . . The situation has been aggravated by the import limitations and export obligations resulting from short-term problems of equilibrium, which have led practically to production instructions. For all these reasons, firms cannot op- timize their decisions and rationally combine their resources (1985, p. 115).

III. THE EXCHANGE RATE, PRODUCT PRICES, AND COMPETITION

According to Lajos Faluvégi, Deputy Prime Minister and President of the Planning Office, the pre-condition of renewed economic expansion in Hungary is that productive activities are increasingly oriented to- wards exports. Preliminary targets for the 1985–90 period call for exports to rise at an average annual rate of 3.5–4.0 percent. Faluvégi notes that reaching this target would permit the growth of national income to attain 3 percent a year during the period while imports would increase 3 to 5 percent a year (1984, p. 1029).

The export target appears rather modest. According to the World Bank's average projection, the manufactured exports of the developing countries would rise by 8 percent a year between 1985 and 1990 (1985). Also, Hungary has considerable possibilities for expanding and upgrading its food exports, provided that export markets are diversified.

Apart from the growth of foreign demand, Hungary could theoretically increase its exports to private market economies by 65 percent if it regained the market shares lost between 1971–73 and 1984 in its trade with these economies. And while regaining market shares takes time, this objective would need to be pursued through the adoption of appropriate policies.

The question arises, then, how can Hungary accelerate its export growth to private market economies. More generally, the question is how can Hungarian firms improve their international competitiveness to permit increasing exports as well as efficiently replacing imports, so as to ease the foreign exchange constraint that limits the growth possibilities of the national economy.

The first condition is to adopt a realistic exchange rate. As shown above, the forint appreciated in real terms by approximately 15 percent between 1978 and 1985. Yet, the external shocks Hungary suffered, and the objective of turning the trade deficit into a surplus, would have necessitated a devaluation.

While adjusting the exchange rate adds to inflation, in providing tax rebates to exports and imposing taxes on imports, the introduction of a value added tax would have the same effects as a devaluation without any inflationary consequences, provided that the tax were to replace profit taxes as suggested below. However, reducing profit taxes by one-half would permit but a 3.5–4.0 percent adjustment (Vince, 1983, p. 3), which would go only part of the way to undo the appreciation of the real exchange rate.

The Hungarian authorities wish to keep the rate of inflation within a 6–7 percent range. In recent years, reductions in consumption subsidies was the principal factor contributing to price increases. In early 1985, the resulting increases reached the presumed annual limit, leading to a virtual freeze on producer prices for the rest of the year.

Although reducing consumer subsidies is desirable in the long term, the rationalization of producer prices is a more immediate objective, when the process of rationalization involves, first of all, setting realistic exchange rates. At the same time, the inflationary effects of a devaluation may be mitigated by simultaneously lowering tariffs. Apart from compensating for the increases in import protection associated with the imposition of the value added tax, one may provide partial compensation for the effects of the devaluation through tariff reductions.[20]

Lowering tariffs parallel with a devaluation would lessen the bias against exports that results from import protection. The bias against exports may be further reduced by increasing export incentives and extending the incentives received by direct exporters to indirect exporters (the manufacturing of domestic inputs for export production) as well.

To begin with, it would be desirable to ensure the automatic and duty free importation of inputs used directly or indirectly for export production. This provision conforms to GATT rules and hence does not invoke retaliation on the part of importers. It has been used to good effect by successful exporting countries in the Far East and, more recently, Turkey.

On the example of these countries, it would further be desirable to extend the credit facilities available to direct exporters to indirect exporters as well while increasing the volume, and improving the terms, of these credits. In particular, providing longer-term credits would contribute to investment in export activities.

Hungary may also follow the example of successful exporting countries in improving the organization of foreign trade. Apart from generalizing the right of direct exportation to all industrial firms, and extending it to agricultural cooperatives, it would be desirable to encourage the establishment of trading companies. Producers, then, would be free to choose among the alternatives of direct exporting, selling through the traditional specialized exporting firms, and utilizing the services of trading companies.

Trading companies have played an important role in the rapid expansion of exports in Japan, subsequently in Korea, and more recently in Turkey. At the same time, experience indicates that, in order to become important factors in exporting, trading companies need incentives, foreign exchange allocation, and capital.

The described measures would provide inducements for exports as well as for efficient import substitution, particularly in industries producing inputs for exports. At the same time, for these inducements to have the desired effects, additional measures would need to be taken to establish rational prices, to provide the carrot and the stick of competition, and to ensure the incentive effects of profits.

Note has been taken above of the use of 'constructed' prices in domestic markets that unfavorably affected industrial exports. To overcome the deficiencies of this price scheme, it was decided to introduce 'genuine' market prices in Hungary. This was to be done first for firms that undertook certain obligations in the framework of the so-called 'price club,' established in 1984, subsequently extended to over one-third of industrial firms in 1985, with further extensions planned in later years.

Membership in the price club required the fulfilment of three conditions: (a) supply-demand balance in domestic markets; (b) domestic prices not to exceed import prices,[21] and (c) potential for export expansion. It was further stated that the extension of the new price scheme was conditioned on equating domestic supply and demand, with domestic prices being bounded by import prices.

In practice, however, there is little domestic competition in Hungary that would ensure the establishment of genuine market prices. Also, as noted by the head of the department responsible for price control in the Materials and Price Board, in the absence of import competition, comparisons of domestic and import prices have considerable information requirements. Thus, "one needs to take account of the product's physical and chemical characteristics, its specifications, durability, the variability of product characteristics, packaging, the rate of delivery, the accepted delivery time, as well as other conditions of sale, such as the size of the order and the servicing, transportation, and financial conditions."[22]

This is a formidable set of requirements and, in his earlier review of criticisms of the so-called competitive price scheme, the then President of the Materials and Price Board, Béla Csikós-Nagy, expressed the view that a "price scheme based on import prices is a practical impossibility" (1983, p. 732). Csikós-Nagy added that "of the several millions of products manufactured in Hungary only a few ten thousand are imported. Thus, not actual but constructed foreign prices would be in the center of price determination, and the comparisons of domestic and foreign semi-manufactures and finished goods would burden price setting with problems that cannot find a solution" (Csikós-Nagy, 1983, p. 732). The same point was subsequently made by the head of the department responsible for price setting at the Materials and Price Board:

> How can an import price that does not exist and is not known in the home market serve as a ceiling for domestic prices? This would be possible under import competition, when the producer is provided with the importing alternative . . . and the potential import price provides a limit to the domestic price. But if the seller knows that he does not have to meet competition from abroad, what is the limit? . . . Without real competition, the import price ceiling cannot provide a limit for the domestic price (1984, p. 4).

At the same time, in the absence of effective domestic and import competition,[23] the freeing of prices raises the danger of monopolistic or oligopolistic price determination. This danger has in fact been invoked in rationalizing the increased role of the Materials and Price Board in setting prices in conjunction with the introduction of so-called genuine market prices.

It appears, then, that the lack of competition in Hungary has not permitted the establishment of genuine market prices and has led to increased price controls. It is further apparent that in a small country, a situation approximated by Hungary, the efficient allocation of resources would require adopting world market prices and specializing in response of these prices.

While one may adopt world market prices, for standardized products, which have well-defined specifications, most manufactured goods are differentiated products where import competition would be needed to align domestic prices to world market prices. Under present conditions, this is not in the realm of possibilities for Hungary. Such being the case, one should first take measures to intensify domestic competition, with the gradual opening of the domestic market to imports.

In 1980–81, several trusts and large enterprises were broken up, leading to the establishment of 167 new firms. Still, Hungary continues to have a very centralized industrial structure. To increase competition, it would be necessary to continue the process of deconcentration, by breaking up firms that have several factories producing identical or similar commodities. Such is the case, in particular, in the steel, machinery, textiles, clothing, and shoe industries as well as in construction and commerce.

Breaking up large firms is a necessary but not a sufficient condition for effective competition. The break-up of the food canning trust has not led to price competition in the industry, for example. Rather, the newly-established firms have colluded in setting prices, which have then been reviewed by the Materials and Price Board. Central price setting, however, does not provide an appropriate solution as noneconomic considerations, such as the desire to limit price increases, affect the outcome.

A more appropriate solution would be to establish anti-trust legislation and to rely on the courts to ensure that cartels are not formed. While this would require a transformation of the way the courts presently operate, it would represent an extension of the role currently being assigned to them in the economic sphere in handling cases of bankruptcy. At the same time, such an arrangement would permit limiting interference in the firms' activities by central authorities.

The courts may also be given a role in breaking up large firms that have monopoly or quasi-monopoly positions in Hungary. Moreover, in order to minimize the possibilities for interventions on the part of the ministries, one may wish to transfer their newly-acquired responsibility for supervising the legality of the firms' actions to the courts.

Domestic competition could further be increased if the measures taken in 1981 and 1982 were followed by additional steps to provide inducements for the establishment of small and medium-size enterprises. These enterprises could also play a role in replacing imported parts and components by domestic production and embark on direct exportation. Appropriate measures may include increasing the number of workers that can be hired by private firms, reducing the taxes that were recently increased on such firms, and eliminating the additional taxes imposed on workers' organizations supplying state-owned enterprises.

At the same time, steps would need to be taken to gradually introduce import competition. János Deák, the Director of the Institute of Market Research, suggested that this be done by liberalizing during the 1985–90 period, the imports of products and product groups, where exports are profitable at the existing exchange rate, followed by further import liberalization in cases where international competition can be established during the next five-year period. Deák also suggests closing down activities that could not become internationally competitive (1983b, pp. 11–14).

The implementation of this proposal would permit the gradual liberalization of imports while limiting the cost of adjustment in the domestic economy, when an additional criterion for import liberalization may be the existence of monopoly positions. At the same time, it should not be assumed that foreign competition would necessarily lead to the demise of domestic firms that presently produce at costs in excess of import prices. This is because of the possibilities for improving operating efficiency in Hungarian firms through improved utilization of the capital stock and through reductions in what has been called intra-plant unemployment.

In fact, increased competition from imports would elicit cost reductions through the rationalization of operations and provide inducements for technological change. It would also make exports to private markets more attractive relative to production for domestic markets by lessening the advantages that sellers have over buyers in Hungary. In turn, if particular plants or firms continue to make losses in a competitive environment, they would need to be closed down. While decisions on closing plants may be taken by firm management, the involvement of the courts in bankruptcy proceedings would provide for the orderly closing down of firms.

IV. FACTOR PRICES AND INSTITUTIONAL CHANGE

Further consideration needs to be given to the pricing of productive factors. Several important measures have been taken in this regard in 1985. They include the introduction of a 10 percent tax on labor and a 3 percent tax on own capital for most manufacturing industries, compensated by a net reduction in the profit tax by 3–4 percentage points. At the same time, a number of firms have adopted new wage regulations that treat wage costs as any other cost item and make the ability of firms to pay wages dependent on its income.[24]

The tax on wages is intended to internalize the cost of some of the social policies that are presently financed from the government budget; the tax on own capital provides a payment to the state for the ownership of capital. Both of these changes contribute to the efficient pricing of primary factors while increasing the incentive effects of profits.

In turn, the newly-introduced wage (earnings) regulations improve rationality in firm decision-making by treating all cost items equally. They represent a break with the system of incremental wage regulations, under which increases in wages are financed from increases in profits. Under the incremental wage system, the ability of the firm to raise wages is dependent on its original starting position and inefficiently managed firms could raise wages by effecting some improvements in their operations while highly efficient firms could do so to a lesser extent as their scope for productivity improvements was more limited. Furthermore, as noted above, the incremental wage system has contributed to risk aversion and has slowed the process of technological change for the sake of providing steady wage increases.

At present, the new earnings regulations apply only to a minority of firms that have accepted its introduction; other firms continue to employ the incremental wage system or increases in wages are determined centrally. In view of its described advantages, the application of the new regulations should be extended over a wider sphere.

Under the new earnings regulations, firms that cannot pay the competitive wage will lose labor to other firms. At the same time, the mobility of labor would need to be accompanied by the mobility of capital. This, however, would necessitate adopting appropriate tax and credit policies.

The imposition of taxes on labor and capital increases the interfirm variability of profits. But, for profits to have sufficient incentive effects, the payments made to the budget from profits would have to be reduced. The recent lowering of the profit tax rate represents the first step in this direction. It would need to be followed by a more substantial reduction in profit tax rates, say by one-half, with the revenue loss offset through the introduction of the value added tax. As noted above, the introduction of the value added tax would also improve the international competitiveness of Hungarian exports.

While lowering profit tax rates would increase the amount of funds successful firms have available for investment, firms exhibiting poor performance would have to draw on their amortization funds to finance their losses, thereby leading to the reallocation of capital. Providing credits on the basis of profitability considerations alone would also contribute to the allocation of capital to efficient activities. This, in turn, would require placing increased reliance on commercial principles in bank lending.

The recent establishment of financial institutions and commercial banks represent steps in this direction. Making profitability the dominant consideration for the commercial banks would further call for the establishment of a competitive banking structure.

At the same time, the availability of investment funds to manufacturing enterprises would need to be increased, with additional funds devoted to infrastructural investment aimed in particular at improving transportation and communication facilities. This may be accomplished by devoting an increasing part of the increment in national income to new investments, encouraging private savings, promoting foreign direct investment, raising the share of the industries of transformation in total industrial investment, and reducing the scope of central investments and of central interventions in firm decisionmaking on investment.

Hungary's recent experience with the issue of bonds indicates the responsiveness of savers to interest rates. Establishing positive real interest rates on savings deposits can be expected to attract further private savings. The same effect may be achieved by permitting private individuals to buy shares in small and medium-size firms while encouraging the establishment of such firms.

Promoting foreign direct investment would benefit Hungary through the inflow of capital as well as through the increased availability of technological and marketing know-how. Particular importance attaches to the latter factors as, more often than not, the purchase of foreign licenses has not led to continued efforts to improve technology in Hungarian firms and marketing expertise is needed to ensure the success of the export effort.

Increasing the share of the industries of transformation in total investment would involve reducing allocations to energy and to basic industries. Among other things, it would be desirable to renegotiate the agreement on the joint Hungarian-Czechoslovakian hydroelectric installation on the Danube that would require substantial funds and bring limited benefit as well as potential environmental damage.

The funds available for firm investments may further be increased by limiting the scope of central investments. Such a shift would permit orienting investments toward high profitability uses by relying on firms to make choices on the basis of their evaluation of market possibilities domestically and abroad. This will also increase the responsibility of the firm for its own actions while the central interventions practiced today represent an undesirable division of responsibilities.[25]

At the same time, the introduction of bankruptcy proceedings would need to be accompanied by the strengthening of financial discipline,[26] thereby replacing the 'soft' by a 'hard' budget constraint for the firm. In this way, one may reduce the presently excessive demand for investment credit on the part of firms, with interest rates used to equilibrate credit markets. Also, firms would have more incentive to make placement with banks which would again contribute to the reallocation of capital.

Distortions in product and in factor markets have been said to motivate case-by-case interventions by the supervising authorities that have taken the form of fixing prices, establishing export obligations, setting targets for domestic sales, and modifying ex post the firm's retained profits. Such interventions have grown in scope in recent years as 'manual guidance' has been utilized to re-establish macroeconomic equilibrium.

Reducing distortions in product and factor markets and re-establishing macroeconomic equilibrium would lessen the rationale (or the excuse) for case-by-case interventions. At the same time, the institutional changes under way aim at limiting the opportunities for interventions. Thus, following the earlier consolidation of the industrial ministries into one, sectoral departments have been abolished, the only exception being the energy sector. Furthermore, apart from about one hundred of the largest industrial firms, the ministry only retains veto power over the choice of the firm's manager who is elected by the council or the collective of the firm.

These institutional changes are to be welcomed. But, fears have been expressed that the newly-acquired responsibilities of the Material and Price Board for 'market surveillance' would mean the displacement rather than the abolition of case-by-case interventions. And, while the new legislation provides possibilities for the firm to present its case at the courts for compensation in the event that the Board's actions adversely affect its profits, its dependence on the Board in regard to price setting may make this little more than a theoretical possibility.

The above considerations again point to the importance of freeing prices which, as noted before, is dependent on the establishment of conditions for competition. At the same time, there would be need to reduce the scope of fiscal redistribution that takes the form of ex ante regulations and ex post decisions on a case-by-case basis. As noted above, financial support accounted for 40–45 percent of firm profits, representing a counterpart to the various taxes that took away over 80 percent of the profits.

Apart from actions to assist firms in difficulties, the bulk of financial support has aimed at offsetting the high production costs for firms that cannot profitably export at the existing exchange rate. The adoption of a rational exchange rate would reduce the need for such support, both by shifting upward the threshold of export profitability and by providing possibilities to replace high cost export products through the expansion of low-cost exports.

Correspondingly, fiscal support for exports could be reduced and ultimately eliminated. This had been repeatedly envisaged in the past without, however, establishing the condition for its elimination through the adoption of a rational exchange rate. More generally, all financial interventions should be limited to cases when government actions affect the firm's profits, thereby increasing the financial responsibility of the firm for its own actions.[27] This purpose would further be served by penalizing firms that delay payments to other firms.[28]

Note has been taken above of the changes in the system of appointing managers. Under the new regulations introduced in 1985, in the majority of the firms the chief executive will be chosen by an enterprise council that is, in turn, elected by the workers of the firm. In smaller enterprises, generally those having less than 500 workers, the chief executive will be elected by the general assembly of the workers' collective. Finally, in the largest one hundred industrial firms, the supervising ministry will continue to appoint the chief executive for the time being.

The following discussion will concentrate on the case of firms that have enterprise councils, which account for approximately two-thirds of all industrial firms and for a similar proportion of industrial workers. In turn, only about 2 to 3 percent of the workers will be in firms where the general assembly elects the chief executive, representing about one-sixth of industrial firms. The remaining one-sixth of industrial firms, employing nearly one-third of the workers, will remain under the administrative control of the supervising ministry (Deák, 1985).

Apart from selecting the chief executive, the enterprise council will define the annual plan, approve the annual financial statement, determine the utilization of profits, set up subsidiaries, and decide on the division of the firm into independent units. On the whole, the council will fulfill the function of the board of directors of capitalist firms, with the important exception that the supervising ministry will retain veto power over the choice of managers and its agreement will be necessary for closing down the firm.

At the same time, while in capitalist countries the board of directors represents the shareholders of the firm, in Hungary the council will be composed of the firm's workers. This represents a change compared with the original proposal that called for majority participation by representatives of organizations, such as the supervising ministry, the banks, the Chamber of Commerce, as well as outside experts.

The changes made in the composition of the council make them resemble the Yugoslav system of workers' management. As it is well-known, this system has involved a bias against hiring new workers who would reduce the average product of labor, which is the relevant consideration for the workers' collective that does not equate wages to the marginal product of labor. Also, Yugoslav firms have showed a preference for increasing wages and social benefits over new investment.

There is a danger that enterprise councils in Hungary will follow the Yugoslav example. This danger is enhanced by reason of the fact that the trade unions are playing an important role in selecting the member of the council. Another danger is that the chief executive would dominate the proceedings, thereby perpetuating his stewardship. Such a danger exists since the council will include members of the management team who are appointed by the chief executive.

The above considerations indicate the advantages of the original proposal to have a majority of outside members on the enterprise council. This is not to suggest to have representatives of the supervising ministry on the council, since this would mean combining ownership and regulatory functions. A more appropriate alternative would be to establish an agency, consisting of legal, economic, and accounting experts, that would represent the state qua owner on the enterprise council. But, in order to avoid that such an agency assume excessive powers, its minority participation on the council would be desirable. A possible formula may be to have one-third of the members represent the agency, one-third the other outside organizations referred to above, and one-third the firm's employees on the enterprise council.

One may envisage establishing the described form of enterprise council initially for industrial firms that have remained under administrative control. Eventually, however, all enterprise councils established under the present regulations should be so transformed. Finally, in the case of firms established by banks, a procedure that is supposed to be applied in the future, the banks' representative may have a larger representation on the enterprise councils.

CONCLUDING REMARKS

Following a brief review of the policies applied in response to external shocks, this paper has examined Hungary's adjustment experience in the 1978–85 period. It has been shown that Hungary succeeded in transforming a deficit in convertible currency trade into a surplus during the period. But, this involved the adoption of deflationary policies, bearing chiefly on investment activity, as well as import controls, while Hungary lost export market shares and the rate of economic growth averaged only 1.6 percent a year.

Apart from effecting a shift in Hungary's convertible currency balance, it was envisaged to re-establish the reform process that had begun in 1968. Among the measures initially taken, the introduction of the so-called competitive price scheme in January 1980 did not fulfill its promise and the system of wage setting continued to reflect the application of the basis principle; i.e. increments in wages were linked to changes in the firm's performance.

In the early 1980s, organizational changes were also made in consolidating the three industrial ministries into one, breaking up trusts and a number of large enterprises, and providing for new organizational forms in the public as well as in the private sectors (Balassa, 1983b). While the last-mentioned changes have been given considerable attention, in 1984 the combined output of the new organizations did not attain 2 percent of the output of state enterprises. In turn, although the break-up of trusts and large enterprises created the potential for competition, collusive actions on the part of the newly-established firms hindered the exploitation of this potential. Finally, until 1985, retaining the sectoral departments of the industrial ministry limited changes in its operating procedures.

At the same time, the exigencies of turning a deficit into a surplus in convertible currency trade and the requirements of the reform effort repeatedly came into conflict and, more often than not, this conflict was resolved in favor of the former objective. This involved limiting the firm's freedom of actions, both through binding regulations and through case-by-case interventions.

In turn, the changes introduced in 1985, in particular the establishment of enterprise councils, changes in the tax system, the new wage regulations, and the shift away from the so-called competitive price scheme, represent important new reform efforts. But, for these measures to have their full effect, further actions would need to be taken to rationalize product and factor prices and to increase the freedom of action by the firm. More generally one should create a situation where the firm responds to market signals rather than to ever-changing regulations and interventions. This, in turn, calls for establishing the conditions for effective competition in the domestic economy and, eventually, through imports.

These changes are necessary for the structural transformation of the Hungarian economy that has been hindered by the practice of over-regulations and 'manual guidance.' Such transformation will require investments, more exactly efficient investments that conform to market conditions. In this respect, too, greater scope needs to be given to decision-making by the firm that has to take the risks and enjoy the reward of its actions. One may, then, ensure that 'the new growth path' lives up to its name as adjustment occurs through exports and efficient import substitution, thereby leading to higher rates of economic expansion.

ACKNOWLEDGMENTS

The author is greatly indebted to Hungarian officials and economists for helpful discussions on the subject matter of the paper and to Bela Csikós-Nagy and Ottó Gadó for their incisive comments on the preliminary version. Useful comments were also made by participants at the 9th U.S.-Hungarian Round Table on Economics held in Berkeley, California on June 10–12, 1985. Shigeru Akiyama prepared Table 1. This paper is a revised and updated version of Balassa (1985).

NOTES

1.   Trade is defined to include services other than investment income; unless otherwise noted, all data originate in official Hungarian statistical sources.

2.   The terms of trade loss is measured by taking the difference between Hungary's imports and exports valued in actual prices and in the prices of the 1971–73 base period; the export shortfall is derived by taking the difference between Hungary's actual exports and its hypothetical exports, calculated on the assumption that trends observed in world trade in 1963–73 continued *and* Hungary maintained its 1971–73 export market shares in this trade.

3.   Private market economies provided markets for 39 percent of Hungary's exports and supplied 48 percent of its imports during the period under consideration, with socialist countries accounting for the remainder. About 15 percent of Hungary's trade with socialist countries was settled in convertible currencies but the volume of this trade was circumscribed by state-to-state trade agreements.

4.   Changes in Hungary's market shares have been calculated with respect to the imports of nonfuel primary products, fuels, and manufactured goods by private market economies in the years 1971–73.

5.   Between 1973 and 1978, Hungary's cattle exports to the European Common Market declined from $133 million to $43 million. But, in the same period, Hungary's meat exports to the Common Market increased from $84 million to $149 million.

6.   Changes in export market shares in the commodity groups listed above have been calculated with respect to the 1976–78 period; in turn, the base period for estimating changes in the income elasticity of import demand has remained 1963–73.

7.   The data are expressed in current dollars at fob prices for the United States, Canada, Australia, and New Zealand and at cif prices for Japan and the countries of Western Europe. They originate in International Monetary Fund, *Direction of Trade Statistics*. Lack of information on the commodity composition of exports did not permit applying the methodology utilized in regard to the 1973–78 and 1978–81 periods.

8. In fact, the dollar value of Turkish exports increased by 75 percent between 1980 and 1981, permitting increases in imports of 18 percent while simultaneously improving the balance of payments to a considerable extent. In the same year, the dollar value of exports fell by 6 percent, and that of imports by 2 percent, in Hungary.

9. The data derive from International Monetary Fund, *Direction of Trade Statistics* and *International Financial Statistics*.

10. In 1981, exporters received an extra amount equal to 5 percent of export value if their exports reached $4 million a year and 10 percent if exports attained $15 million. And although these rebates have subsequently been reduced, they provided a strong push for the establishment of trading companies that spearheaded the export expansion.

11. For a detailed discussion of the situation existing in 1981, see Balassa, 1982; subsequent developments are discussed in Balassa 1983c.

12. This has been the case in some developing countries as well, reflecting a confusion between the use of the dollar in denominating exports and imports and the share of trade with the United States. In turn, adjustments in the currency basket to appropriately reflect the geographical composition of trade have led to considerable devaluations in several countries in recent years.

13. Among Hungary's principal trading partners, the forint was devalued by 9 percent vis-à-vis the German mark and by 11 percent vis-à-vis the Austrian shilling while it was revalued by 9 percent vis-à-vis the Italian lira; at the same time, a devaluation of 40 percent occurred vis-à-vis the U.S. dollar.

14. This and the subsequent points apply to domestic sales as well.

15. In an empirical investigation covering all state enterprises, it has been shown that in 1979 and in 1980 the correlation between pre- and post- redistribution profits in Hungarian industry was practically nil (Kornai-Matits, 1983, p. 15).

16. This is the conclusion of a survey of managers conducted by the Labor Research Institute as reported in *Figyelő* (Observer), October 21, 1982.

17. Interview given by Andrea Deák, Chief Economist of the Industry Ministry, as reported in *Figyelő* (Observer), December 22, 1983. p. 11.

18. These are the conclusions of a survey, the results of which are reported in *Figyelő* (Observer) January 5, 1984, p. 12; the difficulties exporters encountered because of the existence of import restrictions were also voiced in interviews by firm managers, reported in *Figyelő* (Observer) August 30, 1984, p. 5.

19. The dangers of providing preferential treatment to large exporters, irrespective of the cost of earning foreign exchange, are noted in Török, 1985.

20. Adjusting tariffs to the same extent as the exchange rate would leave import prices unchanged, and the resulting compensated devaluation would be equivalent to an (implicit) export subsidy. However, with tariffs being relatively low in Hungary, full compensation could not be envisaged.

21. Import prices (or world market prices) refer to the prices prevailing in private market economies. The prices of goods sold to, or purchased from, socialist countries are adjusted by the use of compensating taxes and subsidies to approximate prices prevailing in the (capitalist) world market.

22. Interview reported in *Figyelő* (Observer), October 4, 1984, pp. 1, 7.

23. The importance of competition is emphasized in Csikós-Nagy, 1985, p. 38.

24. Faluvégi (1984), Madarasi (1984) and Medgyessy (1984) describe these changes and indicate the need for further improvements in the system of incentives,

some of which are taken up below. Use has further been made of the review of the system of economic decisionmaking edited by Pulai and Vissi (1985).

25.   This point is emphasized in Kismarty, 1985.

26.   On the question of financial discipline, see further below.

27.   The institution of a list of firms operating with low efficiency, with a view to induce these firms to improve their operations, represents a step in this direction. However, a variety of exceptions continue to be made, providing scope for bargaining (Laky, 1985).

28.   Recent increases in firm-to-firm indebtedness and the lengthening of payment delays are reported in Jánossy, 1985, p. 5.

REFERENCES

Balassa, Bela, *Turkey: Industrialization and Trade Strategy*. A World Bank Country Study, Washington, D.C., World Bank, 1982, pp. vi, 455.

———, "The Hungarian Economic Reform. 1968–81," *Banca Nazionale del Lavoro Quarterly Review,* No. 145, June 1983, pp. 163–84. Republished as Essay 12 in Bela Balassa, *Change and Challenge in the World Economy*. London, Macmillan, 1985, pp. 261–81. World Bank Staff Working Paper No. 506 (Cited as 1983a).

———, "Reforming the New Economic Mechanism in Hungary," *Journal of Comparative Economics,* September 1983, pp. 253–76. Hungarian translation in *Közgazdasági Szemle* (Economic Review), 30:7–8, July-August, 1983, pp. 826–42. Republished as Essay 13 in *Change and Challenge in the World Economy.* pp. 282–309. World Bank Staff Working Paper No. 534 (Cited as 1983b).

———, "Outward Orientation and Exchange Rate Policy in Developing Countries: The Turkish Experience," *The Middle East Journal,* Summer 1983, pp. 429–47. Republished with a postscript added, as Essay 10 in *Change and Challenge in the World Economy* (Cited as 1983c).

———, "The 'New Growth Path' in Hungary," *Banca Nazionale del Lavoro Quarterly Review,* No. 155, December 1985, pp. 347–72.

———, "Adjustment Policies in Socialist and Private Market Economies," invited paper prepared for the Congrès International des Economistes de Langue Française, held in Budapest on May 27–29, 1985 and the 9th U.S.-Hungarian Round Table on Economics held in Berkeley, California on June 10–12, 1985. *Journal of Comparative Economics,* 10:2, June 1986, pp. 138–59.

Balassa, Bela and Laura Tyson, "Adjustment to External Shocks in Socialist and Private Market Economies," invited paper prepared for the Seventh World Congress of the International Economic Association held in Madrid in September 1983. To be published in the Proceedings of the Congress. World Bank Development Research Department Discussion Paper No. 61.

Csikós-Nagy, Béla, "Az árrendszer továbbfejlesztése (The Further Development of the Price System), *Pénzügyi Szemle* (Financial Review), 27:10, October 1983, pp. 723–34.

———, *Arpolitikánk időszerdü kérdései, 1985–1988* (Timely Questions of Our Price Policy, 1985–1988), Budapest, Közgazdasági és Jogi Könyvkiadó, 1985.

Deák János, "Az iparvállalatok teljesitmény- és exportösztönzésének tapasztalatai a legutóbbi években (Experiences with Incentives for the Performance and Exports of Industrial Firms in Recent Years), *Ipargazdasági Szemle* (Industrial Review), 14:2, 1983, pp. 29–39 (Cited as 1983a).

―――――, "A külkereskedelmi egyensúly és az export-import szabályozás (The Equilibrium of Foreign Trade and Export-Import Regulations), *Külgazdaság* (Foreign Economy), 27:9, September 1983, pp. 3–14 (Cited as 1983b).

―――――, "Az iparvállalatok átszervezésének menetrendje" (The Programme of the Reorganization of Industrial Firms), *Figyelö* (Observer), February 7, 1985.

Draviczky, Tamás, "Beruházási hitelezés, export-növelés vagy más?" (Investment Credits, Export Development or Something Else?), *Figyelö* (Observer), August 2, 1981, p. 1.

Dunai, Imre, "A külgazdasági tevékenység állami irányitása, szabályozása (The State Guidance and Regulation of Foreign Trade Activities) in Miklós Pulai and Ferenc Vissi (eds) *Gazdaságirányitás 1985,* op. cit. pp. 91–100.

Faluvégi, Lajos, "Cazdasági hatékonyság—gazdaságirányitás (Economic Efficiency—Economic Management), *Közgazdasági Szemle* (Economic Review), 31:9, September 1984, pp. 1025–43.

Garamvölgyi, István, "Hogyan tovább? Az exportfejlesztésben" (How to Proceed? In Promoting Exports), *Figyelö* (Observer), March 10, 1982, pp. 1, 11.

Héthy, Lajos, *Gazdaságpolitika és érdekeltség* (Economic Policy and Economic Interests), Budapest, Kossuth Könyvkiadó, 1983.

Hoós, János, *Az új növekedési pálya feltételei és követelményei* (The Conditions and Requirements of the New Growth Path). Budapest, Közgazdasági és Jogi Könyvkiadó, 1985.

Jánossy, Dániel, "Fizetöképesség. Vállalatok feketelistán" (Ability to Pay. Firms on the Blacklist), *Figyelö* (Observer), May 30, 1985.

Juhász, Adám, "Versenyképesség és árrendszer" (Competitiveness and the Price Regulations), *Közgazdasági Szemle* (Economic Review), 30:7–8, July–August, 1983, pp. 950–65.

Kevevári, Béla, "A tökeallokációs mechanizmus fejlesztésének lehetöségei" (Possibilities for Developing the Mechanism of Capital Allocation), *Pénzügyi Szemle,* (Financial Review), July 1984, pp. 483–94.

Kismarty, Lórándné, A beruházási döntési rendszer korszerüsitéséröl" (On the Modernization of the System of Decision-Making on Investments) *Pénzügyi Szemle* (Financial Review). 29:5, May 1985, pp. 361–67.

Kornai, János and Agnes Matits, "A költségvetési korlát puhaságáról—vállalati adatok alapján," (On the Softness of the Budget Constraint—on the Basis of Firm Data), *Gazdaság* (Economy), 17:4, 1983, pp. 7–28.

Laki, Mihály, "A gazdaságirányitás és a vállalati valóság" (The Guidance of the National Economy and Firm Reality), *Külgazdaság* (External Economy), 29:5, May 1985, pp. 41–58.

Lakos, István, "A magyar kivitel eredményei a fejlett tökés országokban (The Achievements of Hungarian Exports in the Developed Capitalist Countries), *Külgazdaság* (External Economy), 25:11, November 1981.

Madarasi, Attila, "A vállalati jövedelemszabályozásról" (On the Regulation of Firm Incomes), *Pénzügyi Szemle* (Financial Review), December, 1984, pp. 886–98.

Medgyessy, Péter, "A jövedelem-szabályozási rendszer továbbfejlesztése" (The Further Development of the System of Regulation of Revenues), *Ipargazdasági Szemle* (Review of Industrial Economics), 15:4, 1984, pp. 63–68.

Petö, Márton, "Alacsony és magas jövedelmezöség" (Low and High Profitability), *Figyelö* (Observer), December 15, 1983, p. 3.

Pulai, Miklós and Ferenc Vissi (eds), *Gazdaságirányitás*, 1985 (The Guidance of the Economy 1985), Budapest, Közgazdasági és Jogi Könyvkiadó, 1984.

Rácz, László, "Import korlát—vagy versenyár" (Import Limitation—or Competitive Price?) *Figyelö* (Observer), March 29, 1984, p. 4.

Török, Adám, "A magyar ipar nettó nem-rubel exportjáról" (On the Net Non-Ruble Exports of Hungarian Industry), *Külgazdaság* (External Economy), 29:5, May 1985, pp. 3–17.

Vincze, Imre, "Az értéknövekmény-adó" (The Value Added Tax), *Figyelö* (Observer), September 8, 1984, p. 3.

World Bank, *World Development Report 1985*, Washington, D.C. 1985.

NATIONAL ECONOMIC OBJECTIVES AND THE HUNGARIAN REFORM PROCESS IN THE 1980s

Rezső Nyers

The year 1985 marked the end of the seventh five-year plan period, and, at the same time, a time of major political events in Hungary. Among these the Congress of the Hungarian Socialist Workers' Party and the elections to the National Assembly and to the local councils are the most notable. All that widens the public character of politics entails a long-term evaluation of the economic situation and debates on economic issues bring about the drawing up of a political program for five years and, in its wake, the next five-year plan.

If, based on the issues raised at the Congress, we were to try to outline the issues being stressed in Hungarian politics they might be characterized by the following frequently used terms: "development of socialist democracy," "efforts at national consensus," "continuation of the economic reform process," "improvement in international competitiveness," "relative earnings better related to performance," "increasingly equal chances for education," "development of inter-

33

national relations in all directions.'' Beside these, if briefly, it is always stressed that Hungary is a member of the Warsaw Pact and actively participates in the cooperation of CMEA countries. In his address to the Congress Janos Kadar emphasized, among other things, that the 1968 economic reform has stood the test, and also that the current policy is valid for a long term and its future is secured. He said all that in the name of the Party leadership.

Elections to the National Assembly and the local councils are proceeding in the spirit of expanding democracy. The program of People's Front provides a common political base that expresses the consensus of the Party and of progressively thinking non-party people on the basic problems of development. This program does not demand a full-scope acceptance of the Party's philosophy and politics, as regards either its contents or its character, and thus makes it possible for non-party people to undertake a wider role in public life.

It is a new feature of the current elections that, in general, at least two—and even as many as three to five candidates stand for election in each constituency. In practice, the following alternatives present themselves to the voters: in some cases they may choose from party-member and non-party candidates; in other cases from several non-party people; but it also occurs that party-member candidates compete against each other for the mandate. The change in the electoral system might be viewed as a departure in the direction of a socialist political pluralism. In consequence of the election, the desires and wants or different social strata will be better articulated. Moreover, in accordance with the resolution of the Party Congress and the program of the People's Front the role of elected bodies, namely national assembly and local councils, in controlling the state administration will gain strength.

The control of the economy is characterized by an open-handed, non-dogmatic conception of socialist principles and efforts at pragmatism. The drawing up of the five-year plan for 1986–90 is nearing completion and, parallel to that, the larger firms have begun preparations for compiling their own five-year plans. It seems that the social objectives of the medium-term plan cannot be implemented using the instruments and methods of previous times. A radical change is needed in the behaviour of economic units. Therefore, in harmony with the planning work, the program for continuing the reform of economic control and management has been developed, and economic development in 1985 has started in this spirit. The concerns are different from those of four or five years ago, but they are invariably great.

The government is making greater efforts than before to raise the quality of inputs provided by experts to the planning process while, at the same time, making planning democratic. This is to be achieved by letting different interests and views existing in society confront each other in the course of planning so that they all will have an impact on the plan. The world economic forecast taken as the basis for plan discussions, has several well elaborated variants, the development of relations with CMEA countries and their difficulties have been better assessed, and increased attention has been paid to the social impacts of solutions to economic problems. Nevertheless, there still are some uncertainties both in the plan and in the situation of the economy that can not be clarified in advance but that will demand flexible adjustment on the part of economic control in the course of implementing the plan.

I. PRIORITIES OF ECONOMIC POLICY

The discussions about economic policy and the economy-wide plan have unambiguously clarified the medium-term priorities among the goals. Clarification occurred essentially on a majority basis, but in every case we may speak about a decisive majority. There have remained, however, reservations or even opposing opinions in some part of the economy or political life, so that we cannot believe, if only on this account, that the traffic signals of economic life show a "green light" to the assertion of priorities. Also, the objective difficulties deriving from the existing circumstances are substantial. In the economic policy of the years 1986–1990 the following three goals enjoy priority:

- Preservation of the external economic equilibrium attained in 1984, and its strengthening through improved domestic economic efficiency;
- Revival of economic growth through increased investment and greater efficiency, simultaneously with a moderate encouragement of personal consumption;
- Continuation of the reform of economic control and management, expansion of the possibilities of firms for autonomous operation, and the realization of government control in conformity with the market.

The difficulty of the task mainly lies in the simultaneous assertion of the three priorities, in that each of them should be realized, but in a way as not to thwart the implementation of the other two priorities, or to minimize the conflicts between the three. In the first half of the decade this was not, and could not be, achieved because under the pressure of world economic impacts, which were grave for the Hungarian economy, economic policy assumed a defensive position. All forces were concentrated on improving the external economic equilibrium; this was also aided by a necessary curbing of imports. The growth rate steeply fell on this account and, amidst the central restrictions, reform measures could only be taken in a narrow field, the stimulation of small ventures.

Now, the essential improvement in Hungary's external economic situation in 1981–1984 allows the simultaneous assertion of the three priorities, although it can not be excluded that the past policy stance may have a certain "aftermath" in that circumstances in foreign trade may exert a restricting effect on economic growth and cause difficulties with the very necessary improvement of the system of economic control and management. This danger has to be reckoned with, but the plan must be based on the assumption that this will not occur.

The deficit in the balance of trade attained its peak of $1.1 billion in 1978, falling to $155 million by 1980, but, in addition, there also was a deficit of Rb 524 million in the ruble trade in that year. In the years that followed, great improvements showed in the balances of both convertible-currency and ruble trade in the wake of powerful government measures and considerable efforts by enterprises. In the aggregated balance of the years 1981–1982 there was already a surplus of $280 million, but there still remained a deficit of Rb 914 million. Thus while the dollar balance improved, the ruble deficit did not grow and somewhat diminished in the average of the two years. In 1983–1984 there was a considerable improvement in the balance on both markets. In the aggregated balances of these two years the dollar surplus increased to $1.157 billion, while the ruble deficit fell to Rb 572 million.

In 1984 a balance of trade surplus of $603 million allowed Hungary to meet its debt service commitments as well as to reduce the international debt. The deficit in the ruble balance was only Rb 140 million and in the next one or two years this, too, will become eliminated because the bill for oil imports will cease to grow. Thus, the two balances improved simultaneously, but for different reasons: the dollar value of imports diminished by $1 thousand million, partly because of the strengthening of the dollar, with exports stagnating. During the same period the value of exports to the ruble area increased by Rb 2.5 thousand million, with a somewhat declining value of the ruble, and the growth rate of ruble imports was decreasing. The continuation of the surplus in the dollar balance cannot take place in the future through the forced curbing of imports, but only by boosting exports, mainly of highly processed manufactures. From the market aspect, the volume of exports necessary for improving the ruble balance is attainable but, here too, a more profitable product pattern is necessary.

Hungary's external debt attained its peak in 1980 when, according to the official publication of the National Bank of Hungary, the gross debt amounted to $9.09 billion and Rb 1.224 billion. By the end of 1984 the gross dollar debt had fallen by around $1 billion, and the net debt, reduced by claims and reserves, amounted to $4.1 billion, with the ratio of long-term loans increasing to above 80 percent in the meantime. The sum of gross ruble loans increased in four years by Rb 200 million, because repayment starts only in the next several years. The Hungarian balance of payments on current account showed in 1983–1984 together a surplus of $600 million, and in the ruble balance essentially the planned deficit appeared.

From all of that it follows that a smooth development of external economic relations can be secured with an annual trade surplus of $600 million and a balanced ruble trade; but improved export performances are needed for attaining these. The balance of payments position also allows the smooth transaction of credits. Our situation is on the whole truly characterized by the compilation of the *Institutional Investor* of March 1985, in which the indicator showing Hungary's credit-worthiness increased in a year by almost 3 percentage points, compared to a gain for an average of 109 countries of only 0.5 percentage points, and exceeding the average of all the countries surveyed by 7 percentage points. As regards the future, the requirement of balance of payments and government budget equilibrium are invariably stressed in government policy and, from the scientific aspect, this can only be approved as hardly any doubt on the need for such policies can arise.

The resuming of economic growth and the creation of more favourable distribution proportions have become a political necessity in Hungary, and from the economic point of view they are attainable, although not easily. They have become politically necessary because with the prevailing slow rate of growth the preservation of living standard and improvement of external competitiveness would be jeopardized, while they have become economically possible because, with the adjustment of the main distribution proportions and the activation of the market mechanism, the basic economic conditions for balanced growth have been brought about.

We have put behind us a particular recession period, initiated and controlled by the government because of a gross deterioration in external conditions, that took into account the strong market constraints and the financial emergency. In the years from 1981–1985 Gross Domestic Product (GDP) increased by 2.3 percent on annual average, but, accounting for the continuous terms-of-trade losses, in real terms this only was 1.5 percent per year. At the same time, this increment in output was used almost completely for eliminating the trade deficit and therefore domestic absorption did not grow at all. Investment diminished by 3.1 and personal consumption increased by 1.3 percent on annual average, because of an extensive growth of social benefits, while real wages diminished by 1.2 percent per year. Exports increased by a yearly 5.5 percent, while imports by only 0.3 percent, and, although the import intensity of production was moderated, the difference had to be partly covered by reducing stocks.

According to the presently valid plan concept, in the years ahead we shall attempt to prevent a repetion of the recession and to fight its paralyzing effect. GDP is planned to grow by 2.8 percent per year, domestic absorption may grow at the same rate and, within it, investment by 5 percent and consumption by 2 percent annually. Henceforth, imports may grow at the same rate as exports. The revival of growth is modest, and seems, therefore, attainable, but the change in tendency is highly important.

Some experts have reservations towards the planned resumption of economic growth because they are afraid that, in the framework of such growth, inefficient production may expand rapidly and the domestic and the external market would suffer because of the increase in efficient activities that an acceleration of growth would bring about. Those who observed the past trends aimed at boosting quantity, the neglect of sales, in the 1970s, cannot regard these anxieties as mere carping, with no foundation. Nevertheless, anxieties that obstruct action must not be allowed to prevail. The real problem is whether we can raise the cost and market-sensitivity of firms to a sufficient degree, whether we are able to concentrate investments on technological developments with quick returns, whether we can establish incentives to stimulate higher productivity and capital efficiency in various fields of the economy. In other words, whether we shall be able to correctly implement our ideas of economic control in practice.

It should be clear from what has been said that the attainment of both the foreign trade objective and the growth target decisively depend on the successful continuation of the reform process of economic control and management. This is why the latter is an important priority not only for the foundation of long-term development, but also for the solution of economic tasks in the years between 1986–1990.

II. PRINCIPLES OF THE SYSTEM OF ECONOMIC CONTROL AND MANAGEMENT

It is known that the reform of the Hungarian system of economic control and management stopped short in a semi-developed state in the early seventies, and certain prereform methods were built into the mechanism. Thus the whole system became ambivalent. The idea of renewing and continuing the reform came again into the foreground of the political life in 1978- 1979. The final decisions were taken in 1984.

Relying on profound analyses of the situation and possibilities of the Hungarian economy, and in possession of the results of debates among experts and policy-makers, the Central Committee of the Hungarian Party decided on the further development of the system of economic control and management in April, 1984. The resolution set out from the statement that the principles of the reform introduced with 1968 have been tested and proven to be correct; therefore, they should be further developed in the course of their consistent application, and the whole system of management should be overhauled in conformity with the prevailing and expected situation. It also had to be considered, however, that while in the late 1960s and the early 1970s the reform process could be started under advantageous world economic conditions, in the present period we have to reckon with external circumstances and impacts that are disadvantageous for Hungary. In the previous period no such sacrifices had to be demanded from the population for the implementation of the reforms as is the case today, although it is also true that the load-bearing capacity of strata having above-average incomes essentially exceeds that of the late 1960s.

What is the substance of the trend sometimes called in the West "the Hungarian mode of economic control and management?" Some people use this adjective when they compare the Hungarian reform to economic changes implemented in Yugoslavia, or with those again discussed in the Soviet Union and Bulgaria, or with those aimed at in Poland, and not infrequently also when they examine the interrelations between the economic reform-campaign under way in China and the seventeen-year-old Hungarian reform process appearing in two waves. On the other hand, some other Western experts speculate whether an autonomous Hungarian solution has any justification at all within the socialist world, whether the community of CMEA member countries is "receptive" to intensive cooperation with a national economy that builds the market mechanism into its own system.

Experience of the past seventeen years has convincingly proven that contrary to the scepticism that lasted for years in Eastern Europe, as well as in the West, a national economy applying the market mechanism in the Hungarian manner is capable of intensive planned cooperation with national economies whose economic decisions are centralized. It has also become clear to the Hungarian leadership that the criterion of adjustment to the CMEA is not the extent to which the role of the market mechanism is reduced by the cooperating country, but much more by whether, beside the market mechanism, adequate economic "bridges", meaning commercial, price and financial instruments, are built out for drawing the autonomous enterprise sphere into cooperation with foreign trade activities. Although the problem of the criterion for foreign trade decisions has remained undecided in the theoretical sphere in all the socialist countries, practice has decided it in an unambiguously positive manner. Thus, it may be considered as settled that the Hungarian solution is "CMEA-conforming" even if the other countries do not use similar methods.

Developments during the last few years have had a modifying impact on reasoning all over Eastern Europe. It is increasingly recognized in the European socialist countries that intensive economic growth, soon to present itself almost everywhere as a necessity, demands a system of economic control radically different from that established in the period of extensive development. Yet, except for a few common characteristic features such as the dominating role of socialist ownership relations; the principle of economy-wide planning; the state monopoly of foreign trade and foreign exchange management; economic control and management are no longer subject to a monolithic economic theory or practice. Several kinds of approaches have developed, there is a regular exchange of experience among countries about the impacts of the different methods, and an acceptance of the principle that there is no possibility of devising a uniform model of management for all countries. The several kinds of solution will, in all certainty, persist for some longer period, because this is advantageous from the viewpoint of work seeking ways for elaborating the most expedient mechanism. However painful this will be for philosophers and political economists who have already conceptually "developed" the model of socialism, we cannot avoid a new, relatively slow period of searching for ways aimed at devising concrete methods; we must be able to cope with this task.

In the course of the current further development of the Hungarian system of economic control and management we are proceeding essentially towards the "target model" worked out in 1966, implementing its principles, building on but going beyond had been implemented from it in the system introduced in 1968. The basic principle is invariably to organically link central planning with the market mechanism in a single uniform system. That is, it is out of question that the national economy would be divided into two spheres with their own laws, and in one of them planned control would prevail while in the other the self-regulation of the market. The central planning has a full-scope impact at the macroeconomic level and, through economic and legal regulations, it exerts a directing role on microeconomic actions to the necessary depth. The participants in economic life act in the micro-economy under market circumstances, on a market regulated by economic instruments, and the impacts of their activities are "fed back" to the central control. The substance of the present further development is to improve economic regulation, to enhance its "market-conformity," as well as to find a more rational solution for the "feed-back" of market effects.

The principle of an economy with several sectors, in which different forms of ownership can be found, has been confirmed. This, too, is a principle from 1966–1968, but in the 1970s some uncertainty arose in its interpretation, particularly whether it should be employed for a shorter time, to revive business, or whether it should be a lasting concomitant of socialist economy in Hungary. It should be noted that the necessity of having several sectors had been acknowledged also by the traditional socialist economic philosophy as a principle valid for the period of transition to socialism, but in socialism it was already considered as unnecessary and a waste of resources. The Hungarian solution has now repeatedly and unambiguously taken a stand for having several sectors in socialism and, in contrast to the earlier assumption, precisely in the interest of a rational management of resources.

In the course of the now ongoing extension of the reform the original concept of the economic reform will become consolidated and expanded so that the interest of the socialist economy will not be simply derived from a so-called "central will," but rather that a national economic interest truly expressing the social consensus should come about by integrating partial interests differing from each other in short-term questions. According to the elaborated program this concept is more consistently applied, and in a more practical manner, in the course of the present further development than was the case earlier.

Work is in progress aimed at the development of the bodies representing the interests of enterprises and cooperatives; at letting producers'
and consumers' interests conflict with each other; at bringing into
harmony the interests of economic units with those of the financial
agencies; and at the development and smooth operation of a democratic mechanism for the reconciliation of interests.

A new solution is applied in the present process to the exercise of
ownership rights over state enterprises. Enterprises will have ownership structures depending on whether they perform public state services or operate in a situation where they depend on the market. In the
former case the tasks of the owner are fulfilled by government agencies
or by local councils, in the latter by enterprise councils in larger firms
or by the assembly of employees in smaller firms. The expectation is
that this new structure of ownership rights will be more effective in
demanding the efficient use of social capital and will stem the tendency
to waste capital in state enterprises.

The immediate goals of the present reform process are to consolidate
the external and the domestic economic equilibrium by the end of the
1980s, to achieve some excess supply on the greater part of the domestic market and a smooth operation of the market mechanism, and to
strengthen the effectiveness and market-conforming nature of central
control. In economic policy planning it is considered likely that, as in
the foreseeable economic processes, there will be a two-stage development also in control: in 1985–1987 the completion of the consolidation
period will dominate, with a partial and gradual enlivening of the
market mechanism, while in 1988–1990 the economy will already
start developing along a new path, under more advanced circumstances
of market relations and a completely market-conforming system of
economic control.

III. WHAT HAS HAPPENED AND WHAT IS GOING TO HAPPEN

At the end of 1984 a true avalanche of legal regulations came to light in
Magyar Kozlony the official Gazette of the Hungarian People's Republic. With January 1st, 1985, 58 new or modified legal rules came
into force that provide a complex framework for the conditions of
economic management and harmonize the modifications introduced in
various fields. Let us survey, in somewhat more concrete terms, what
the Government has regulated by issuing this package of legal rules:

- 4 legal rules treat the possibility of expanding competitive economic relations and the delimitation of desirable enterprise behavior. At the same time they declare illegal the issue of economic superiority at the expense of other enterprises or consumers. The scope of government economic control is outlined, for the firms operating in the competitive sphere, as legal supervision, financial regulation and market surveillance. With this the "umbilical cord" has been abolished that allowed government interference with the operation of enterprises.

- 9 legal rules provide for the expansion of the legal and economic autonomy of enterprises and cooperatives. The autonomy of enterprises in decisions on production, capital management and the use of income is growing. The relationship between government bodies and enterprises is placed on a strictly legal basis. If, in the case of government interference the firm suffers damage, it can assert its claims for damages to the courts.

- 13 legal rules specify modifications in the power of the pricing authorities and in the tax system. The scope of official price limitations has become somewhat restricted and the procedure itself will be simpler. The substance of the change in the tax system may be summed up in two measures. The first increases the taxes of productive and service enterprises to be paid on resources, wages, capital, investment, while simultaneously reducing the rate of the profit tax. The other shifts the weight of taxation from the production phase to sales, thus increasing the weight of the turnover tax in the system.

- 14 legal rules provide for the general order of income distribution in the enterprise sphere, for the taxes to be paid, the state subsidies, the enterprise funds as well as for the general rules of investment and capital management. These measures give enterprises greater freedom in using their income and in investment than they had previously.

- 9 legal rules deal with labor regulation problems and the order of regulating earnings in enterprises. Both regulations allow a greater assertion of enterprise interests than was the case earlier, and reduce government constraints. The enterprises may decide themselves which of the three possible systems of earnings regulation they wish to apply.

- 9 legal rules comprise the measures affecting state and enterprise finances as well as the further development of banking system. The provisions separate the scope of state and enterprise manage-

ment more clearly from each other, increase the autonomy of the
banking system vis-à-vis the state budget and regulate the financial relations among the three spheres in a more transparent way.
In connection with the banking system the rules comprise two
essential changes: on the one hand they emphasize and exactly
describe the task of the National Bank of Hungary as the bank of
issue, also leaving for it the tasks of a credit bank, on the other
hand they make possible the founding of further financial institutions and affiliates according to need.

We must add to these new laws the fact that in 1984 the process of
change affecting the economic system had already asserted itself in
practice. Three important things should be mentioned. First the many
new small ventures, small cooperatives and a large number of other
small businesses that have quickly penetrated into the ''market gaps''
and, in spite of their relatively small number, strongly stirred the
''stagnant waters'' of the overregulated domestic market. Second, the
reestablishment of the bond market, in the framework of which two
submarkets are coming to life: one for the bonds of enterprises and
public bodies, in which enterprises participate, and one for the population, where the issuing bodies are communities. Third, the beginning
of inflows of foreign equity capital, productive and banking capital,
true, for the time being only to a modest extent.

What is still going to happen in the 1980s? According to the con-
cepts, between 1985–1987 the introduced system and the principles
already applied will gradually evolve. Thus the transitory favours
granted to enterprises to mitigate market impacts, exemptions and
''brakes'' will be abolished, the system of taxation will be further
developed, the profit tax reduced, and the wage taxes increased, and
the organizational system of the economy will be modernized. A certain number of large enterprises will be decentralized, the expansion of
small ventures will continue and the monetary and banking systems
will develop in the present order.

In the second stage of development, 1988–1990, the two-level
banking system may be brought about, and beside the central bank of
money emission a network of independent commercial banks may be
created. In this period it will also be possible to introduce a personal
income tax, and thus to realize the joint taxation of incomes from
diverse sources. Also, a major part of social net income may be re-
grouped into the sphere of turnover, and consumer price subsidies may
be reduced to a rational level. Preparations will be made to work out a

value-added tax system for Hungary, and better conditions will be created for the long-term interest of firms in the value of assets.

IV. A "BIRD'S EYE VIEW" OF ECONOMIC CONTROL: GOVERNMENT CONCERNS AND EXPECTATIONS

The recognition, palpable in the reform of 1968, that is today politically commonplace in Hungary is that for intensive development and for efficient management a new, greater driving power is needed than was the case earlier. Driving power is insufficient if leaders and the working people have to be stimulated to better work through political campaigns, or if the government must raise the presently relatively low rate of investment, since in the 1970s both these driving forces were applied together and yet the efficiency of the economy could not be improved substantially. Sufficient driving power can only be secured for the economy by enlivening and channelling into the right direction ventures based on individual and collective interest. This recognition is powerfully present in today's government policies and manifests itself in the initiation and stimulation of the continuation of the economic reform process. Both the present situation and the forecasts about the future speak for the reform, and thus the reform process relies on an objective situation and on objective interests. As such, it is essentially an irreversible process in Hungary.

The government's reform concept is characterized by the recognition, based on facts, that low-efficiency production can gradually be rendered more efficient with better work in enterprises; in this field there are large reserves that can be exploited even in a short time. As a matter of fact, this concept expresses the basic truth that in the past the government did not always find the expedient method for tapping these reserves and that previously it expected results too quickly. For example, the restrictive economic trend of the years 1979–1984 was expected to raise enterprise efficiency significantly, based on the fact that the rate of investment remained at 22–24 percent of GDP even during this period of restraint, and that the "socialist pressure" exercised through the regulators would force enterprises to increase efficiency rapidly. This expectation did not come true, and it could not, because the internal market pressure and a satisfactory freedom of maneuvering of enterprises were missing. Both of these were largely eliminated by the domestic application of the instruments of the restrictive policy. The concern now is to produce these two missing factors and to reinterpret "socialist pressure," to apply, instead of a firm by firm restriction, a general one directed against low efficiency. This is no easy task, but by all means one to be endorsed.

In recent years the government has fully adopted the concept of the 1966 resolution on the reform that an efficient economy needs sectors with different kinds of ownership relations, and that room must be given to economic competition of rational dimensions both among and within sectors, particularly since the latter has proven to be as important as the former. In 1982 the government took a significant step by permitting various small ventures in a wide range of activities, and their evolution has exerted a highly positive effect on the present situation. This process is double-faced. On the one hand it makes the earlier already legalized forms, agricultural small-scale production, handicrafts, retail trade, economically more advantageous. On the other hand, it provides a legal form for such activities that earlier had found their place in the illegal or semilegal "second economy." The process evolving under the slogan "with small ventures against the second economy" has been unambiguously successful despite the accompanying concerns and problems, but for their completely smooth incorporation into society more time is needed, and for the complete suppression of the second economy market relations need further development.

The government has a further possibility along the sectoral line, and that is the drawing in of foreign equity capital into the Hungarian economy. This idea may be implemented mainly through companies in mixed ownership, as joint property, but in a given case also a venture with exclusive foreign ownership may be licensed. In principle the government agencies fully accept the idea of expanding such ventures. At present the practical possibilities are being weighed, setting out from the fact that a compromise between two different interests has to be found: promotion of the Western interest, above all access to the CMEA-market, and the Hungarian interest, which is improving the balance of trade in convertible currencies.

Among the concerns of the government related to economic control the following ones are the greatest and the most difficult to solve:

- A gradual reduction of the rate of inflation, first from 7–8 percent per year to 6 and then to the order of 4–5 percent, simultaneously with stimulating growth. The task is difficult because the danger of deterioration in the terms of trade still exists, consumer price subsidies can be reduced only slowly, the ratio of social benefits can hardly be diminished, and excess demand prevails in a considerable part of the market. The solution is helped, on the other hand, by the necessary corrections already made in respect of the main proportions of the national economy.

- The creation of income differences between enterprises that reflect differences in efficiency ought to be promoted, financial favors should be reduced and, in general, by strengthening the observance of normative rules, special measures taken for individual firms or branches should be constrained to a very narrow scope. This concern cannot be solved by a kind of "sword-stroke" either.

- A stronger than the presently prevailing central impact ought to be exercised on personal incomes, partly in order to better remunerate more qualified work, partly to draw away high "windfall" incomes coming about in small ventures, but mostly in the second economy. The first can be attained by reducing the rigidity of central earnings regulations, the second one by the introduction of personal income taxation.

V. ECONOMIC CONTROL "VIEWED FROM BELOW": CONCERNS AND EXPECTATIONS OF ENTERPRISES AND ENTREPRENEURS

Viewed from below, the economic processes present a different picture of the same situation, one in which a variety of partial but very specific views of the situation predominate. Sometimes the macroeconomic contradictions can hardly be recognized in enterprise problems, while at other times the constraints on economic action appear to be much greater in the microsphere than is evident to the government agencies that are attempting to solve micro-level problems. The two approaches already may confront each other in an institutionalized form in the framework of the Chamber of Commerce representing the interests of its member firms, and also related to the extensive nation-wide activities of the Hungarian Economic Association and the Federation of Technical and Natural Scientific Associations. This is one of the important aspects of the evolving democracy of the Hungarian economic life, a particular kind of pluralism which channels thinking and activity, in the last resort, towards a more clarified integrated social interest.

The greatest concern of enterprises today is that in financial and foreign exchange matters the government does not yet provide satisfactory freedom of action for the evolution of entrepreneurship. Many firms have made comparative calculations about the weight of taxation in developed industrial countries and it has turned out that, in the same branches, the Hungarian ratio of the total tax burden is one and a half times that in the market economies examined. Foreign exchange management, and in this context the transaction of imports and, not infrequently, of exports, is extremely sluggish from the viewpoint of the enterprises and, because of it, useful deals are settled more slowly than is necessary. As a consequence, it is an established opinion in enterprise circles that in this field there are strong brakes on management and that they ought to be eliminated at the earliest opportunity.

A great many socialist enterprises put up grudgingly with the idea of developing economic competition if it endangers the safety of their own market. However, beside this otherwise understandable aversion, frequently concrete objections are also raised in connection with the poor conditions for strengthening enterprise competitiveness. The main argument is that the socialist enterprises still are overregulated in both legal and economic respects, and that this prevents them from responding rapidly to market changes. Another hindering factor is the limited availability of loans that can be raised for business purposes. Enterprises object to the slow development of the infrastructural network serving production and sales with no less justification, either.

The gradual introduction of democratic management methods in 1985–1987 will cause a transitory period of uncertainty in the life of enterprises. In 1985 Enterprise Councils were formed or enterprise assemblies were convoked in one-third of the firms in order to formulate the development strategy of the firm and to elect the management. Where no such new enterprise organs are as yet organized, we frequently find a feeling of uncertainty among managers and a consequent avoidance of risk-taking. In enterprises where the new organs have been established, they have had a positive impact on the enterprise atmosphere from the start, but they can as yet hardly carry on their activities according to their true goals. Many enterprise managers fear that the new organs based on the principle of partnership will be inclined to interfere with the rights of enterprise management to make decisions regarding operations. These anxieties are, obviously, not unfounded. Still, they are more of a psychological nature, since, after a period of "running-in," the new forms of "democratic enterprise management" are expected to produce better enterprise operation.

In spite of the extraordinary briskness in the formation of small ventures, much hesitation is still felt here on part of entrepreneurs. For a majority of people there still is a feeling of provisionality regarding these ventures, although one may say that "in general and in principle" it is unjustified, since even the Party Congress took a stand for the maintenance and even development of this sector. Yet "in concrete terms and in practice" it still is justified. There is a certain provisionality also in Hungarian market relations, because, in the case of several products and services, it cannot be foreseen whether or not the socialist firms will still be capable of taking over the task of meeting the demands of the market or whether there will be strong competition from imports on the market. But the problem is more substantial because of the uncertainties of material supply and taxation, as well as because the government has yet not established a policy in connection with this sector, from the viewpoints of either mitigating the "boom" or protecting against a possible decline.

VI. THE REFORM PROCESS OF ECONOMIC CONTROL AND MANAGEMENT AND THE POLITICAL SPHERE

The question is asked at times both abroad and in Hungary whether an economic reform can be consistently implemented without a political reform; and the answer always is, naturally, that in general and in principle, it can not. If the question is put in the concrete terms of the present-day Hungarian reality, it may be formulated in about the following manner: is the Hungarian political structure and practice of today suited for carrying out the economic reform process? In considering this question it is important to distinguish the ideological content of politics from the functioning of the institutional system and from the style of political practice.

As regards the ideological content, it seems that the bases of adequate ideology are already established, although not everything is as yet complete in the system of ideas. The Hungarian solution to economic control and management relies on two "ideological pillars" or principles, and today both of them are already strong ones. One of the principles is the necessity of intensive development and the consequent need for systemic change to bring it about. The other principle is that the socialist economy is a commodity producing economy and commodities cannot be managed efficiently on social level in physical terms. Intensive economic development, rapid technical progress and the necessity to confront inputs with results also lead to the necessity of commodity production. On the basis of these principles the Hungarian economic solution can be fitted into the political economy of socialism, because the category of commodity production is distinct and separate from the category of capitalism. Nevertheless, to date this new interpretation of the substance of socialist society has not, or has not sufficiently, penetrated into wider masses of Hungarian society.

No political reform will take place in Hungary that would basically change the political objectives or the conceptual structure of the political system, nor is such change a condition for the consistent and successful implementation of the economic reform process. However, the development of a system of political institutions appropriate to Hungary's current and future needs is and will remain on the political agenda. Similarly, the development of an appropriate style of policymaking is and will continue to be a priority task. The general trend is to work out a national consensus within the framework of a strengthening and developing democracy. This demands that interests of specific social groups be integrated from time to time, and in this integrative process the main role will continue to be played by the Hungarian Socialist Workers' Party. At the same time an important role in creating this consensus will be assigned to the People's Front, the cooperative movement and the representatives of local politics.

The development of the political system manifests itself in the more democratic form of the election system, in the substantial expansion and consolidation of the system of self-government of the local councils, in a freer assertion of the principle of representation of various interests, in the ever more open handling of political questions, in the diminishing difference, initiated from both sides, between ''official'' and ''non-official'' public lives. The concept of Marxian philosophy of political freedom is compatible with an even higher degree of freedom than the present one and also with more meritory democratic methods. It would be wrong to assume that the present-day ''official philosophy'' prevents greater democracy, but, under the given realities, a more advanced system and practice of politics can only evolve gradually, through a longer process. From the viewpoint of the economic reform process the Hungarian political system is not a hindering but rather an aiding factor, and the decisive criterion is that the tendency of development should point to a stronger democracy.

The development of democracy is characterized, in Hungary too, by its making divergent interests more open in concrete and short-term questions. Thus, it has to be accepted that certain parts of the reform process produce different effects and evoke at times sympathy, at times aversion from individual social strata. Consequently, with strengthening democracy not only the driving power of the reforms gathers momentum, but, simultaneously, also the braking powers. The two forces act alternatingly also in the trade union movement, where at times the increase in the degree of freedom of enterprise management is greeted, and at other times the steps taken by the government with a view to achieving economic equilibrium are viewed with suspicion. Trade union solidarity sometimes becomes spontaneously confronted with the political leadership also when some reform measure serves efficiency, but makes difficult the situation of a specific group of workers. These problems may be solved within the trade union movement through the confrontation between the short-term interests of a narrower worker community and the long-term interests of the wider community. This situation necessarily introduces more politics into the trade union movement than is the case at present and demands the development of the internal democracy within the movement.

For the implementation of the socialist objectives of social and societal policy it is fundamentally important that the central controlability of macroeconomic processes should not diminish, but rather, it ought to increase amidst the economic reform process. The array of policy instruments has on the whole been adequately developed and requires only refining and improvement: The political instrument of policy, the mechanisms for the reconciliation of interests, and for creating and nurturing the social consensus, are already being developed and the completion of this task will be attained in the near future. The driving power of the progression of the reform process may, and hopefully will, be the authoritative majority establishing itself in society.

RECENT CHANGES IN THE PLANNED CENTRAL MANAGEMENT SYSTEM OF HUNGARY AND THEIR BACKGROUND

Ernó Zalai

The reform of the economic management system in the centrally planned economies cannot be a single act but must be an evolutionary process that transforms basic behavioral patterns and institutions. This process began in Hungary in the late 1950s and some recent changes are aimed at giving a new impetus to it. This paper briefly overviews Hungary's past experience with economic reform and against this background describes the main goals and essential features of some recent changes.

I. THE NATURE AND TASKS OF THE ECONOMIC REFORM PROCESS IN HUNGARY

The basic goal of the economic reform has been to establish an environment in which enterprises and households are in most cases automatically forced to produce and consume more efficiently and to bear fuller responsibility for their decisions and actions. The word automatically is used here as the opposite of the extensive direct involvement of governmental and other higher authorities in lower level decisions.

There has been only one such automatic regulatory institution in the recent history of mankind, the competitive market. It is not surprising therefore that the theoretical model of pure competition has had a major impact on economic reform ideas in Eastern Europe. In this sense there is a close spiritual tie between some neoliberal ideas in the West and the reform ideas in Eastern Europe since both advocate the increased role of competition and market forces in economic decisions. It would however be a mistake to overexaggerate this superficial similarity. [1]

Thus, the simulation or reestablishment of a regulated market mechanism has been a major element of the Hungarian economic reform ideas and measures as well. I want to stress this point, because this in itself explains many of the inherent difficulties encountered by the reform, as well as the somewhat disappointing fact that one can only expect a slow evolution, rather than sudden changes. One should not forget either that the creation of a quasi-competitive environment is an extremely difficult task in Hungary for several reasons. Attention should be called to a few of them here.

Without much exaggeration one might state that competitive markets have almost no tradition in Hungary. Before the socialist revolution, in a feudo-capitalistic Hungary, markets fell very far from the ideal of pure competition. Monopolies, bribes, corruption on the one hand, and autarchic, inward-looking traditions on the other hand distorted competition and limited industriousness in Hungary. Thus, the task is not to reestablish, but rather to newly create quasi-competitive markets in those sectors where they are feasible.

The history of developed market economies also tells us that it takes a long time and large costs to create a relatively stable and globally efficient competitive environment. It indicates also that cultural and ideological values such as the Protestant ethic or Japanese cultural traditions are very important factors among those determining the success of this process. Neither the remnants of previous cultural values, nor the behavioral patterns shaped by later developments provide a very favorable ground for competitive institutions in Hungary.

Among cultural values one should not forget the inertia of historical processes and their tendency to become reversible only slowly. Socialism in Hungary began by adopting the then existing overcentralized planning and management system of the Soviet Union as well as its theoretical and ideological underpinnings. Among these was the doctrine that central planning and markets are mutually exclusive. Moreover, due to the special circumstances and tasks of the era, the above system proved to be quite successful and almost irreplaceable in many ways. For example, it achieved in a relatively short period of time the transformation of the out-of-date macroeconomic structure by facilitating industrialization, raising the rate of accumulation, eliminating the feudal structure of agriculture, and reducing extreme social differences. To many minds this concrete form of socialism has assumed strong ideological values that are hard to change.

For these and similar reasons the goals set by the economic reform can be realized even under favorable conditions only in a long period of time. It is also natural that some of the earlier reform ideas are bound to change in the light of new experience and that the evolution of the economic management system will not be a linear one. The past two decades of the Hungarian economic reform illustrates well how slow and unstable, sometimes even reversible this process can be. Although this period is yet too short for us to be able to judge what the ultimate outcome of this evolutionary development will be, and although it is also too early to try to objectively assess what exactly has happened, most economists in Hungary tend to agree that the reform measures introduced so far have not yet been able to release the forces of competition and industriousness on a large scale. This goal has therefore remained the number one objective of the recent reform measures as well.

II. SALIENT FEATURES OF THE INDIRECT CENTRAL MANAGEMENT SYSTEM

Before turning to some details of the recent changes, it is necessary to characterize briefly the salient features of the existing central planning and management system of Hungary that has evolved since the launching of the New Economic Mechanism. While there is no need to describe the earlier directive planning and management system in detail here in order to highlight the distinctive characteristics of the present system we must briefly recall some essential features of the earlier one.

The early central management system operated on the basis of rather detailed and compulsory plan indicators. This, in turn, necessitated a hierarchical organizational structure and information flows. Horizontal links, typical of decentralized market systems, were almost completely absent or regulated by the centers. Planning was done mostly in physical terms and prices played very limited roles. They did not reflect scarcity or market values. Planning gradually evolved into an iterative, multi-level, hierarchical bargaining process about targets and resources. Almost every decision was made or at least sanctioned at the central level. Central planners apart from a few macroeconomic priorities, did not have adequate information on which to base their decisions and had to rely on the extrapolation of average tendencies and on the biased information provided by lower echelons. As a result, the achieved basis assumed a decisive role in planning so that decisions focused on the redistribution of incremental resources (status-quo planning). The system guaranteed the survival of economic units regardless of their efficiency and without significant differentiation in incomes or wages.

It quickly became evident that this system failed to coordinate efficient economic decisions and to harmonize appropriately individual and collective interests. The partial economic reform measures of 1957 and especially the introduction of the celebrated NEM were major steps towards a qualitatively different type of central planning and management system. Decentralization and monetarization are probably the two words that best describe the essence of the direction of changes. The theoretical basis of the new economic mechanism was generally weak; it contained the elements of both a self-regulating market system and parametric central regulations along the lines of Lange's model of competitive socialist economy. In the absence of balanced market forces and institutions the system inevitably evolved into an indirect, monetarized central management system. In this indirect management system, central planning and decisions have essentially retained their importance and dominance. As a matter of fact, the evidence shows that even the hierarchical bargaining character of the earlier planning system has remained virtually unchanged, but shifted to the sphere of economic regulators.[2] The real qualitative change has taken place in the sphere of central regulation, where the detailed compulsory plan targets were replaced by economic regulators such as prices, income regulations, credits, etc.

This change affected the nature and conditions of central planning in several ways, but it did not essentially change them. Central planning continued to rely on rather detailed plan calculations that cover the entire scope of socioeconomic development. Decisions related to the key areas of further development, such as investments, major technical innovations, structural changes, and international cooperation and trade, remain very much under direct central control. The detailed plans, however, do not become compulsory targets for economic units, but rather provide a basis for determining the actual values of economic regulators and for monitoring plan implementation. This indirect management system is based on the belief that the central authorities can design a regulation and motivation system that will induce economic units to make decisions that coincide with central objectives. At the same time it is hoped that the increased freedom of decision-making and material-financial self-interest will better mobilize resources and increase efficiency at the micro level.

In the light of past experience it is evident these beliefs and hopes are only partially correct. In the negative sense the indirect management system has justified itself. Compared to some other centrally planned economies employing a more directive management system, the Hungarian economic performance is not worse and as a matter of fact its comparative advantages have shown up in many areas, especially in the field of consumer goods supply. On the other hand, many of the earlier maladies of the economy have continued to exist. As one should expect, the opponents of economic reform want to see this fact as evidence of failure, whereas its proponents blame the continuing presence of directive instructions and the unfavorable external conditions for the inability of the reform to achieve greater success. The past two decades have also witnessed several major revisions of the concrete forms of the management system, 1985 being only one such example. The inherent difficulty and the experimental character of designing an appropriate regulation system, the sometimes drastically changing external economic and political environment, shifts in the internal political power structure are not negligible factors explaining these changes. Moreover, many economists in Hungary have shown convincingly that the very nature of the present indirect central management system is itself a major cause of these regular revisions.[3] And this cause is deeply rooted in the fact that this system tries to simulate but does not create real market institutions, and that it has retained many aspects of the previous hierarchical organizational and information structure.

The crucial difference between a decentralized self-regulating or regulated market mechanism and the present indirect management system is that the coordinating "hand" in the former is less visible, whereas it is all too visible in the latter. The environmental conditions in this latter system do not appear as objective, natural forces to which

economic units have to adjust in order to secure their survival. Therefore they naturally seek ways to manipulate these conditions in their
favor rather than adjusting to them. This is a well known phenomenon
in all economies, but it is especially strong in a formerly overcentralized economy where this instinct is predominant. The slow progress in
achieving structural change and technical development and in increasing productivity, the large portion of redistributed enterprise income
and the resulting weak correlation between profitability and income
retaining capability, and the lack of bankruptcies are clear evidence of
the success of these efforts to manipulate the norms of behavior and of
the bargaining power of Hungarian enterprise. It is not only the enterprises that are interested in distorting the uniform character of economic regulators. Political interest groups and state authorities also
exert pressure in this direction. As a result enterprises are pressed to
fulfill obligations that might be contrary to their own interests, as for
example, unprofitable supply obligations and various social responsibilities. In the spirit of NEM these enterprises have to be compensated for fulfilling these otherwise unprofitable tasks.

As a result of these pressures and because of the failure to achieve
central plans with sufficient precision through the use of uniform economic regulators, the regulation system contains too many special
rules and exceptions. Even if some major revisions restore its normative character to some degree, the tendency of introducing special
measures starts anew. Then when the regulation system again becomes
too complicated and unmanageable its revision again becomes inevita-
ble. Thus, the indirect central management system that has evolved in
Hungary is inherently unstable and therefore cannot provide an adequate basis for long term enterprise decisions.

This short characterization of past Hungarian experience with economic reform illustrates the motivations and considerations that lie
behind the recent changes that are described in the next section. The
main objectives of these measures can be summarized as follows:
further decentralization and strengthening of market forces; strengthening the uniformity of the regulation system; and further limitation of
direct governmental involvement in enterprise decisionmaking.

III. RECENT CHANGES IN THE REGULATION
SYSTEM

In 1985 many elements of the Hungarian economic management system were modified in the light of the previous experience and changes

in national priorities. These modifications affected both the institutional and the regulatory system. With regards to the former, we want to call attention here first of all to the changes in the central control and supervision of state enterprises and to the introduction of some new forms of enterprise management. The aim of these measures is to further increase the independence of enterprise decisionmaking and to make clearer their ownership rights and responsibilities.

The complex revision of the economic regulation system also resulted in major changes. The changes affect most of all the so-called competitive industrial sphere, where market forces are as yet rather weak and their strengthening has been given high priority. The rest of the paper will review the main characteristics of these changes in the various subsystems of economic regulation.

Producer's Price System

Hungary has already gone a long way ahead in modernizing its price structure so as to make prices better reflect domestic and international market values. The growing share of freely-negotiated prices, the introduction of the so called competitive pricing rule[4] in 1980, the gradual decrease of price subsidies, the changes in exchange rate policy, the efforts to bring producers and consumers price structures closer to each other are some examples of these efforts. The longer term goal of price policy in the competitive sphere is to leave the determination of prices to the market. This can, however, be achieved only if the conditions for the effective functioning of markets improve. Therefore, in the short run various forms of administrative price controls will continue to be applied. One of these is the law on "unfair prices," the enforcement of which is part of the new governmental market supervision function. This legal arrangement replaces the former one on "unfair profit's," and this change in term deserves special attention. This law covers an area broader than price formation alone. It summarizes the basic rules of economic competition in addition to defining cases in which prices or pricing behavior is regarded as unlawful. A separate resolution attached to the law lists examples of unfair pricing, mostly situations in which the rules of fair competition are violated.

In the competitive manufacturing sector the so-called competitive pricing rule has been maintained but modified so that only the export price level and not its profit margin limit domestic price movements. At the same time, it is envisaged that by 1987 only 15-20 percent of enterprises in manufacturing industry will remain under such administrative price controls. A parallel development is the separation of enterprise cost calculation from central price planning. About 60 percent of industrial products will be exempted from the obligation of detailed price calculation which used to provide the basis for administrative price control. The "fairness" of prices will be judged against the observation of general pricing rules. Cost calculation is to become part of the economic activity of the enterprises rather than that of central price planning and control.

Consumer's Prices

Reducing the differences between producers' and consumers' prices has been a major goal of Hungarian price policy, especially since 1979. Except for a few areas such as food, medicines, public transport and cultural services, subsidies in the consumer's prices will be gradually eliminated. In connection with the reform of the tax system it is planned that in the near future turnover taxes as well as personal income taxes will play a more significant role than before in generating revenues for the state budget. At present turnover taxes are planned to fall into one of four categories, 0, 11, 22 and 30 percent, and in the case of some luxury items special consumption taxes will be applied.

State Enterprise Income Regulation

The longer term changes in the tax system are aimed at lowering the tax burden on enterprise profits. Under current rates of taxation on such profits there is insufficient differentiation of net enterprise incomes according to enterprise performance. Larger enterprise income differentiation combined with greater freedom in deciding on the use of retained income as well as further limitations on the redistribution of profits among enterprises are viewed as crucial in transforming the enterprise motivation system into one better meeting the requirements of a regulated market mechanism.

The shorter run, transitory changes already point in this direction. In order to decrease the amount of profit-proportional taxes, new factor-proportional taxes were introduced in 1985. The enterprises have to pay a 10 percent tax on wages and other labor related expenses and a 3 percent tax on enterprise property. These taxes have to be paid from retained net income. They also make labor more expensive to the enterprises and thus motivate them to better economize it. The calculation of the enterprise gross profit for purposes of taxation takes into account subsidies, tariffs, and taxes on enterprise activities. From the profits a single reserve fund can be formed, whereas earlier several types of reserve funds were allowed, and the enterprises can freely decide on its size. There is a 15 percent local tax and a 35 percent state tax levied on enterprise profits. Certain activities will continue to be supported by tax exemptions.

The major change in the enterprise income regulation system is that the obligatory apportionment of the enterprise funds into development and bonus fund has been eliminated. The profits retained after paying the above mentioned taxes and the full amount of amortization, a part of which was earlier centralized, make up a single enterprise fund, the further use of which is freely determined by the enterprise.

Depending on the use, investment, saving or payment of bonuses to which profits are put, enterprises must pay additional taxes according to fixed schedules. Savings, for example, are tax exempt, for most investment outlays enterprises have to pay an 18 percent accumulation tax. The taxes levied in cases where net earnings are used to pay wages and bonuses are described below. It also should be mentioned here that the income regulation of enterprises in public services is different from the one described here. For example, they are exempted from taxes on wages, property and investment as well as from local tax obligations.

The Regulation of the Earnings of State Enterprise Employees

This element of central regulation has provoked much criticism in the past and has been frequently changed. This is the field where most of the problems stemming from the lack of real markets, unclear ownership rights and from the absence of long-term incentives are concentrated. At present there is strong pressure towards increasing personal incomes through higher wage payments. In the past various measures were tried to ensure that personal incomes, average or total, would grow only to the extent that the enterprise performance improved. This regulation acted in opposition to raise productivity and had undesired effects on employment policy. Less rigid regulation in this field can only be introduced if the general economic environment fundamentally changes the motivation of the enterprise leadership and the workers. This can not be achieved in the near future, and therefore the regulations introduced in 1985 are only cautious steps toward giving greater freedom for the enterprises in determining wages.

Since 1985 three alternative forms of earning regulations have been applied. The most flexible one is the so called earning-level regulation. Under this regulation enterprises pay taxes based on a progressive tax schedule on the total earnings, wages and bonuses of their employees. This tax is calculated individually for each employee, and not on total earnings. In this system the possibility of increasing earnings depends basically on the actual performance, or tax-paying capacity, of the enterprise. For a transitory period, according to recent plans lasting until 1988, additional taxes are applied to discourage enterprises from increasing earnings faster than value added. About 60 percent of the enterprises are expected to be subject to this form of regulation, but they have the right to choose, under specific conditions, one of the other two forms as well.

The second form is called the incremental earning regulation. In this category the enterprises pay additional taxes on earnings only if their average per-worker earnings increase from one year to the next. The third form is the central earning regulation in which the enterprises can increase per-worker earnings without increased tax liability up to a given percentage, and then they pay progressive taxes only above this level. A special version of this regulation applies to those enterprises that are assigned another form of taxation but which want to put themselves into this one. In this case the tax-free increase in per worker profits is only 2 percent and total increase is limited to 3 percent.

Changes in Monetary Regulation

The above measures, especially the effort to strengthen market considerations and relations are to be supported by appropriate monetary regulations in financing both operating and development activities. The envisaged changes, to be introduced only gradually, increase the scope of monetary policy and it is hoped that they will mobilize and flexibly reallocate enterprise financial resources. An important step towards the modernization of the credit system is the introduction of commercial bills. The regulation of these bills is based on internationally accepted rules. Enterprises, cooperatives and individuals may, by means of commercial bills, grant credit to each other from their own financial resources. It is expected that the introduction of commercial bills will reduce superfluous cash flows, strengthen financial discipline and make the general credit system more flexible.

Commercial credits can not be given for a time period longer than a year or for financing of investment. The terms of the credit are decided by the involved parties and are only indirectly regulated by means of interest (discount) rate charged by the refinancing bank. Refinancing depends solely upon the credit-worthiness of the borrower, as judged by the bank.

Another new development is the introduction of so-called current account credits. This means that the banks can provide the creditworthy enterprises with a certain amount of money within the limits of which the enterprises can arrange for their due payments without applying for individual credit to the bank. The amount of credit and its terms of use are determined by contracts made between the bank and the given enterprise. The period of the contract cannot exceed one year, but it can be renewed if the enterprise maintains its creditworthiness. The introduction of current account crediting is expected to enable the enterprises to flexibly adjust their credit stock to their actual demand for money. The same interest rate is applied to the current account credit as the one charged on other short-term debts.

During the preparation of the recent changes the expanded use of shares and shareholding companies was discussed but it was not deemed timely for both theoretical and technical reasons. Consequently their role will be rather limited in the near future. Significant capital reallocation and creation will mostly remain the task of the government and banks, although some forms of capital lending and borrowing between enterprises has been already earlier allowed for. Enterprises can lend capital to each other on the basis of freely negotiated interest rates or rents, and it is also possible to receive a share of the profit of the business receiving the capital. For some years it has been also possible to issue bonds in order to obtain financial resources, so far limited usually to investments in the communal sphere (gas supply, telephone network and so on). Production enterprises cannot as yet issue bonds for purchase by individuals.

All these envisaged changes will increase the role and responsibility of the banking system. The banks, through their credit policy, must closely monitor the activities, profitability and creditworthiness of enterprises, and assume more of the functions of commercial banks. We would like to recall that the 1968 economic reform was primarily concerned with the decentralization of decision making in areas related to current or short-run use and production of commodities, whereas it maintained to a large extent central control over investment decisions. The centralized, one-level banking system inherited from the past has not been changed, for it seemed to be a suitable institutional arrangement for securing central control over structural (investment) decisions. With increased emphasis on market building and profitability it became gradually a widely accepted view that these developments call for business-oriented commercial banking system. Therefore it has been decided that from January 1, 1987 the present one-level Hungarian banking system will be turned into a two-level one. The central bank (the Hungarian National Bank) maintains the tasks of the bank of issue and in this capacity it is expected to strengthen monetary policy and control. The commercial banking functions will be taken over by some already existing and newly established banking institutions. They are expected to operate in a competitive, profit-oriented manner. They include five larger general commercial banks, several smaller specialized banks, a special development financing institution and a saving bank for the population.

IV. CONCLUDING REMARKS

In this short paper we could only give a brief overview of the current changes in the Hungarian economic mechanism. We want to stress that these changes decided in 1984 were based on a complex analysis of the working of the indirect management system that had evolved by the early 1980s.[5] The main conclusion of this analysis was that there was no need to revise the principal guidelines of the 1968 economic reform but rather to strengthen and further develop them in some specific areas. According to this analysis the main tasks facing the future development of the central economic management system are further decentralization, strengthening of market forces and relations, and parallel increase of the efficiency of central control.

Thus, in the mid-1980s the declared political will supported the further development and introduction of the 1968 reform ideas. The paternalistic tendencies of the socialist state and shorter run economic and political considerations have tempered this will in the past and slowed down the reform process. The past two years have not been too different either. Many of the intended measures described above have either been postponed or introduced only partially, together with individual regulations. At the same time the resources needed for the transition to a ''new economic development path'' have been considerably reduced in the past few years. Therefore, the eventual success or failure of the newest reform wave remains to be seen later.

NOTES

1. There are, of course, very different interest (political) groups who are supporting economic reform in a given period of time on various grounds. The renewed wave of reform measures in the late 1970s, for example, seemed to have been supported by both what might be called the 'market-socialists' and 'plan-dirigists' in Hungary. The latter group might have found the impersonal forces of market a useful tool in carrying out the prolonged task of painful structural changes, which were successfully blocked by the involved parties in the hierarchical plan-bargaining system.

2. For a more elaborate discussion of the plan-bargaining issue see, for example, Antal (1981), Laki (1979).

3. The historical development of economic reform ideas and the economic management system is thoroughly analyzed by Antal (1985).

4. The competitive pricing rule was introduced to relate domestic relative price changes to those in world market prices in the tradeable sectors. This rule in the case of energy, raw materials and intermediate products means that their domestic price level followed the corresponding price movements on convertible currency world markets. In the case of manufacturing industrial products domestic price level was limited by the export price level, but at the same time the domestic profit margin could not increase faster than that on export either. For more details on this and related issues see Vissi (1985).

5. For a more detailed and authentic account of this analysis see Havasi (1984), Vissi (1983).

REFERENCES

Antal, L. (1981). "Historical Development of the Hungarian System of Economic Control and Mangement." *Acta Oeconomica*, Vol. 27 (3–4).

Antal, L. (1985). *Our Economic Management and Financial System on the Way of Reform*. (in Hungarian), KJK, Budapest. (Original title: Gazdasdgiranyitasi es penzugyi rendszerunk a reform ritjan).

Havasi, F. (1984). "Further Development of the System of Economic Control and Management in Hungary." *Acta Oeconomica*, Vol. 32 (3–4).

Laky, T. (1979). "Enterprises in Bargaining Position." *Acta Oeconomica*, Vol. 22 (3–4).

Vissi, F. (1983). "Major Questions of the Improvement of Economic Control and Management in Hungary in the Mid-Eighties." *Acta Oeconomica*, Vol. 30 (3–4).

Vissi, F. (1985). "Changes in the Economic Mechanism in Hungary." *Keizai Kenkyu*, Vol. 36 (4).

PART II

ECONOMIC REFORM AND ENTERPRISE BEHAVIOR

THE ROLE OF SMALL
VENTURES IN THE
HUNGARIAN ECONOMY

György Varga

On the basis of legal regulations promulgated in Autumn 1981, small-scale forms of enterprise have developed from 1982 on at a rate exceeding expectations (Table 1). Although the mode and directions of development have corresponded to expectations in every respect, the creation of new forms of ventures has been a highly significant step from the social and economic viewpoints.

Besides 7200 enterprises and cooperatives, 1.6–1.7 million small-scale organizations perform complementary production and service activities in today's Hungarian economy. Most of the small organizations operate in agriculture. More than 90 percent of the small-scale enterprises are accounted for by the 1.4–1.5 million families engaged in small-scale agricultural production beyond their work done on large-scale farms. A further 0.6–0.7 million families carry on agricultural production as a hobby, basically for their needs. These private agricultural activities represent an additional source of income for 56–58 percent of the population.

Almost 25,000 people hold private retail licenses and 139,000 carry

Table 1. Number and Staff of Small Organizations

	At the End of			
	1982	*1983*	*1984*	*1985*
Small cooperatives	145	255	393	713
Specialized industrial and service cooperative groups	477	1243	2424	2805
Economic workteams in enterprises	2775	9192	18178	21153
Private economic workteams	2341	4741	7873	10118
	Number of employees and members (1000)			
Small cooperatives[a]	4.9	9.1	14.5	30.7
Specialized industrial and service cooperative groups[b]	—	41.3	79.8	92.5
Economic workteams in enterprises[b]	29.3	98.0	200.0	241.5
Private economic workteams[b]	11.1	23.7	42.5	55.3

[a] Average yearly staff
[b] Number of members at the end of the period
Source: Magyar Statisztikai Zselkonyv (Hungarian Statistical Pocket Book) 1985. Budapest.

on licensed handicrafts activities. Out of the latter, 62,000 are retired people or individuals who pursue these activities in addition to their full-time employment. The number of private retailers has risen by 10,000 over 1981, that of handicraftsmen by 35,000 between December 31, 1980 and December 31, 1981.

I. FORMS OF VENTURES

This paper will be restricted above all to the new, small-scale forms of ventures whose establishment was legalized at the beginning of 1982 (Table 2).

The small cooperative is a cooperative carrying on productive, service or other socially useful activities, except for agricultural activities, in an organizational frame-work that is simpler than the one prescribed for traditional cooperatives. Its organization and the forms of self-government reflect its small membership which is restricted by law to at least 15 and at most 100 members. In cooperatives with less than 30 members it is not necessary to elect a board of management nor a supervisory committee, and the chairman exercises the right of management. In small cooperatives the general assembly is indeed the most important forum of cooperative self-government, since it has

Table 2. New forms of organization

Form of Ownership	Form of Organization	Possibility of Their Establishment since 1982
State	1. Small enterprise	X
	2. EWPE[1]	X
	3. Contract, leasing in retail trade and catering	
Co-operative *a/* Agricultural		
	4. *Auxiliary units* performing nonagricultural activities in agricultural co-operative farms	
	5. Specialized agricultural group	
b/ Non-agricultural (industry, construction, services)		
	6. *Small* industrial and servicing *co-operative*	X
	7. *Specialized groups* of industrial and servicing co-operatives	X
	8. EWPE[1]	X
Private	9. Small-scale (artisan) industry	
	10. Retail trade	
	11. CLP[2]	X
	12. EWP[3]	X
	13. Agricultural household plot and auxiliary farm	
	14. Private peasant farm	

[1] Economic Business Work Partnership within the Enterprise (Hungarian abbr.: VGMK)
[2] Civil Law Partnership (Hungarian abbr.: PJT)
[3] Economic Business Work Partnership (Hungarian abbr.: GMK)

exclusive authority in the most important questions, such as expulsion of members, approval and modification of the statutes, preliminary consent to major contracts, etc.

The autonomy of the small cooperative and its exemption from bureaucratic restrictions is also reflected in the rules governing its business operations. The small cooperative assumes increased financial risk since, if it incurs losses or loses its funds, no rehabilitation procedure, such as receivership, may be initiated, and the cooperative cannot be "resuscitated" with help from outside. If it can not cover the loss with its own resources, or perhaps with credit granted to it, it will be dissolved by the body exercising legal supervision over it, and a liquidation procedure will take place.

The small cooperative differs from large cooperatives also in the special rules affecting membership relations. The small cooperatives may have not only full-time members, but also part-time members who may be employees of other firms or cooperatives who work at the small cooperative beyond their legal worktime, undergraduates of higher institutions of education and even retired people (Table 3).

The legal regulations affecting the small cooperatives lay great stress on the collective ownership rights of the cooperative members. The small cooperative can only be founded if the so-called starting wealth or assets, are available for starting the activity defined in the statutes and for providing a financial foundation for the continuous activity in the first year. The establishment of such financial security requires an increased financial contribution by members. On the basis of personally performed work and the financial contribution made in the form of subscribed shares, personal income is due to each member from the income of the small cooperative. In the case of a loss, the personal incomes of members will diminish (Table 4).

The income regulation of the small cooperative is based not on profit but rather on gross income. Consequently, the small cooperative does not pay a profits tax, but a 28 percent, or, beginning with January 1, 1985 a 35 percent, income tax. The tax rate of small cooperatives services for consumers has been reduced from 18 to 15 percent. The personal income of the small cooperative members is not guaranteed and only as much personal income can be paid out as is left over in the so-called "disposal fund" after taxes have been paid. If the small cooperative incurs losses, or if its disposal fund is less than the personal incomes paid to members in the course of the year and the latter have not paid back the uncovered personal income then it has to draw on its own assets to cover the lack of funds. In case the small cooperative is incapable of covering the insufficiency or loss from its own resources, it cannot count on central help, and it must be wound up.

The specialized group is an organization of citizens operating within the framework of a cooperative, with self-government, economic autonomy and independent economic accounting. The specialized group is not a legal entity. Such a group may be formed in the framework of any industrial, agricultural, sales etc. cooperative, state farm and economic association belonging to the scope of agricultural income regulation, if this is desired by at least five such members, who must be over the age of 15 and who possess the financial means necessary for operation and if the parent organization approves the formation of such a group. The specialized group may undertake commodity production or provide services, primarily for the population, and complementary activities, mainly for the parent organization, according to the rules relating to the small cooperatives.

Table 3. Types of Employments in Different Forms of Small Enterprises

Form of Ownership	Form of Organization	Form of Occupation			The Organization May Employ	
		Full-time		Part-time	Paid Labour	Family Members
I. *State*	1. Small enterprise	X				
	2. EWPE			X		
	3. Contract, leasing leader	X			X	X
	employee	X	or	X		
II. *Co-operative*						
a/ Agricultural	4. Auxiliary unit	X				
	5. Specialized group	X				
b/ Non-agricultural	6. Small cooperative	X	or		X	
	7. Specialized group			X		
	8. EWPE			X		
III. *Private*	9. Small-scale industry					
	artisan	X	or	X	X	X
	employee	X	or	X		
	10. Retail trade					
	small shopkeeper	X	or	X		
	employee	X	or	X		
	11. CLP	X	or	X	X	
	12. EWP	X		X		
	13. Household plot and auxiliary unit				X	
	14. Private peasant farm	X		X		X

Table 4. Sales, Profits, and Taxes of Small Organizations
(million forints)

	Sales			Profits or Net Incomes			Taxes		
	1983	1984	1985	1983	1984	1985	1983	1984	1985
Small cooperatives	3875	7400	14604	813[a]	1288[a]	2764	—	—	—
Specialized industrial and service cooperative groups	4289	10408	14148	1615	3804	4786	340	717	1273
Economic workteams in enterprises	4960	11331	14833	2985	7145	8896	786	1667	7501
Private economic workteams	4490	9719	13387	1255	2725	3627	625	1278	1911

[a] profit

Source: A nem-job szemelyiesequ tarsasaqok tevekenysegenek elemzese/Analysis of the activities of associations that are not legal entities/, PM Ellenorzesi foigazgatosag/ Head Office of Auditing of the Ministry of Finance/, 1985.

The major internal rules relating to the operation of the specialized groups have to be laid down in the rules of operation. Such rules govern the main principles relating to the carrying on and development of activities, of using profits, the value limit beyond which the specialized group may conclude a contract only with the preliminary consent of the leaders of the cooperative, as well as the basic rights and duties of the members. The highest forum of the specialized group is the meeting of members which has exclusive authority in questions of fundamental importance such as electing and dismissing leaders, approving the annual plan, evaluating management and the winding up of the specialized group. In addition there is an executive committee and a chairman, both elected for a set term. (The term is set individually, it is not regulated by law.) In its operations the specialized group relies on the financial contributions of its members and on money and other assets ceded for its use by the parent organization. The members are only responsible for the debts of the specialized group up to the amount of their financial contribution. If a member leaves, he may reclaim his financial contribution, provided that it has not been used for covering a possible loss.

The specialized group covers the production costs and its other outlays from its receipts. If the specialized group behaves in a manner harmful to the interests of the parent organization or if it squanders the assets it received from the latter, the parent organization may dissolve the group.

The taxation of groups operating in industry and service cooperatives is identical with that of the economic workteams and differs from that of the groups in agriculture.

The most peculiar type of new small-scale organization is the economic workteam in enterprises.[1] Its organization is very simple. It is a collective venture formed from among the employees and retired workers of a state enterprise. For its creation and operation the approval of the enterprise management is needed. The number of members may vary between two and thirty (Table 5). In general, it uses the assets of the state enterprise, for which it pays a fee, but the assets of the members may also be used. In legal respects it differs from the general economic workteam in that the responsibility of members is restricted in that the members are only at risk to the extent of the income earned in the workteam and the assets contributed, and beyond that the operating firm stands surety for their committments.

The income regulation of the workteam is separate from that of the enterprise, and those active in the workteam get for their work per-

Table 5.   Size of the Small Organizations

Form of Ownership	Form of Organization	Membership for Ownership
I. *State*	1. Small enterprise	"smaller"
	2. EWPE	30 members
	3. Contract, leasing	
	retail shops	5 members
	catering units	12 members
II. *Co-operative*		
a/	4. Auxiliary production unit	not limited
	5. Specialized group	not limited
b/ Non-agricultural (industry,	6. Small co-operative	"smaller"
construction, services)	7. Specialized group	not limited
	8. EWPE	30 members
III. *Private*	9. Small-scale industry	13 members
	10. Small retail trade	
	11. CLP	not limited
	12. EWP	30 members
	13. Agricultural household	
	plots and auxiliary farms	1 household
	14. Private agricultural farm	

formed an "entrepreneurial fee," on which, beginning with the current year, a 6 percent corporate tax is levied instead of the earlier 3 percent, and, instead of a monthly accident insurance premium of Ft. 250, a 10 percent social insurance contribution has to be paid. (Both corporate tax and social insurance contribution are levied on entreprenuerial fee—e.g. turnover—less costs.) After these payments, the members of an economic workteam of an enterprise pay a progressive income tax according to the general rules affecting private craftsman.[2] The fee paid for the activities of the workteam by the enterprise is not counted as part of its wage costs and is subject to agreement between the ordering party and the workteam, taking into account costs, financial prescriptions and market relations.

A new form of organization and management is operation under contract. This has been introduced mainly in trade and catering. Beginning with 1982 industrial and service enterprises also may give out contracts for the operation of some shops or workshops that employ at most 15 persons. Operation under contract is a particular combination of great autonomy within the firm and small venture. The fixed assets of the shop or workshop continue to be handled by the enterprise and the workers remain employees of the enterprise. But the individual asking to use these facilities concludes a civil contract with the enterprise valid for at most five years. The economic content of this relationship is a venture to operate the shop or workshop with such profitability as to allow the payment of a fixed monthly sum to the enterprise. The size of this amount is determined through competitive public bidding where those applying for the leadership of the unit in question win through their bidding. The lump sum covers those overhead costs of the enterprise related to the operation of the unit, the charges for the use of assets, machines and equipment and buildings, for the wages to be paid to the workers of the unit, who remain employees of the enterprise, and also comprises the enterprise's share of the profit of the unit in question. The income above the lump sum belongs to the leader. On this amount he must pay a general income tax and he has the right to use it to complement the income of the employees. The leader organizes and directs the unit in the name of the firm, but at his own risk and responsibility.

All these regulators create a strong entrepreneurial interest in the profitable operation of the unit. The manager has a high degree of autonomy in procuring materials, in determining the microstructure of production, in choosing the working schedule, etc.

The lump-sum-system is intended to reduce bureaucracy and foster the evolution of the initiative and enterprising spirit of collectives and brigades in cooperatives. Units of industrial and agricultural cooperatives employing at most 15 persons, and carrying on industrial production or providing consumer and other services may be transformed into sections operating under a lump-sum-system. If this system is employed the worker or workers undertake the payment of a definite lump sum, and in return they are exempted from rendering account to the cooperative item by item and need not implement instructions of the employer. The agreement has to include the following: a detailed description of the scope of activity, the expected annual receipts as determined by the results of the preceding years, the related costs, the lump sum to be paid, the means of procuring raw materials, and the rules relating to the maintenance of fixed assets. For example in a barber's shop the potential receipts might be worked out on the basis of the figures of the preceding years. Within these receipts the main services, haircuts, shaves, washing etc., as well as the materials to be used and the wage costs would also be projected. The unit does not pay the total price of each service to the cooperative, but only the difference between the price charged and direct plus wage costs. This payment covers, among other things, the general overhead costs of the cooperative and also contribute to its profit.

The lump sum must also be paid if the receipts do not cover wages and direct costs. In such a case the worker may terminate the contract beginning with the next month, and continue working according to the traditional order. If the worker earns a surplus income above the expected annual receipts as laid down in the agreement, he pays the taxes on this surplus according to the rules of the general income tax. If there are several workers in a unit, they may make a separate agreement simultaneously and together. In such cases they collectively undertake the payment of the lump sum to the unit.

Among the forms aiding the evolution of organized ventures, the simplest one is the economic workteam, community, or partnership. In this form the founding members are not separated from each other either organizationally, or legally, or from the viewpoint of responsibility. In this work organization it is possible to combine full-time and part-time, temporary participation as well as long term activity.

For example it was the formation of economic workteams that provided an opportunity to people engaged in remote controlled aircraft modelling to undertake the chemical weed-control and spraying of small parcels of land. By fitting small cans onto the models it became possible to cultivate small lots in a modern way, without polluting the environment and avoiding large-scale waste. The aircraft-modellers thus became "entrepreneurs."

The economic workteam is the association of private persons without their constituting a legal entity. For its creation the conclusion of a contract of association and its approval by local (municipal) district or city councils is necessary.

Economic workteams may provide a consumer with other services, such as car repairs, undertake small-scale production such as shoe repair, or engage in an activity complementing the work of economic organizations by, for example, the series production of parts, or by providing organizational assistance such as market research. The economic workteam may not pursue commercial activities but a workteam may be created for the promotion and organization of such activities, for example in the form of an information service to help the exploitation of tourist accommodations.

Activities to be performed under official license, for example an industrial trade license, can be performed by private persons, private craftsmen included, only in the framework of an economic workteam.

It follows that private craftsmen also may become members of economic workteams, but on such occasions they may also continue their activities as independent craftsmen.

Observing the general regulations of the Civil Law Code, practically anyone may found an economic workteam. Employed people and co-operative members also may participate in economic workteams. An economic workteam may be founded at least by two and at most by thirty persons. The workteam may also have employees and their number adjusts to the number of members, but their total may not exceed ten people. The members of the economic workteam pay taxes in a way identical with that of the enterprise economic workteams, and similar to that of private craftsmen.

A new form of cooperation between small-scale craftsmen and the large-scale sector is leasing out to private craftsmen. Larger economic organizations may lease out their smaller industrial or service units, mainly producing for the population, to a private craftsman. In this case the craftsman and his fellow-workers operate assets in state ownership and thus pay a rent according to an agreement. The socialist sector of trade is a particularly important field for such ventures. At the end of 1984 nearly 15,000 shops and catering units operated under leasing or other contract in some other profit-motivated form. In shops employing at most five persons, and in catering units with at most 12 employees, contractual operation was introduced as a new form and the system of leasing was significantly modified on January 1, 1981.

The substance of the contractual form is that the shop manager carries on, against the payment of a fee, independent commercial activity in the shop of the firm, and partly with its assets, for a definite term. The right to operate the shop can be won at an auction-like competitive bidding, announced in advance. The manager of a shop operated under contract decides autonomously on every question related to the operation, maintenance and management of the shop, his scope of authority being only restricted by legal rules and the contract concluded with the firm. The manager may freely dispose of the income remaining after having made the payments due to the enterprise.

There is a difference between the shops leased out and those operating under contract in respect of the legal status of the manager and the employment status of the employees, namely whether they are employed by the lease-holder or by the enterprise.

Medium-sized units of retail trade may operate in an income-motivated system beginning in 1983. The independence defined by the commercial firm extends to the procurement of commodities, sales,

the management of stocks, labor, wages, assets and costs, and even to
sales prices. The shop manager and the other employees drawn into the
system of income motivation only get their basic wages uncondi-
tionally. For the attainment of a predetermined "result-requirement" a
premium is due, and a certain part of overfulfilment is given to the
entrepreneurs as benefit above wages, that is, the assertion of financial
stimulation is not restricted by the limitations of wage control.

The above three forms covered 27 percent of the shops, 33 percent
of the total commercial staff and 26 percent of turnover at the end of
1984. Among them the income-motivated system is the most popular
one in retail trade, while in catering it is the contractual operation.

In various areas of the Hungarian economy, for example in agriculture, further experiments at enterprising are going on. Their scale is
fairly wide, they reach from the collective forms of venture to the
system of "socialist individual entrepreneurs" hallmarked by the
name Tibor Liska.

Table 6.   Distribution of Sales of Small Organizations
in the First Half of 1984
(in percent)

Kind of Activity	Small Cooperative	Specialized Industrial and Service Coop Group	Enterprise Economic Workteam
Manufacturing	44.1	18.0	15.0
Industrial services	20.5	28.7	56.0
Construction	25.3	40.9	18.0
Agricultural and sylvicultural activity	—	0.4	0.4
All other activities of which:	10.1	12.0	16.0
Data processing, computer technical activities and organization	1.1	0.5	2.2
Personal and household services	1.1	0.6	1.7
Business services	1.7	1.7	1.0
Housing and public utility services in towns and villages	0.0	0.6	0.7
Total	100.0	100.0	100.0

II. GROWTH AND STRUCTURE

The number of small organizations[3] has been increasing at a relatively fast rate since 1982. According to the data of the Central Statistical Office the number of small organizations approached 29,000 and their employment 337,000 by the end of 1984. The development of small organizations is well reflected by the data on sales, profits and taxes.

While the total net sales of enterprises and cooperatives increased in 1984 by 7.4 percent, that of the small organizations grew by more than 110 percent. At the same time, their share in total gross output increased from 0.4 percent in 1983 to about 1–1.2 percent.

The income of the decisive majority of association members is Ft 35,400 annually, but the maximum may even reach Ft 200–250,000.

It may be seen from Table 6 that the activity of small organizations is aimed mainly at the production of manufactures and at industrial services such as maintenance, as well as at construction activity. In the first half of 1984, 3.3 percent of the enterprise economic workteams performed some kind of service for the population. With specialized industrial and service cooperative groups this ratio was 14.6 percent.

III. THE ECONOMIC WORKTEAM IN ENTERPRISES (EWE)

It is worthwhile to treat this form of small enterprise activity separately because EWEs constitute the decisive majority of small ventures that have come into being; this form has produced the most controversy; and because an expedient way of bringing about entrepreneurship within the enterprise is being sought all over the world. Orginally, the EWE was expected to use, through a joint venture between the enterprise and its employees, the insufficiently exploited productive assets of the enterprise to reduce the shortage of commodities, or to satisfy new demands. This assumed that there would be a financial contribution by EWE members to creating the conditions for such undertakings.

It was hoped that with the spreading of this form of venture a new kind of cooperation would develop between the enterprise and its employees so that as Terez Kaly writes: ". . . the wage-labor relationship would be replaced by a partnership relation between those who established cooperation with the firm."[4]

The EWE, as originally conceived, carried in itself the possibility of a venture which presumes autonomy, risk undertaken in the hope of profit, and the right of autonomous decision about the fate of the venture. But the possibility which existed in principle, could not be or could only partially be implemented. As a matter of fact, for example, an autonomous choice between feasible activities no longer assumes a relationship between employer and employee, but rather a common decision by partners with equal rights who assume risk and responsibility together. This implies the evolution of a whole system of small autonomous organizations with independent rights of decisionmaking within the enterprise organization built up according to rigid hierarchical rules. But the majority of enterprises support this hierarchy and therefore have at least up to now, rejected every new development, including the joint venture, that could undermine the internal "order." Enterprises have, therefore, made efforts to engage the capacities of the EWEs for themselves so that the latter do not work "outward" and become autonomous actors on the market. It follows that the EWE cannot decide on what kind of work to undertake, since it faces a single "buyer," its own firm, on the "market." Thus, it can only decide on, and negotiate with the firm about, whether it undertakes the work offered or not and at what price. In the last resort, the enterprise can refuse to commission the EWE.

The EWE members were nowhere expected to invest money, there was no way nor need for that, as they do lease the machines, do not buy materials, and do not pay for the overhead costs. All that is superfluous, since the firm only claims their worktime and labor power. Therefore, the EWE members only contribute the costs needed for their establishment. Finally, nobody expects the EWEs to take risks. At most they risk a minor or major part of the surplus worktime. The activity of the EWEs is characterized by a short-term approach to matters because in general, they do not risk capital and have no interest in assets. This is also indicated by the fact that at some enterprises the EWE members overstrain the machines.

While the firms are not interested in organizing EWEs of entrepreneurial type, they are all the more interested in having the EWEs operate as a collective task force, or as a work brigade. Thus, participation in the EWE is primarily not entrepreneurial behavior, but that of an employee, aimed at increasing personal income by sacrificing leisure time. The EWEs and most of the specialized industrial cooperative groups have become work brigades essentially because enterprises are not interested in introducing internal ventures. Their interests have remained attached to results attainable with the usual operation, under the conditions determined by the relation of worker dependence with relatively narrow limits to autonomy.

What advantages derive for the enterprises from the operation of the EWEs? Above all, their ability to retain their manpower improves. It is a fact that the EWEs have mitigated labor fluctuation and the flow of manpower away from industrial firms. The exploitation of machinery and equipment can be more intensive and this may moderate the per unit capital costs of highly capital intensive firms. The EWEs also can improve the opportunities of enterprises for a flexible adjustment to the market. Finally, although the cost of labor in the EWE exceeds that of labor employed during the legal worktime, it is less than the fee that would be charged by subcontractors or by foreign labor. This is indicated by Table 7.

It has been estimated that the fee paid to the EWEs secures for the enterprise increased output at least equal in value to these payments. Experience has borne out that the quality of work done by EWE members is frequently higher than that performed by external entrepreneurs. It should be mentioned that the money paid out in the form of wages is the "hardest" forint for the enterprise because of strict regulations over the wage bill. This is why they were also looking for methods such as the EWE for increasing performance which they did not need to finance within the strict restrictions imposed by wage controls, but rather from "softer" general overhead costs. Thus, by resorting to the EWE form the enterprises reduce reliance on the earlier means of increasing labor inputs overtime, part-time jobs, giving out work to the complementary workshops of cooperatives, etc.[5]

Consequently, organizing workteams the enterprise may obtain additional performance without increasing wage costs, while the wages

Table 7. Cost of One Man-hour by the Source of Labor Power in
a Large Engineering Firm
(in Forints)

Enterprise worker, during legal hours	50–60
EWE	100–110
Complementary workshop of cooperative	120–130
Subcontracting firm	200
Guest worker	300

Source: Figyelo, No. 10, 1985.

of its workers increase. The enterprises' interests coincided with the desire of workers to create an opportunity for raising their income at their own workplace. It is an undeniable achievement of the EWE that, although during the regular hours of work the worker has no active role in organizing his own work, in the EWE, where time is money for him, he does have such a role. The rational organization of his work becomes the immediate interest of the EWE member.

It follows that the selection of members of the EWE serves as a highly effective screening process which excludes poorly performing workers and elects its own leaders in a democratic manner. The collective may relieve the leader at any time. In the EWEs, collective feeling and mutual support strongly assert themselves. It is thus understandable that every forint paid to the EWEs produces an increase in national income of about 5–6 forints, while the corresponding ratio is: 1:2–3 during the regular hours of work according to computations of the Research Institute of the Trade Unions.

In 1984 the income of EWE members, above the wage earned during regular work hours, increased by 23.8 percent over the preceding year and reached Ft 35,700 per capita. For comparison the average earnings in industry increased by 7.4 percent in 1984 and exceeded Ft 67,000 per worker. Firms attempted to maintain hourly net income of EWE members at 2.5–3 times their regular hourly wages. Considering that the performance of EWE members are 120–150 percent of the output of an average worker, as well as the 60–70 percent overtime supplement, that would be paid if the work were done through overtime labor, the income of EWE members is equitable and proportional to their performance.

The substance of criticism related to the EWEs is that there exists the possibility of ''smuggling'' a smaller or greater part of the work to be done during regular worktime into the EWE. This is particularly possible with intellectual activities and maintenance work where the effort of the workers is difficult to measure and separate. It is also argued that antagonisms arise between EWE members and workers remaining outside them, and that the cost of higher income is self-exploitation. These criticisms are partially true. Examples can be found where work was commissioned in EWEs that could have been performed during regular hours. However, in most enterprises the workteams win the orders and commissions of the enterprise at public biddings. The form of the bidding is an auction where the entrepreneurs in effect bid down the proposed price, reduce the time required for the completion of the job.

It is possible, of course, for the EWEs to form a cartel and thus prevent the "erosion" of entrepreneurial fees. Cost-sensitive firms try to protect themselves against such oligopolization of the internal enterprise "market" by encouraging the formation of new EWEs and thus increasing labor supply. They also invite fewer tenders than required by the amount of work to be done. Nevertheless, it is true that in some fields an EWE may effectively enjoy a monopoly position. A mitigating factor is that against the financial interests of the EWEs the firm can put forward moral and ethical factors. The reason that moral as opposed to economic factors are used by the firm stems partly from the relative insensitivity of firms to costs and partly from the fact that the modernization of the internal accounting system of the enterprises has not kept pace with the development of internal ventures.

The possibility of unfair manipulations by or of the internal ventures could be suppressed if the collective exercised democratic social control over the invitation of tenders and handing out of commissions and if the equal chances of participation could be improved. This seems to be a much better solution than the practice followed in some enterprises, namely that they maximise the annual overtime and the attainable income.

The EWEs seem to have become a permanent part of the division of labor in the enterprise because enterprises are unwilling to give up the improved performance provided by EWEs. A solution of the currently existing contradictions is only conceivable if the EWE itself could be transplanted into the main job and the regular worktime. Such experiments have recently been started in a few big firms where a large number of EWEs are operating. The substance of these experiments may be compared to the contractual operation applied in home trade. The results of the experiment can not yet be appraised, but success can only be expected if the venture can be segregated from the traditional, petrified work organization during regular legal hours. Existing EWEs have attained outstanding performance precisely because their work was separated from the work organization based on hierarchical dependence relations.[6] We can not yet see today how the new forms of enterprise management, which will certainly rearrange internal enterprise relations, will affect the economic and social conditions for organizing internal ventures during regular worktime. If the cost-sensitivity of firms increases strongly, if the relative hardness of the wage-forint diminishes, that is, if the firms can renumerate greater performance with higher wages, it is likely that the ratio of work performed at the expense of leisure time will diminish and a part of the EWEs will automatically cease to exist, or internal ventures will develop in such new fields where they can be found today only in insignificant numbers, for example in product development, product planning etc.

IV. THE SMALL COOPERATIVE

Industrial cooperatives underwent an organizational centralization similar to that of the state enterprises. In 1975 the number of industrial cooperatives was still nearly 800, but by 1979 their number had fallen to 673, largely because of mergers, which also increased their size. In 1975 there were more cooperatives than enterprises in industry, but in 1979 statistics already showed 29 more industrial enterprises than cooperatives.[7] As a result of this growth in their size, the management, decisionmaking and the system of motivation in inudstrial cooperatives increasingly began to resemble the methods applied in state-owned industrial enterprises. Their cooperative character was pushed in to the background and the cooperative members increasingly took on the role of employees.

At the turn of the decade it was partially the same economic forces that called to life other forms of ventures that also created a possibility for the formation of small cooperatives. The legislators were partly led by the desire to create a new framework for cooperation, based on the voluntary principle, in which the ownership motivation of the membership would assert itself and where cooperative democracy would have real content and would truly operate.

It is worth noting that the founding of small ventures, above all of small cooperatives, started in the cooperative sector of industry more hesitantly and more slowly than in the state sector.[8] The existing industrial cooperatives sought only to be as flexible as other cooperatives so that they could remain competitive. In many cases they were headed by elderly chairmen who did not want to make changes and, initially, the bodies representing cooperative interests did not stimulate the foundation of small cooperatives.

A considerable part of the small cooperatives came about through transformation of already operating traditional cooperatives. Cooperatives with a membership of less than 100 were stimulated to undertake such tranformation above all by the interest in gross income which offered an opportunity to break out the limits of wage control. Also, several specialized industrial and service cooperative groups which had operated in the framework of farming cooperatives but believed that they might attain more advantageous income positions as small cooperatives were transformed. Finally, private persons founded small cooperatives, but in relatively smaller numbers. Some of the members of the latter, however, have not given up their earlier main, full-time jobs.

The profitability of small cooperatives significantly exceeds that of the traditional ones. Against the 11.7 percent (return on sales) profitability of the latter in 1983 and 10.5 percent in 1984, the small cooperatives attained 21 and 18.8 percent. The number of small cooperatives running into loss was three in both years.

The small cooperatives sell almost 60 percent of their industrial output and services to other industrial users, indicating that they operate mostly as subcontractors. Partly, however, they perform such activities as had not been earlier performed by industrial cooperatives. The proportion of products requiring high intellectual labor input and of those turned out in small series is relatively high. This is possible because small cooperatives have concentrated a relatively large intellectual capacity which quickly responds to the market. The fortuitous linking of market pressure with the flexibility inherent in the small organization is the source of good economic results.

At the beginning of this chapter the importance of consolidating the cooperative character was mentioned. In this respect there is a difference between the small cooperatives having come about through the transformation of and/or separation from the traditional cooperative and the new ones founded by citizens. In the majority of the transformed cooperatives the traditional bodies of self-government continue to operate. In the small cooperatives created through separation, the old methods of management and control are less adhered to. Since in these cooperatives the membership is smaller, they avail themselves of the opportunity for simplification and change. In the newly founded cooperatives the number of members does not reach 30. Thus, no elected bodies were mandated for them, and self-government has thus become simpler and more direct. The majority of presidents also do some other kind of work. Members exercise proprietary management and their democratic rights at the general assembly. Mutual information is continuously exchanged in daily practice and proprietary interests and behavior asserted. Experience to date suggests that in these organizations the good cooperative traditions, collective feelings, mutual support and the educative power of the community, revive.

It should be noted that it is mainly in the small cooperatives coming about through separation and in the newly founded ones that work is undertaken at the expense of holidays. Not infrequently, members work even 200–250 hours a month. Beside the lack of the "wage-brake" this fact, and, of course, higher efficiency, contribute to the personal incomes which are 20–50 percent higher than those of workers in the traditional cooperatives. Outstanding high incomes occur first of all among people performing intellectual services such as technological development, engineering, computer techniques. Their monthly incomes were between Ft 16–29,000 in 1984.

It is noteworthy that a part of the small cooperatives is only nominally small because there exists a possibility for small cooperatives to operate specialized groups, and while the membership of the small cooperative is limited by law, that of specialized groups is not. It is thus possible to found a small cooperative consisting of the necessary minimum of 15 members which de facto employs 100–150 people in the form of specialized groups. The activity of such small cooperatives is essentially restricted to the management of the specialized groups. These organizations are not full-scope cooperatives in nature, and their cooperative features can develop but in a restricted scope.

The small cooperative is part of the socialist sector. This is due not so much to the economic aspects of the organization as to the nature of the social relations developed within the work organization. As a matter of fact, up to now it has not been compulsory for the small cooperatives to form indivisible cooperative property. The behavior of small cooperatives is diversified also in the respect that while in cooperatives coming about through transformation, indivisible cooperative property as well as personal incomes are increased, a number of the newly founded cooperatives spends all of their net income, or a considerable part of it, on raising personal incomes. Some small cooperatives raise funds for their development by issuing special-purpose shares.

We have witnessed remarkable changes since the beginning of 1985. Up to the end of March, 107 small cooperatives were formed, almost as many as in 1984. Thus the number of small cooperatives can now be put at about 500. The majority of these new organizations came into being through the transformation of traditional cooperatives or by separation from them. The explanation for this phenomenon may be found above all in the risks related to the new system of wage and earnings control and the increased tax burdens. The forms introduced in 1985 to control earnings are not advantageous for labor-intensive activities. Recognition of this has induced a lot of cooperatives themselves into the small cooperative form. As has been mentioned, at the beginning of this year the corporation tax and the social insurance contribution of small ventures have been increased and a 10 percent surtax levied on the economic organizations purchasing from small ventures. The latter measure particularly reduces the competitiveness of small ventures, above all in such fields where the labor supply has kept pace with demand for labor. Therefore, a part of the specialized groups dissolved in order to avoid tax disadvantages although some of them reformed as small cooperatives.

V. EXPECTATIONS, REALITIES AND CONCLUSIONS

The small ventures started to evolve in a period of Hungarian economic development when many difficulties had to be faced. The rate of economic growth slowed down after 1979, and real wages have been decreasing for half a decade now. But some of the employees did not resign themselves to declining living standards and sought opportunities for earning additional income in the so-called second economy. The government recognized that for additional income earned through work done at the expense of leisure time additional performance can be won for the economy in bottleneck areas, above all in the fields of personal services and subcontracting. The legalization of the second economy was expected to include the accumulated savings of the population into the ''blood circulation'' of the economy, thus somewhat mitigating the disadvantages deriving from the lasting decline of investment. The small ventures were expected to revive competition and to mitigate price rises, at least in some areas. There also was an idea that in consequence of the decelerating economic growth, enterprises would make efforts to get rid of superfluous labor, and, understandably, of unskilled labor or that of people with low qualification, and that these would be absorbed by the developing small ventures. The relatively fast spread of small ventures has proven first of all that people have not lost their enterprising spirit and if they are given a chance that they can react with surprising rapidity.

About 340,000 people, that is more than 6.5 percent of the population of working age, participate in associations and small cooperatives. The growing number of small ventures and of people participating in them also are a yardstick of the confidence they place in economic policy.

The average annual income of members in associations excluding small cooperatives was Ft 42,375 in 1984. In addition to the members, these incomes influence the living standards of another 6–700,000 people. Thus, the associations influence decisively the living conditions of about one million people, or at least play an important role in them.

The development of small scale ventures is a large-scale social experiment that has proven that people's labor elan and creativity will evolve if the link between income and performance becomes direct and close, and also that labor intensity and productivity will grow significantly. The small ventures hold, so to say, a mirror to the large firms in that they prove that the organization of work based on direct interest and spontaneous activity may be on average of higher standards than to be found in enterprises operating in the traditional framework of work organization and interests. In this the voluntary discipline plays an important role. The first breach in the petrified enterprise organization structure was made by the intra-enterprise small ventures. Up to now, no persuasion, central decision or resolution could achieve as much in the loosening of the overcentralized and hierarchical enterprise organization systems as the small venture. The final consequences of this impact cannot yet be foreseen, but there can be no doubt that firms where EWEs are operating in relatively significant numbers were forced to introduce decentralization of varying degree in the decision, accounting, and motivation systems of the enterprise. It is a fact that, as a result of intrapreneurial ventures, the earlier hierarchical relations are gradually being replaced by relationships based on bargaining.

In certain fields, for example, construction designing and building, in computer technical and personal services and in the knitwear industry, the new forms of venture definitely strengthened competition and this has also had a moderating impact on price trends. The new organizations are build up on the basis of economic rationality. As a rule, combined work organizations have become established which resolve the rigid limits of specialization. These new organizations provide more favourable chances for the emergence of organizing and leading personalities and for the assertion of talents than the traditional enterprise organizations. From the viewpoint of ownership forms and enterprise size structure the new organizations diversify the socialist economy and strengthen market relations, first of all the markets for individual factors of production, especially for labor. From among the small organizations it is the small cooperatives, the independent economic workteams, as well as the contractual units and those specialized groups that can be considered to be true ventures, where the participating members undertake financial and existential risk.

Certain expectations towards the small organizations have now been met. What are these?

1.   A part of small ventures have not become autonomous market actors, but a considerable part of them have become built into the large-enterprise order, thus strengthening their autarkic nature. For the low-efficiency firms and those in the so-called crisis branches the EWEs are a form suitable for retaining their workforce. With this, the market pressure for the renewal of the production structure and for the elimination of uneconomical activities is weakened.

2.   Most of the new organizations do not mitigate shortages of consumer goods and services or in the subcontracting sphere, but they do help in exploiting the capacities of large firms. In choosing the field of operation the decision of the big firm giving the commission and the opportunity to realize income play a great role. It follows that the market-sensitivity of these new organizations is consequently highly differentiated.

3.   It seems to have been a naive idea that the new organizations would absorb the surplus labor released by the enterprises. As a matter of fact, in three years merely 30,000 people have left the socialist sector to become independent small entrepreneurs. Against expectations, primarily qualified employees have joined the small ventures and the consequence is that the less qualified labor becomes more valuable to large enterprises.

4.   The fact that the majority of associations are internal ventures allows enterprise managers to handle employees in a differentiated manner so as to make venturing possible for some workers and employees groups and to exclude others from this opportunity. This is indicated, for example, by the fact that in 30 percent of the firms none or only one or two small ventures are operating.[9]

5.   The hopes attached to the mobilization of savings by the population have been only partially realized. Although the capital of associations and small cooperatives doubled between 1983 and 1984, their total value is only Ft 13 billion. The financial contribution by members was Ft 770 million at the end of 1984.[10] The total contribution by members to an average association was about Ft 28 thousand.[11] Thus, today the population risks its own savings only to a small extent. The consequence is a preservation of the handicraft character of small-scale production and wasteful consumption. The basic cause of abstaining from investment is the frequent changing of economic regulators, and the confusion in the social judgement of rent-like incomes from invest-

ment. The small volume of members' wealth invested in the ventures, the relatively weak interest in property, and the legal over-regulation favor primarily those who seek opportunities for quick enrichment.

Experience shows that society and the institutional system have not been prepared adequately for the development of small ventures. This is indicated by the sometimes passionate debates about them. It is a fact that the introduction of ventures into the social fabric caused certain ideological disturbances. These bear a ghostlike resemblance to the ideological confusion produced at a previous time by the support given to the household-plot farms. Many people feel that values have been lost because accustomed career paths have become modified, egalitarianism has weakened, a greater mobility of labor and organizations may create greater instability etc. There also are people who point to the very high incomes of some individuals, generalize and claim that ventures are unfair trickeries and phenomena foreign to socialism. Thus, ventures and, in a wider sense, the economic reform, render certain values, earlier considered to be everlasting, anarchronistic, while they enrich the socialist system of values with new elements.

Ideological clarification is not promoted by the fact that the system of economic control and management gives the feeling sometimes of loosening, sometimes of tightening rules on small venture behavior. In this respect, the tax-raising package introduced in February 1985 can be justly criticized, particularly so the measure that levies a 10 percent surtax on enterprises which commission various small ventures, EWEs and specialized cooperative groups. This latter kind of tax also conflicts with the spirit of the Act on the Prohibition of Unfair Economic Activity. The last items of section (2) of paragraph 12 of this Act states: ''. . . the prohibition of restricting economic competition refers . . . to restricting the choice between sources of procurement and sales possibilities.'' Many managers consider the introduction of the surtax as a kind of signal and exhibit a cautious behavior towards small ventures. The impact of the criticisms levelled at the high incomes and of the ''income adjustment'' attainable though the higher taxes might be that small ventures submerge into the illegal sphere and the monopoly position of the remaining legal ones will be strengthened.

With regard to the political judgement of small ventures, a rather unambiguous situation has been brought about by the 13th Congress of the Hungarian Socialist Workers' Party. In its resolution a separate section is devoted to small ventures and, among other things, it is stated that: "Such complementary and auxiliary activites that fit into the system of socialist management will be supported also in the future."

It is a source of concern that the decisive majority of small organizations are not legal entities. It will be expedient to handle the EWE separately as a particular intra-enterprise collective undertaking. However, with market organizations, the establishment of a form of private association which prescribes the limited financial responsibility of members and which is a legal entity, ought to be considered. In such a form of organization the minimum of financial contribution could be prescribed; there would be a way to tax entrepreneurial and personal incomes in a differentiated manner; and settlement of the rules for liquidating such organizations could strengthen the investment propensity of potential investors and lenders. Such legislation is also needed because the majority of associations were founded by creative people willing to take risks, but who have no starting capital.[12] It is also desirable to consider the establishment of credit-granting, market research, management consultancy, accountancy advising organizations that would specialize in aiding small ventures.

Another source of the ideological and economic conflicts is the particular duality of the economy. That is, the socialist sector of decisively large-scale nature and the sector of small-scale plants and small ventures based either on collective or individual management are operating according to different principles and are regulated in different ways. This economic behavior, differing in nature, is of course also reflected in social relations, that is, in the system of social contacts of the two spheres. For example, the small organizations do not have a representation of interests of their own. Within the Chamber of Commerce a section for small business has been brought about but small entrepreneurs can only be members as individuals, as ventures they cannot become members of the Chamber. It follows that, up to now, no uniform representation of interests of small ventures has come about.

This duality of the Hungarian economy and, of course, the lack of resources is an explanation for the particular situation characterizing the relationship between the small ventures and the large firms. While the large firm is dependent, as has been shown, on the products and services of the small firms, it often also is at war with them, first of all for the factors of production, especially labor. The large company justly feels that in wage policy a socially sensitive field, it is at a disadvantage relative to the small ventures, while the small ventures justly protest that they are in a de facto disadvantageous situation in respect of material supply and credit conditions. It follows that in the contemporary Hungarian economy we can witness a curious competition mainly between the large firms and the small ventures, partly on the market for commodities and services, but first of all on that for resources.

The causes of the ideological confusion, and in a sense, also of the duality of the social system of values, and of the just criticisms of small ventures are mostly those indicated above. The key to a lasting solution may be found in a consistently implemented reform of the large-enterprise sphere, as a result of which the profit-motivated or self-governing socialist firm, operating as a venture sensitive to the market and costs, would become the basic unit of the economy, and shortage phenomena would cease.[13] This is a basic condition for the consolidation of the existence of small ventures, for transferring the intrafirm ventures in large enterprises to the regular hours of work, and for establishing smooth cooperation between large companies and small-scale businesses.

There also exists an opinion according to which it is sufficient to introduce the modern methods of capital allocation, institutional credit granting, government control with guaranties, etc., and then the small enterprise sphere can be made viable. It is my conviction that a reform restricted to the scope of small entrepreneurs, and leaving the sphere of large firms, which basically determines the nature of the economic environment, intact, would offer no solution. In my judgment, the negative features of the present situation are natural concomitants of a huge social experiment pointing to a progressive direction. This process started in 1982, without antecendents and experience, and nobody foresaw the new opportunities and contradictions arising from the appearance of small ventures. The dialectics of development will open the way for wide economic and institutional reform and not for retrograde forces. In contrast to the problems mentioned above, there is a lasting process that can be characterized by the development of entrepreneurship and entrepreneurial organizations consistent with the socialist system.

NOTES

1.   The enterprise economic workteam is similar to but for reasons to be explained, not identical with the western intra-preneurial group. It is a subtype of the economic workteams discussed below.

2.   The taxation rules entering into force in January 1985 are valid for all small ventures.

3.   By small organization or small venture is meant henceforth the small cooperative, the specialized industrial and service cooperative group, the economic workteam in enterprises and the private economic workteam. The latter three are associations that are not legal entities.

4.   Laky, Terez: Enterprise business work partnership and enterprise interest.

5.   It is to be noted that it was the difference between the "soft" and the "hard" forint that stimulated many agricultural cooperatives to transform their complementary activities into specialized industrial and service groups.

6.   Laky: ibid.

7.   *Ipari Zsebkonyv (Industrial Pocket Book),* Central Statistical Office, Budapest, 1980, and *Magyar Statisztikai Zsebkonyv* (Hungarian Statistical Pocket Book), Central Statistical Office, Budapest, 1984 and 1985.

8.   From this viewpoint the situation was more favourable in the agricultural, sales and consumers cooperatives, because they already possessed some experience with ventures.

9.   A nem jogi szemelyisegu tarsasagok tevekenysegenek elemzese/ Analysis of the activity of associations which are not legal entities/, PM Ellenorzesi Foigazgatosag/ Head Office of Financial Auditing, Ministry of Finance/, Budapest, 1985.

10.   The data only refer to associations.

11.   Ibid.

12.   The majority of people in household plots and complementary farms, private craftsmen and retail dealers as well as of EWE members are elderly people.

13.   Gabor, R. Istvan: Masodik gazdasag: a magyar tapasztalatok altalanosithatonak tuno tanulsaga/ The second economy: lessons of the Hungarian experiences that seem liable to generalizations/, *Valosag,* No. 2. 1985.

ENTERPRISE SIZE, BEHAVIOR AND PERFORMANCE IN THE REFORMED HUNGARIAN ECONOMY

Leyla Woods

I. INTRODUCTION

This paper examines some of the characteristics and consequences of the size structure of Hungarian industry. The discussion focuses on state-owned industry, and on the larger industrial enterprises in particular, for several reasons. In 1982, state industry accounted for 84 percent of total industrial employment, 97 percent of gross fixed assets employed in industry, and 93 percent of industrial production (1982 Statistical Yearbook), so the performance of this sector is of decisive importance to the performance of the Hungarian economy as a whole.

The behavior and performance of large industrial firms under the New Economic Mechanism (NEM) has attracted considerable attention in both academic and official circles in Hungary. Economists have argued that excessive concentration in Hungarian industry constitutes a significant obstacle to the successful implementation of economic re-

form. The concentration of production and employment in large enterprises and the relative scarcity of small and medium-sized firms has
endowed many large firms with monopolistic or quasi-monopolistic
status; impeded the development of a "background industry" of subcontractors and specialized firms; restricted domestic competition in
all but a few sectors; encouraged the resumption of bargaining over
regulations and state financial aid between large enterprises and central
agencies; and reduced the flexibility and innovative capabilities of
Hungarian industry. Some observers have even asserted that most
large enterprises are of necessity anti-reform and have informally exerted their considerable influence to obstruct or undermine the reforms.[1] Official concern with the bargaining, inflexibility, and other
undesirable consequences of the predominance of large firms in Hungarian industry has led to a number of measures to ameliorate the
problem, including the consolidation of the industrial branch ministries
into a unified Ministry of Industry, the breakup of larger firms and
trusts, and the adoption of new regulations to encourage the creation of
small firms and the establishment of subsidiary and joint enterprises.

The paper is organized as follows. Section II reviews the evolution
of the state industrial structure. Section III considers the motivations
and objectives of central actors and enterprise managers. On the basis
of the preceding discussion, Section IV provides a stylized description
of size-related enterprise behavior and hypotheses about consequent
enterprise performance. These hypotheses are empirically tested in
Section V. Section VI presents the conclusions of the paper, indicates
the direction of future research, and offers some further considerations.

II. EVOLUTION OF THE INDUSTRIAL
STRUCTURE

Prior to the nationalizations of 1948–49, Hungarian industry exhibited
a dualistic structure characteristic of many late-industrializing countries. Over 50 percent of the industrial firms were very small, employing fewer than 20 workers, but the few largest firms accounted for
about half of the total labor and capital employed in industry.[2] Industrial concentration ratios in Hungary in the interwar period were among
the highest in the world (Schweitzer, 1982). Furthermore, average
establishment size was fairly large compared to establishments in other
industrialized and industrializing countries.

The major effect of the nationalizations in 1948–49 was to increase greatly the number of medium-sized and larger industrial firms and to reduce substantially the total number of firms.[3] This was accomplished primarily by merging the smaller firms, although in a few cases some units of large industrial complexes, such as the Ganz and Csepel works, were split off to form independent enterprises (Schweitzer, 1982). Some "experimental" mergers during the 1950s further reduced the number of industrial enterprises, from 1632 in 1949 to 1309 in 1961. During the 1950s, the average size of establishments also increased considerably (Erlich et al.).

The second major merger wave occurred in 1962–64, decreasing the number of state industrial enterprises to 853 by 1964. These enterprise consolidations were predominantly horizontal, amalgamating enterprises in the same sector or subsector. Some enterprise mergers, however, were based on vertical integration, geographical proximity, or the ability of the enterprise directors and deputy directors affected by the mergers to get along with each other. Additional mergers brought the number of state industrial enterprises to 811 by 1968. Average establishment size continued to grow during this period, as did the number of establishments per enterprise.

The motive for the 1962–64 enterprise mergers was the improvement of central direction and control. Enterprise consolidations were expected to improve directive planning by allowing a reduction in the number of bureaucratic layers between central planners and enterprise managers, and by ameliorating problems of coordination between firms in the same sector or in a vertical relationship. The monopoly or quasi-monopoly positions acquired by many large firms as a result of the amalgamations were also expected to improve industrial operation since the managers of monopolistic firms now faced the full demand curve and could vary their production in accordance with the demands of all consumers. Many large enterprises were in fact designated as "responsible for supply" in their particular sector.[4]

Whatever the perceived or actual benefit of a highly concentrated industrial structure in a directive planning system, many economists have pointed out that such a structure is extremely ill-suited to the needs of a reformed market-oriented economic system that relies on domestic competition and flexible enterprise response to changing market conditions. Bauer offers a contrasting view: the enterprise amalgamations of 1962–64 were undertaken with an eye to subsequent economic reform in which the economy would be managed without either plan directives or a self-regulating market. Instead, economic management would be based on a consensus between central agencies and enterprises charged with "responsibility for supply" (Bauer).[5] Similarly, Kornai has characterized the reformed Hungarian economy as a vegetative system in which extensive redistribution of enterprise profits is used to maintain the existing structure of enterprises and production (Kornai).

Establishment size and distribution were affected not only by the merger waves, but by other policies as well. In the 1950s, new establishments were created or existing small factories expanded in smaller towns and villages to utilize local labor and raw materials in pursuit of extensive and rapid industrialization and full employment. As new, and usually very large, heavy industrial plants were built in small towns, local light industry and handicrafts establishments were created or expanded to employ the wives of the men who worked in nearby heavy industry. In the 1960s, enterprises were encouraged to shift their operations to the provinces in an effort to reduce industrial concentration in Budapest. After the mid-1960s, enterprises themselves sought to shift their production out of Budapest in response to growing labor shortages in the capital.[6]

Enterprise managers in the 1980s have inherited the unwieldy industrial structure developed in preceding decades. For the largest enterprises, this entails a large number of establishments. The establishments themselves are large and often geographically distant from headquarters and the other establishments.[7] Efforts to rationalize and consolidate production are often stymied by labor shortages and difficulties in raising the investment funding necessary to build and equip a new factory.[8]

Another inherited problem confronting enterprise managers is the over-diversification of production.[9] Hungarian firms exhibit very high levels of both vertical and horizontal diversification. In a study of diversification in state manufacturing firms, Bago found that, on average, 56 percent of enterprise employees worked in activities outside the firm's main line of business.[10] Of this 56 percent, 48 percent worked in areas related to the main line of business and 52 percent in activities in another industrial branch. High levels of diversification are also characteristic of establishments. Most of the production outside the firms main sector of activity is devoted to in-house production of direct and indirect inputs for the firm's main product lines. This vertical diversification is often the result of supply difficulties traceable to the lack of a domestic "background industry" of subcontractors and small specialized firms; continuing shortage conditions, which make suppliers unresponsive to buyers' demands; and the delivery, quality, and specification problems frequently encountered in regard to inputs or machinery imported from other CMEA countries. The significant horizontal integration is the consequence of the earlier merger waves as well as more recent enterprise decisions to begin manufacturing new products in order to keep labor and capital employed despite a fall in demand for the enterprise's traditional products.[11]

III. OBJECTIVES OF MANAGERS AND CENTRAL AGENCIES

Rationalization of the Hungarian production structure is impeded not only by "market" factors such as labor shortages and the lack of alternative sources of production inputs, but also by the conflicting objectives of the central agencies and enterprise managers. In consonance with the aims of the NEM, the center generally wants enterprises to adjust their product mix and marketing patterns and work with the greatest possible efficiency in order to maximize enterprise profits. More specific central objectives sometimes conflict with the profit maximizing objective. The central agencies are committed to maintaining the availability of certain kinds and classes of consumer goods. If these goods cannot be imported, Hungarian firms must produce them, even if this production is relatively or absolutely unprofitable. Similarly, unprofitable production for hard currency and CMEA export must be continued. Hungarian firms must also accept CMEA imports of intermediate goods and machinery, even if these goods are less suitable than domestic or western products.

One can imagine central agencies putting pressure on enterprises to accede to these profit-reducing requests or offering them financial inducements or recompense to agree with central desires. These interactions would involve the larger firms, since it is easier to deal with one or two large firms than with several small ones and only larger firms would have the capacity to fulfill central objectives and commitments. It is more likely, however, that large enterprises usually anticipate the central agencies' wishes.[12] Large enterprises' willingness to change or maintain their production and marketing patterns, even at the cost of foregone profits, in accordance with central desires can be ascribed to several factors. If enterprise acquiescence to central agencies' desires leads to the brink of bankruptcy, the enterprise can count on central rescue.[13] Short of this stage, the enterprise's contribution to the fulfillment of central objectives can be used as a bargaining chip to induce central agencies to give the enterprise additional financial aid or exempt it from some binding regulation. Other large enterprise bargaining chips include the threat of unemployment of the enterprise's large workforce, the cessation of vital production, the low prices the enterprise is compelled to set for its products, and central agencies' partial responsibility for past investments, if these have contributed to present problems. Until recently, the Ministry of Industry appointed, dismissed, set the salaries, and determined the bonuses of the enterprise director and his two or three top deputies, so the director's salary and career prospects depended on his fulfillment, and preferably anticipation, of ministerial objectives.

Managers' decisions to maintain less profitable production and marketing patterns are the result not only of managers' efforts to satisfy ministerial superiors and maintain the regard of central agencies, but also of the managers' internalization of the goals and outlook of central actors (Szalai, 1981). This internalization of the central outlook is the cornerstone of "consensus management" (Bauer) based on the "system of responsibility for supply" (Schweitzer, 1981). The identity of outlook is reinforced by three factors: managers' previous experience working in central agencies, ministries, and the Party apparatus (Angyal); managers' relatively long tenure at their present enterprises (Granick, Laky, Hethy); and the ideological and social commitments implied by managers' membership in the Party (Angyal).

IV. STYLIZED DESCRIPTION AND PREDICTIONS

The considerations reviewed above and the discussions in the Hungarian economic literature lead to the following hypotheses regarding enterprise behavior and performance. Larger enterprises are likely to be less profitable than smaller firms for several reasons. First, large enterprise size and the large size and number of its constituent establishments lead to diseconomies of scale in coordination and administration. Secondly, larger enterprises' efforts to fulfill central and ministerial objectives lead to the maintenance of relatively or absolutely unprofitable lines of production. Through bargaining with central agencies, on the basis of the enterprises' employment, vital exports, fulfillment of central objectives, or other characteristics, larger enterprises receive proportionately higher subsidies and pay proportionately lower taxes than do smaller firms. As a result of past bargaining with central agencies, larger enterprises enjoy preferential access to investment allocations, so they tend to be more capital intensive than smaller enterprises. Despite this higher capital intensity, the difficulties of managing large and complex enterprises and the decisions to maintain unprofitable production lead to lower labor productivity in larger firms. Larger enterprises also tend to pay higher wages (Szalai, 1982) and face more stringent price controls (Szalai, 1982), Angyal, author's interviews) that, ceteris paribus, also lead to lower profitability. Finally, larger enterprises may be less profitable than smaller ones because, knowing that the center will bail them out of any difficulties, they do not try as hard or because managers devote more time and effort to bargaining than to improving enterprise product mix, efficiency, and marketing.

By contrast, smaller firms lack access to the ear and the pocket of the center, so they are forced to modify their product mix and marketing strategies in response to market forces and to work as efficiently as possible in pursuit of profit maximization. Unlike larger firms, they are subject to less central interference, overt or implicit, in their production decisions, so they can respond more readily than larger firms to the imperatives of the market.

V. EMPIRICAL RESULTS

Several least squares regressions were used in an initial assessment of the empirical evidence for the above hypotheses in three industrial sectors. The sectors were analyzed separately and as a pooled group. In the pooled sample, the observations for each sector were standardized by dividing each observed value by the average sectoral value of the variable over the 1980–82 period. Despite this standardization procedure, the larger enterprises in different sectors may not be really comparable because a larger enterprise's bargaining power is probably at least partly dependent on its sectoral affiliation.

The observations are drawn from a set of annual statistics for the three year period 1980–82. The data set covers only the state firms under the direct supervision of the Ministry of Industry. The sample thus includes 8 of the 11 state-owned aluminum metallurgy firms, 13 of the 16 state-owned telecommunications and vacuum technology firms, and 11 of the 25 state-owned apparel firms. In addition to the ministerially supervised firms, there were 3 local council supervised firms and 1 cooperative in aluminum metallurgy, 3 local council and 6

Table 1. Regression Results for Individual Industrial
Sectors and Pooled Sectors
(t statistic in parentheses)

	Apparel		Telecommunications and Vacuum Technology	
	Const.	Firm Size	Const.	Firm Size
Dependent Variable:				
Profitability	0.18	$-2.65(10^{-5})$**	0.13	$-2.83(10^{-6})$**
	(12.49)	(−5.45)	(10.46)	(−2.49)
Profit Adjustment	−3.36	0.002**	0.07	$-1.17(10^{-5})$
	(−1.15)	(2.54)	(1.50)	(−2.71)
Budget Subventions	−0.68	0.0001	−0.75	$-1.55(10^{-5})$
	(−2.58)	(1.67)	(−4.56)	(−1.00)
Labor Productivity	101.46	−0.009**	137.54	−0.0001
	(15.98)	(−4.34)	(16.31)	(−0.15)
Assets per Worker	91.14	−0.004	225.69	−0.0006
	(13.35)	(−1.69)	(11.02)	(−0.33)
Worker Income	3536.21	0.03	4141.59	−0.0004
	(47.37)	(1.27)	(42.66)	(−0.04)

	Const.	Firm Size	Assets per Worker	Const.	Firm Size	Assets per Worker
Labor Productivity	72.76 (4.61)	−0.008** (−3.77)	0.31* (1.97)	113.68 (6.65)	$-5.36(10^{-5})$ (−0.07)	0.11 (1.59)

	Aluminum Metallurgy		Apparel, Telecommunications and Aluminum (Pooled)	
	Const.	Firm Size	Const.	Firm Size
Dependent Variable:				
Profitability	5.78	−0.0005	1.23	−0.23*
	(1.91)	(−0.37)	(8.52)	(−2.10)
Profit Adjustment (Telec. & Appar. only)	N.A.	N.A.	−5.49	6.49**
			(−2.23)	(3.60)
Budget Subventions	−1.29	0.0003	1.15	−0.15
	(−2.32)	(1.09)	(4.16)	(−0.70)
Labor Productivity	223.45	−0.005	1.04	−0.04
	(3.62)	(−0.17)	(14.90)	(−0.81)
Assets per Worker	671.35	0.23**	0.97	0.03
	(6.11)	(4.27)	(17.55)	(0.70)
Worker Income	5648.73	−0.13	1.00	−0.005
	(33.21)	(−1.60)	(73.50)	(−0.44)

	Const.	Firm Size	Assets per Worker	Const.	Firm Size	Assets per Worker
Labor Productivity	251.78 (2.43)	0.005 (0.11)	−0.04 (−0.35)	0.92 (6.35)	−0.05 (−0.88)	0.13 (0.98)

(continued)

Table 1. (*Continued*)

Notes: ** indicates significance at the 1 percent level.
* indicates significance at the 5 percent level.

Number of observations in each sample:

Apparel	33 observations
Telecommunications and vacuum technology	39 observations
Aluminum metallurgy	24 observations
Pooled sample	96 observations

Definitions: Gross adjusted profits = profits inclusive of all firm payments to the state budget and all state budget subventions to the firm.

Balance sheet profits = profits inclusive of normative firm payments to the state budget and normative state budget subventions to the firm, but exclusive of non-normative firm payments to the budget and non-normative budget subventions.

Profitability = gross adjusted profits/net sales receipts.

Profit adjustment = (gross adjusted profits − balance sheet profits)/ gross adjusted profits.

Budget subventions = (normative budget subventions to the firm − normative firm payments to the budget)/gross adjusted profit.

Labor productivity = net output/total number of workers.

Assets per worker = year-end gross value of firm assets/number of workers.

Worker income = average monthly income of all workers.

cooperative firms in telecommunications and vacuum technology, and 11 local council firms, 2 firms supervised by the Ministry of Justice, and 97 cooperatives in the apparel industry. The annual statistics, taken directly from the enterprises' balance sheets, are routinely reported to the Ministry of Industry.

In the regressions, employment was chosen as the most satisfactory measure of firm size. Net sales receipts and gross or net assets are both subject to ambiguities due to price regulations and the methods used to value and depreciate fixed assets. However, all the measures of firm size are highly correlated. The regressions are based on pooled cross section data, with separate observations for every firm in each of the three years.

Table 1 presents the statistical results. The regression results indicate that the smaller firms tend to be more profitable than larger ones, at least in the apparel and telecommunications industries. (The aluminum metallurgy firms are part of a trust, which may affect the profitability-size relationship in this sector.)

However, several of the ancillary hypotheses discussed above are not supported by the results. Budget subventions are the sum of normative state budget support for the firm and normative firm payments to the state budget. Here, there is little evidence that larger firms receive preferential state treatment. The profit adjustment indicates the extent of non-normative state additions to or subtractions from firm profits, after normative budget payments and receipts. Although the coefficient of size for apparel firms is significant, indicating that larger apparel firms benefit more than smaller apparel firms from non-normative central financial aid, the sign of the coefficient is wrong for the telecommunications sector. The labor productivity variable has the right sign for all three sectors and the pooled sample—indicating higher labor productivity in smaller firms—but is significant only for the apparel sector. Capital intensity—measured by assets per worker—tends to be higher for larger firms in the aluminum metallurgy industry; for the other two sectors, the assets per worker variable is negatively related to firm size. There is no evidence that monthly incomes of workers are higher in larger firms. Holding assets constant did not improve the relationship between firm size and labor productivity.

VI. CONCLUSIONS AND SOME FURTHER CONSIDERATIONS

The regression results for the three industrial sectors analyzed above either fail to provide evidence for—or contradict—some of the hypotheses about the relationships between the size and the behavior and performance of state owned firms. Only the inverse relationship between enterprise size and profitability seems to hold across all three sectors. The results for the apparel firms provide more evidence for the hypotheses than do the results for the other two sectors. In the future, other statistical tests will be used and the study will be extended to other industrial sectors to see whether these preliminary results are indicative of Hungarian state owned industry as a whole. Further work will also be needed to determine why the results reported here apparently diverge from empirical evidence reported elsewhere (Fenyovari, Csanadi, and Szalai, 1982) that indicates support for the hypotheses on enterprise size and performance.

Another problem for future study is why some larger firms exhibit good performance, at least relative to the smaller firms in their sector. Possible reasons for good performance by a larger firm include: successful implementation of previous investments; good use of western licenses and cooperation with western firms; outstanding management; and luck in the form of the fortunate circumstance that goods already produced by the firm are in demand and fetch good prices on western markets or in CMEA trade.

With regard to the future performance of a few of the smaller and many of the larger firms, a number of questions arise. Production profiles can be streamlined and the diseconomies resulting from horizontal overdiversification reduced only if alternative sources of supply can be found or if the central agencies are willing to countenance some disruption in supply and reductions in the range of goods available domestically. If central agencies are unwilling to relax their commitment to the maintenance of present levels of domestic supply, larger firms cannot drop their unprofitable production lines unless similar goods are imported from the west or from CMEA countries or manufactured by new small Hungarian firms. These alternative sources of supply are all problematic: Hungarian hard currency indebtedness precludes any significant increase in western imports in the near term; comparable goods may not be available in other CMEA countries; and new small firms' assumption of the production of the goods depends on the future development of this still very limited sector and the foreseeable profitability of this production.

The recent spinoff of some productive units into independent firms and the splitting up of some large enterprises and trusts has certainly helped to reduce overdiversification at the enterprise level. It remains to be seen whether these two processes and the creation of new small firms and subsidiaries will have any effect on diversification in production at the establishment level.

Reducing vertical overdiversification also presents problems. It will be difficult to break up firms whose establishments are vertically integrated and to reduce establishment level diversification unless the shortage and cooperation problems which induced this diversification are also solved.

Finally, the experience of public enterprise in West European countries is instructive. Several economists have pointed out that these public enterprises can be expected to operate efficiently only if a number of conditions are fulfilled. The conditions include the presence of strong domestic or international competition; a clear understanding that the state will not be the rescuer of last resort, so there is a real threat of extinction; the independence of public enterprises and their freedom from direct governmental or ministerial supervision, aside from regular government audits; subsidization that is not open-ended, but instead clearly set to cover the extra costs of the enterprises' social tasks; and a comprehensive and unambiguous statement or ranking of the objectives and tasks of the enterprise according to which its performance will be judged and its managers rewarded. At present, none of these conditions prevail in Hungary, and the achievement of any one of them is likely to prove very difficult.

NOTES

1. See for example Hegedus (1984a), Szalai (1982) and Szalai (1984).

2. For example, in 1938 firms employing fewer than 20 workers accounted for 53.4 percent of industrial firms; firms employing 50 workers or fewer accounted for 76.2 percent of all industrial firms (Schweitzer, 1982, p. 30). There are no comprehensive data on firm size in interwar Hungary, but the concentration of production in large firms can be inferred from the data on establishments. Out of a total of 3000 establishments, the 100 largest accounted for 43 percent of the labor and 52 percent of the machinery employed in industry (Berend and Ranki, p. 311). Also see Erlich et al.

3. Between 1938 and 1949, the percentage of firms employing fewer than 50 workers fell from 76.2 to 49.6. Firms employing 51–100 workers accounted for 10.9 percent of all firms in 1938 and 13.3 percent of firms in 1949; firms employing 101–500 workers accounted for 10.1 percent and 26.5 percent of all firms in 1938 and 1949, respectively. The proportion of large firms (over 500 workers) rose from 2.8 percent in 1938 to 10.6 percent in 1949. The total number of industrial firms fell from 3911 in 1938 to 1632 in 1949 (Schweitzer, 1982, p. 30).

4. See, for example, Schweitzer (1981 and 1982) and Szalai (1982).

5. French planners also preferred to work with highly concentrated sectors. Mutual coordination and bargaining were feasible only in sectors where the top 20 percent of firms accounted for 80 percent of output, and the planners needed to deal only with a few directors of the largest firms.

6. Most enterprises expanded their provincial workforces by expanding existing establishments or creating new factories rather than by taking over smaller provincial enterprises. As Laki's thorough description of the merger patterns between 1971 and 1979 shows, comparatively few mergers occurred among enterprises in different counties.

7. For example, in 1970 the average state firm in light industry encompassed 4.16 establishments, compared to 1.10 establishments per firm in Switzerland (1965 data), 1.18 establishments per firm in West Germany (1967 data), and 1.46 establishments per firm in the United Kingdom. In heavy industry, Hungarian state firms had an average of 7 establishments, compared to 1.12 establishments per firm in Switzerland, 1.20 in West Germany, and 1.51 in the United Kingdom. The average size of establishments in state industry ranged from 3424 workers employed per establishment in ferrous metallurgy (compared to an average employment of 192 in Switzerland and 662 in France) to 579 employees per establishment in woodworking (compared to averages of 30 workers per establishment in Switzerland and 40 in France) (Erlich et al., pp. 126-139). Also see Bago.

8. Such labor and capital problems are not unique to Hungary: analogous considerations have also contributed to the preservation of multi-plant organization in American and West European firms (Scherer et al.).

9. Out of the 398 state manufacturing enterprises in 1981, only 54 (13.6 percent)

specialized entirely in one industrial subsector. By contrast, 84 enterprises (21.1 percent) worked in 6–10 subsectors and 27 enterprises (6.8 percent) worked in 10 or more subsectors (Bago, p. 695).

10. By contrast, a study of U.S. firms in 1972 shows that only 33 percent of the total operating employment of manufacturing firms worked in areas outside the firms' primary industry category (Scherer, pp. 75–76). The results of the U.S. study and Bago's analysis are not strictly comparable since Bago's analysis covers only state-owned industrial firms and excludes the food products industry while the U.S. study covers all U.S. manufacturing firms. In addition, Bago's analysis divides enterprise and establishment employment into 247 subcategories of industrial production while the U.S. study distributes firm employment among 207 subcategories covering manufacturing, mining, construction, trade, and services.

11. On this latter point, see Laki (1984).

12. See for example Szalai (1981) and Laky.

13. Actually, small enterprises may be liquidated or merged with other firms, but large enterprises are always rescued.

REFERENCES

Angyal, Adam. "A nagyvallalat szindroma." *Kozgazdasagi Szemle,* 1984, 5. sz.

Apro, Eva. "Kollektiv felelosseg vagy kollektiv bunbak?" *Kozgazdasagi Szemle,* 1984, 5. sz.

Bago, Eszter. "Specializacio es diverzifikacio iparunkban." *Kozgazdasagi Szemle,* 1984, 6. sz.

Bakos, Zsigmond. "Megjegyzesek Hegedus Andras A nagyvallalatok es a szocializmus' cimu gondolataihoz'." *Kozgazdasagi Szemle,* 1984, 3. sz.

Bauer, Tamas. "The Contradictory Position of the Enterprise Under the New Hungarian Economic Mechanism." *Eastern European Economics,* Fall 1976.

Bauer, Tamas. "The Second Economic Reform and Ownership Relations." *Eastern European Economics,* Spring-Summer 1984.

Baumol, William, ed. *Public and Private Enterprise in a Mixed Economy.* London and Basingstoke: Macmillam Press, 1980.

Berend, Ivan and Gyorgy Ranki. *Economic Development in East-Central Europe in the 19th and 20th Centuries.* New York and London: Columbia University Press, 1974.

Csanadine, Demeter Maria. "A vallalatnagysag, a jovedelmezoseg es a preferenciak nehany osszefuggese." *Penzugyi Szemle,* 1979, 2. sz.

Erlich, Eva et al. *Establishment and Enterprise Size in Manufacturing: an East-West International Comparison.* Vienna: The Vienna Institute for Comparative Economic Studies, June 1982.

Fenyovari, Istvan. "Vallalatnagysag es jovedelmezoseg az iparban." *Penzugyi Szemle,* 1982, 5. sz.

Hegedus, Andras. "A nagyvallalatok es a szocializmus." *Kozgazdasagi Szemle,* 1984a, 1 sz.

Hegedus, Andras. "Megvalaszolasra varo kerdesek." *Kozgazdasagi Szemle,* 1984b, 9. sz.

Hegedus, Zsuzsa and Marton Tardos. "Some Problems Concerning the Role and

Motivation of Enterprise Executives." *Eastern European Economics*, Winter 1974–75.

Hethy, L. "Selection of Enterprise Executives in Hungary: A Case Study." *Acta Oeconomica*, 1979, Vol. 22, nos. 3–4.

Hoch, Robert. "A maxi es a mini." *Kozgazdasagi Szemle*, 1984, 9. sz.

Kornai, Janos. *Economics of Shortage*. Amsterdam, New York and Oxford: North Holland Publishing Company, 1980.

Laki, M. "Liquidation and Merger in the Hungarian Industry." *Acta Oeconomica*, 1982, Vol. 28, nos. 1–2.

Laki, M. "The Enterprise Crisis." *Acta Oeconomica*, 1984, vol. 32, nos. 1–2.

Laky, T. "Attachment to the Enterprise in Hungary." *Acta Oeconomica*, 1976, vol. 17, nos. 3–4.

Laky, T. "Enterprises in Bargaining Position." *Acta Oeconomica*, 1979, vol. 22, nos. 3–4.

Milanovics, Szvetozar. "A (nagy-)vallalatok es a szocializmus." *Kozgazdasagi Szemle*, 1984, 3. sz.

Peto, Marton. "Az alacsony es a magas jovedelmezosegu iparvallalatokrol." *Kozgazdasagi Szemle*, 1984, 6. sz.

Pryor, Frederic. *Property and Industrial Organization in Communist and Capitalist Nations*. Bloomington and London: Indiana University Press, 1973.

Revesz, G. "Enterprise and Plant Size Structure of the Hungarian Industry." *Acta Oeconomica*, 1979, vol. 22, nos. 1–2.

Scherer, F. M. *Industrial Market Structure and Economic Performance*. 2nd ed. Chicago: Rand McNally College Publishing Company, 1980.

Scherer, F. M. et al. *The Economics of Multi-Plant Operation*. Cambridge, Massachusetts, and London: Harvard University Press, 1975.

Schweitzer, I. "Some Interrelations Between Enterprise Organization and the Economic Mechanism in Hungary." *Acta Oeconomica*, 1981, vol. 27, nos. 3–4.

Schweitzer, Ivan. *A vallalatnagysag*. Budapest: Kozgazdasagi es Jogi Konyvkiado, 1982.

Szalai, Erzsebet. *Kiemelt vallalat—beruhazas—erdek*. Budapest: Akademiai Kiado, 1981.

Szalai, Erzsebet. "A reformfolyamat uj szakasza es a nagyvallalatok." *Valosag*, 1982, 5. sz.

Szalai, Erzsebet. "A reformellenesseg strukturalis okai." *Kozgazdasagi Szemle*, 1984, 9. sz.

THE DIFFUSION OF NUMERICALLY CONTROLLED MACHINE TOOLS IN HUNGARY

Steven W. Popper

A major object of the reforms introduced in Hungary beginning in 1968 was to increase the efficiency of production at the level of the enterprise. In particular, the drafters of the reforms hoped to resolve the problems that tended to retard innovation and the introduction of new technology (Friss, 1969). The principal means of effecting change was to devolve a greater share of economic decisionmaking upon the enterprises themselves. This paper is part of a larger project seeking to ascertain through case studies of diffusion of process innovations the extent to which the post-1968 system of economic regulation has affected the pace of technological change in several branches of the Hungarian economy. The emphasis is upon the balance of forces affecting the decision of an individual enterprise when deciding whether to adopt a newly available process technology.

The first section will present the historical evidence on the diffusion of numerically controlled machine tools (NCMTs) and compare the Hungarian experience with that of other countries. The two following sections will first consider institutional arrangements serving to reduce the willingness of the individual firm to adopt NCMTs, and second, review factors related to the internal constitution of the enterprise that would lead to disappointing results in the use of NCMTs that could in turn have a great effect upon the overall pace of diffusion. The final section is based upon data collected from fifty enterprises responding to a questionnaire survey sent out to eight-five firms identified as users of NCMTs. Though preliminary in nature, these findings provide some insight into several of the points raised in the paper.[1]

I. THE HISTORICAL RECORD

The diffusion of NC technology in Hungary was affected in its early stages by the decision taken in the late 1950s that the country was not to merely consume, but to be a producer of NCMTs as well.[2] Experiments with numerical control were conducted in several enterprise research departments and institutes under the auspices of a central program pursued jointly by the old KGM (*Kohaszat es Gepipari Miniszterium*) the Ministry for Machine-building and Metallurgy, and the OMFB (*Orszagos Muszaki Fejlesztesi Bizottsag*) the National Committee for Technical Development. The first NCMT used in production was not obtained by Hungary until 1964 and was imported from Switzerland (SPE, 1982). Through the end of 1971 there were only eleven NCMTs operating in Hungary. Five were of Western origin, five were various domestically produced prototypes, and one was imported from Czechoslovakia. The majority of these were used by the plants directly involved in the attempt to develop a local NCMT capability, although two NC lathes with Hungarian control systems were installed in a large state enterprise in the electrical equipment sub-branch in 1969. For the present purpose, the date 1966 is taken as that best serving to mark the first commercial adoption of NC technology in Hungary since the machine introduced in 1964 was most likely intended to serve the purpose of facilitating reverse engineering. The machines that began to be purchased in 1966, however, were placed in a facility designed to test the application of NC technology to production. This date represents a lag of 11 years from the first introduction by the innovating country, the United States. This may be compared with lags in the United Kingdom of one year, France, two years, Sweden, three years, Italy, five years, West Germany, seven years, and Austria, eight years (Nabseth and Ray, 1974). The USSR and Czechoslovakia first showed domestic NCMT prototypes at international trade fairs after lags of three and four years respectively (Amann, Cooper, Davies, 1977). These, therefore, are probably close to the actual dates for lags in first use.

The data on the membership of the SPE, the Machine Tool Programming Association (*Szerszamgep Programazasi Egyesules*), a voluntary association of virtually all industrial enterprises as well as research and instructional institutions that utilize NCMTs, indicate 912 NCMTs having been installed from 1964 until the end of the first quarter, 1984. Of these, 34 were emplaced in research or instructional institutions, and another 32 had either been decommissioned or else transferred to organizations outside the purview of the SPE source material. The number of NCMTs covered by the SPE sources in use in Hungarian industry in early 1984 was, therefore, 846. Table 1 indicates the yearly gross increment to the NCMT stock by area of origin. The data indi-

Table 1.   Gross Addition to NCMT Stock by Year
(number of machines)

Year	All NCMTs	NCMTs Used in Industry[b]			
		Total	By Origin		
			Hungary	CMEA	West
1964	1	1	0	0	1
1966	1	1	1	0	0
1967	4	4	0	0	4
1969	2	2	2	0	0
1970	2	1	1	0	0
1971	1	1	0	1	0
1972	11	11	4	1	6
1973	15	13	4	1	8
1974	26	25	6	8	11
1975	48	48	14	19	15
1976	42	41	9	20	12
1977	67	64	16	19	29
1978	101	97	17	22	58
1979	81	79	41	10	28
1980	105	98	42	9	47
1981	164	161	107	16	38
1982	119	111	77	11	23
1983	77	75	45	13	17
1984[a]	45	45	32	10	3
Totals	912	878	418	160	300

[a]   First four months only
[b]   Excludes NCMTs in educational and non-production entities
Source: SPE data

cate that the initial period of diffusion was quite drawn out and only gradually developed momentum. The peak year for NCMT acquisition was 1981 with subsequent additions to the national stock decreasing in the following years.

As noted above, certain central organs played a large role in encouraging the development of a domestic NCMT industry. It was recognized that in the absence of a significant level of domestic use, the local manufacture of NC equipment and its subsequent export would be severely handicapped through an inability to obtain sufficient information on practical applications. Thus the KGM-OMFB program (and particularly those aspects administered by the OMFB) addressed itself, in part, to increasing the rate of diffusion of NCMTs in Hungary. The aid actually extended may be characterized as being of two types: direct financial assistance to enterprises to aid in the acquisition of NCMTs, and investment in central programs of education and service (particularly with respect to control programming) in order to reduce the threshold of sophistication required by a firm considering the installation of this technology. The former characterized the first period of NCMT diffusion, from 1972 through 1975. This was effected through a competition for central development monies which were available on favorable terms. The KGM and OMFB undertook to cover half of the purchase price of machines by enterprises. Of this aid, 60 percent was to be repaid to the central organs by 1980. Eventually, ten of nineteen enterprises which applied to the competition were chosen to be recipients of the aid (83–11NP).[3] However, during this period approximately thirty enterprises installed their first NCMT. The program itself affected the financing of only 55 percent of the NCMTs installed during this period.

In the second phase of development, from 1976 onward, it was felt that such direct aid was not the most productive program and instead efforts were shifted to establishing a satisfactory service and education background in order to aid adopting enterprises in the use of NCMTs. Since the mid-1970s there has been no specific program of aid contributing directly towards defraying the costs of installing NC technology in specific enterprises. During both these periods, however, there has been a considerable transfer of financial resources to enterprises through the taxation and subsidy mechanism. This has had the indirect effect of supplying external credits towards the purchase of capital equipment.

It is difficult to say with specificity what the potential equilibrium level of diffusion of NCMTs in a given setting is. However, we can gain some insight into the nature of the diffusion process in Hungary by comparing data on the speed and level of diffusion in other countries. Table 2 compares the level of diffusion between countries at specific times. The number of years since introduction refers to the time elapsed since the technology was first introduced in each country. The data on the six western countries are from 1969, while those for Hungary are reported for the end of 1982. The Hungarian column presents two values. The first is the value arrived at by considering only metal-cutting machine tools while the second, in parentheses, indicates the value if all NC equipment is considered. The data on western countries derive from a study (Gebhardt and Hatzold, 1974) that does not define what is meant by the term, "national industry." The Hungarian calculations, therefore, employed data on employment in heavy and light industry. These do not include the food processing industry since these were judged to have little likelihood to employ NCMTs. The figures indicate a generally lower level of NCMT utilization in Hungary given the number of years since introduction of the technology. The figure for NCMTs per sample firm compares favorably with that of the United Kingdom after a similar number of years, but this measure is skewed by the fact that the typical Hungarian enterprise is larger than its United Kingdom counterpart. The normalizing measure of NCMTs per thousand employees in sample firms indicates a low level of use.

This low measure may be said to be partly a reflection of differing labor practice. In Hungary, where labor is relatively inexpensive, there has been a tendency for enterprises to accumulate a labor reserve that frequently operates obsolescent equipment but whose primary purpose is to protect the enterprise from potential manpower bottlenecks as well as to lower the average wage for tax purposes. This having been said, it must be emphasized that thirteen years separate the data collected for the western nations and those for Hungary. During that period the usual pattern of post-innovation evolution in the basic technology had served to alter the nature of the decision facing firms by reducing the objective, or technical risk to the employment of NCMTs. This process can be decomposed into three aspects. The first of these is that the passage of time had served to make better and more ample information available to the potential adopter. Second, the production of the technology had been rendered more routine and had been rationalized thus serving to lower the cost of producing, and hence acquiring, the technology. Finally, the technology itself had undergone transformation that had tended to widen the area of potential

Table 2. Comparative Levels of NCMT Usage[a]

	Austria	Federal Republic of Germany	Italy	Sweden	United Kingdom	United States	Hungary[b]
Years since introduction	6	7	9	11	14	15	16
							(number of NCMTs)
NCMTs/sample firm	4.4	8.2	5.1	8.5	6.0	21.4	7.4[c] (8.1)[c]
NCMTs/thous. employ. in national industry	0.1	0.2	0.1	0.4	0.3	0.9	0.5 (0.6)
in sample firms	3.5	1.1	3.9	2.5	3.2	9.6	1.7 (1.9)

[a] Data on Western firms from 1969
   Data for Hungary from 1982
[b] Includes only metalcutting NCMTs
   (includes all NC machinery)
[c] NCMTs/industrial enterprise in SPE listing

Sources: Nabseth and Ray
   SPE data
   Survey data
   Stat. Evkonyv

116

application and to reduce the problematic aspects of NCMT use. This latter process has been especially strong in the instance of the NCMT. The basic technology has been applied to an ever wider range of uses, and has itself undergone such changes as to make it qualitatively different from its initial embodied forms. As an example, the development of both computer numerical control (CNC) and direct numerical control (DNC) had not yet occurred when the data on the Western users were collected, but these were the main thrust of the industry by 1982 whence the Hungarian data derive. When viewed in this light the Hungarian data suggest that the process of diffusion has proceeded less rapidly in Hungary than in the west.

The data presented above may be disaggregated to present more detail on the effect of firm size among the sample firms. Table 3 shows that grouping data in this fashion does not alter the basic conclusion stated above. When the number of NCMTs per enterprise is normalized by enterprise size, the Hungarian figure is consistently below the western average in each size grouping. The second series of comparisons, showing the number of NCMTs per thousand employees, again normalized by enterprise size, seem to suggest that the production program in larger enterprises is more likely to be of the mass production variety which is less suited to the application of NC technology so Hungarian practice in this respect is more in line with that of the West. The comparison of NCMT density at levels below 5000 employees is unfavorable for Hungary.

The Hungarian data will not support a comparison of the contribution of NCMTs versus traditional machine tools in the share of output produced. However, it is possible to consider the share which NCMTs represent in terms of national machine tool capacity through the proxy of a comparative analysis of the proportion of NCMTs in the national machine tool stocks. Comparison of absolute numbers of machine tools with figures for other countries would not be illuminating due to the difference in size of the engineering sectors between Hungary and most developed industrial countries. However, one such comparison might be mentioned in passing. According to the data contained in Gebhardt and Hatzold, Austria possessed four NCMTs in 1966. At that time Hungary had also installed two, according to SPE data. By 1970, Austria had 115 NCMTs operating while Hungary had only ten, not installing the 115th NCMT until 1976.

A more analytically satisfactory comparison can be arrived at by considering the percentage of NCMTs in the national machine tool park. Ray (1984) provides the following information. In 1976, the

Table 3.   NCMTs by Size of Firm[a]

	(1) Austria	(2) Federal Republic of Germany	(3) Italy	(4) Sweden	(5) United Kingdom	(6) United States	(7) (1–6) average	(8) Hungary[b]
Years since introduction	6	7	9	11	14	15	na	16
Per enterprise by number of employees							(number of NCMTs)	
1–499	—	—	2.5	1.5	2.6	—	2.9	1.0 (1.0)
500–1499	5.8	4.5	7.7	5.8	3.9	9.5	5.8	3.5 (3.5)
1500–4999	2.5	8.6	4.0	11.0	6.9	27.0	8.6	6.2 (6.6)
5000 and over	—	11.4	—	32.5	13.8	51.5	20.2	14.3 (17.5)
Per thousand employees by number of employees								
1–499	—	—	10.8	8.3	8.3	—	10.6	2.6 (2.6)

500–1499	7.7	5.5	9.0	7.5	6.0	12.1	7.2	3.6 (3.7)
1500–4999	0.9	4.0	1.3	—	3.2	—	3.7	2.2 (2.3)
5000 and over	—	0.5	—	1.7	1.9	8.5	1.2	1.4 (1.7)
Averages								
per enterprise	4.4	8.2	5.1	8.5	6.0	21.4	8.5	7.4[c] (8.1)[c]
per thous. employees	3.5	1.1	3.9	2.5	3.2	9.6	2.3	1.7 (1.9)

[a] Data on Western firms from 1969
Data for Hungary from 1982
[b] Includes only metalcutting NCMTs
(includes all NC machinery)
[c] NCMTs/industrial enterprise in SPE listing
Sources: Nabseth and Ray
SPE data
Survey data

percentage of NCMTs in total stocks of machine tools in Sweden, Japan, and the United States was approximately 1.5 percent in each, although, naturally, the share by value was much higher. The data for Japan and the United States are unavailable after this date, but in Sweden the percentage had risen to 3 percent by 1980. A similar figure for the United Kingdom was 2.6 percent in 1982, and for West Germany, 2.2 percent in 1980. In Hungary, NCMTs represented only one percent of the machine tool stock in the narrowly defined engineering sector in 1983 (Horvath, 1984). To place this in perspective, it should be borne in mind that the engineering branches are traditionally more advanced in NCMT usage. For example, in the United States in 1973 the shares of NCMTs in the engineering branch and in all industry were 1.13 and 0.91 percent respectively while similar figures for the Soviet Union were 0.45 and 0.27 percent (Amann, 1977). If we make the conservative assumption that the stock of all machine tools in Hungary remained constant at the 1975 figure of approximately 100,000 machines, then the SPE data indicate that the share of NCMTs in the national machine tool stock in 1983, nearly 20 years after introduction, was 0.75–0.79 percent. These figures further serve to suggest that the process of diffusion of NCMTs in Hungary has been slow by international standards.

A measure of the disappointment engendered by this performance can be inferred from the fact that the program originally conceived by the OMFB as being necessary to ameliorate the uncompetitive nature of the machine-building industry called for 820 NCMTs to be in place by 1980, 25–30 percent of domestic origin, and a full 3500 to be installed by 1985. By 1990 the program called for 8600 NCMTs, representing 7 percent of the total machine tool stock, 49 percent by value (Hajos, 1976). In the light of actual performance this would appear overly optimistic. However, if we consider the fact that the projected 1990 level implies a total machine tool park of 122,800 machines of all types, this base figure can be used to suggest that the OMFB projections can better be characterized as hopeful rather than unrealistic. The target figure for 1985 suggests that by that date the Hungarian planners hoped, in effect, to reach a level no closer than a half decade behind the intensity of utilization actually exhibited by the leading industrial countries in that at a level of 3 percent they would equal the Swedish performance of 1980. Although such projections are subject to innumerable potential disturbances, the levels of utilization for Sweden in 1976 and 1980 suggest that by 1990 the value of 7 percent may well represent the level of usage found in western industrial countries.[4] In the light of the comparative data presented before, the Hungarian performance must be considered slow compared to the experience of the industrial West, and in view of the program framed in the 1970s, the performance with respect to the adoption of this technology has been disappointing to the domestic authorities. In the following section of this chapter, Hungarian performance will be analyzed in order to elucidate the forces which have served to frustrate the national design for technological development in this area.

II.   FACTORS AFFECTING NCMT ADOPTION IN HUNGARY

Influence of Investment Cycles

The explanation most readily offered for the slow diffusion of NCMTs in Hungarian heavy industry is that the process was occurring at the same time that the nation was being forced to belatedly adjust to the unfavorable realignment of factor prices and terms of trade that had occurred in the 1970s. These had been effectively postponed from affecting domestic industry due to the policies of insulation earlier pursued by the government. The belated impacts began to apply with full effect in virtually all branches of the economy at the time of the liquidity crisis of early 1982. One of the measures employed by the central authorities was to restrict investment except in areas where it could be demonstrated that it would improve the export position of the enterprise or the energy efficiency of production.

Table 4 explores the relationship between investment barriers and NCMT adoption. The data are indices arrived at by normalizing the relevant values, in current prices, to the appropriate values for each preceding year. This procedure was employed to ensure that any NCMTs acquired during this period whose values were not included in the SPE data would not skew the relationship, assuming that the trend in purchases for these machines corresponds to the one applying to those for which we have value figures. The data suggest that while a relationship between general investment trends and NCMT purchases exists, it is not a simple one. The series on economy-wide investment indicates slackening growth in 1979 with an investment cutback in 1980. The data on the value of new NCMTs, derived from the SPE, show that there was a sharp curtailment of nearly fifteen percent in 1979, the year before the beginning of the general investment rollback.

A consideration of the series on investment in the machine building industry (*gepipar*) alone shows a flattening of the trend in investment beginning in 1978 with a drop of over 5 percent the following year. This would more clearly correspond to the fall-off in NCMT purchases observed for 1979. However, in the two following years, 1980 and 1981, when total investment in the machine industry declined to 84.0 and 88.2 percent respectively of the value of each preceding year, the purchase of NC equipment actually rose. If we consider only NCMTs that were installed in productive enterprises of the machine industry in those years the data still indicate a rise of more than 37 percent in value installed in 1980 and a decline of less than 5 percent of the gross 1980 value in the year 1981.[5]

Considering the time generally required to successfully install a piece of capital equipment, the date reflected in the SPE listing, after deciding upon the investment, it might be more revealing to consider the series of NCMT values with a one year lag after the investment series. This reveals a greater synchrony between the machine industry investment cycle and the series for NCMT installation in that the direction of the trend each year is more or less consistent, but it is not without anomaly. It is difficult to see a consistent mechanism behind a process that would translate a virtually unchanged level of investment in 1978 into a 21 percent decline in NCMT installation in 1979, nor a falling investment trend in 1979, 94.7 percent of 1978, into the 37.5 percent increase in new NCMT value in 1980 noted above. Of course, the mechanism employed by the center to control investment activities need not necessarily be consistent in its operation from year to year in

Table 4.   Indices on Investment and NCMT Addition by Year

Year	Socialist Sector Investment	Value of New NCMTs	Investment in Machine Industry	Value of New NCMTs in Machine Industry
				(*preceding year = 100.0*)
1977	119.3	216.1	147.6	222.6
1978	108.9	189.5	99.8	195.9
1979	103.2	85.6	94.7	79.0
1980	93.0	123.4	84.0	137.5
1981	96.4	103.0	88.2	95.2
1982	101.6	73.7	105.0	77.7
1983	101.2	102.2	101.9	106.3

Source: Calculated from data in Statiszt. Ev. and SPE data.

order to affect this process. Indeed, one of the most persistent problems faced by planners on the enterprise level has been the very inconsistency and variability that such policies have exhibited in Hungary in recent years. In any case, the data that have been presented do not suggest that vagaries in the investment cycle have had an unambiguously decisive impact on the acquisition of NC technology.

This interpretation can be supported further by considering that not since 1975 has there been any formal program directed from the center to foster the diffusion of NC equipment by aiding individual enterprises directly. This means that while the investment figures cited above cover outlays from all sources and for all purposes, the financing of capital equipment such as NCMTs can be considered as falling under the heading of investment initiated and, to a greater extent, financed by individual enterprises as opposed to those projects characterized by state or National Bank primary input or control. Unfortunately, data on enterprise-led investment disaggregated by branch are not available. The data on such investment outlays for all material branches show an increasing or flat rate of growth through 1979, when there was a drop of about 1 percent from the previous year, a decline of eight percent in 1980, and then renewed growth of 2 and 3 percent respectively in the two following years. If we look only at that proportion provided by the enterprises out of their own sources, from 1976 through 1982 there was an average annual increase of over 13 percent, despite a downturn from this source as well in 1979 (Sokil, 1984). This is of some significance in that the questionnaire survey of NCMT-using sample firms showed that the proportion of bank credits used to finance the first purchase by each enterprise was, on average, 35 percent, with a further 6 percent coming from state credits. These figures include both the period of relatively easy credit through 1976 and the more stringent period from 1977 on. For those firms which first introduced NC technology between 1966 and 1976, the proportions of credits for the purchase of the initial NC equipment were 27 percent bank and 14 percent state. For those adopting from 1977 on, these proportions were 40 percent and 1 percent, respectively. Thus the bulk of funds used for first purchase, certainly in later years, came from the source that has shown the least volatility during the course of the recent investment checks.

Of course, these data are merely suggestive and can not eliminate investment cycle downturns as a cause of the slow acquisition of NC technology. Among other things, it is quite obvious that an increase in a value in current terms does not suggest that there has been an increase in real terms.[6] Of more moment is the criticism that a series indicating a steady increase in the funds provided by enterprises from their own sources does not necessarily indicate that enterprise resources overall are not coming under pressure. Such an increase could, and probably does, indicate a response to the gradual dwindling of resources received from the center. The enterprises may have been substituting away from the purchase of NCMTs to provide funding for investments for which they had previously received aid or credits. But if this were indeed the case, the question becomes why the enterprises would be willing to consider such a substitution given the increase in productivity that the literature suggests can be achieved with NC technology.

If, in fact, NCMTs were achieving their full potential in use in Hungarian enterprises and the principal factor retarding diffusion was only scarcity of investment funding, then a steady increase in the relative value of NCMT purchases as a proportion of total machine tool investment that did, in fact, occur could be expected. The reasoning on the part of enterprises in the absence of institutional constraints might be that if the acquisition of capital equipment was, and would continue to be, problematic, the enterprise had best employ technology which is efficient, versatile, and most likely to retain its value in ensuing years. In other words, the total value of equipment purchased might be constrained but not necessarily its assortment. If it were not the case that NC equipment claimed an increasing proportion of machine tool investment, it would suggest that either the NC technology failed to demonstrate its practical superiority on the shop floor or that other factors peculiar to the operation of the enterprise or the supporting economic system must enter the discussion.

That such additional factors were at work is suggested by the information in Table 5. The percentage of NCMTs in new machine tool purchases has fluctuated, never passing beyond the value of 16.5 percent in 1981. The proportion does not exhibit a monotonic increase over time.[7] Further, considering the relative prices of NCMTs as compared to traditional machine tools, a proportion of fifteen percent by value added in a given year would translate into a proportional addition of NCMTs to the national machine tool park at a marginal rate of less than two per cent of the total number added — well below the intended pace. As a further comparison, it should be remembered that the plan for utilization by 1990 called for a machine tool stock with NCMTs accounting for 49 percent of (presumably net) value. To the extent that enterprises are choosing to make the bulk of their newly emplaced

Table 5.· NCMTs as a Percentage of Yearly MT Additions

	1976	1977	1978	1979	1980	1981	1982	1983
							(percentages)	
Value of NCMTs/ All New MTs	3.3	5.0	10.1	9.7	14.8	16.5	11.2	12.5

Sources: Statisztikai Ev.
      SPE data

machine tool capacity traditional as opposed to NC, thereby maintaining and updating the vintage of the non-NC machine tool stock, this target figure will most likely prove to be well above the actual level.

Several additional points may be mentioned briefly in mitigation of the proposition that the existence of centrally-mandated investment stringency is sufficient explanation of the lag in NCMT adoption. The first of these is to reiterate that the purchase of NCMTs has been largely financed by funding sources internal to the enterprise. Interviews conducted at NC utilizing enterprises confirmed that such purchases could in most cases be adequately covered from the development fund created from after-tax profits and that up until 1979, investment funds and hard currency were both available on relatively easy terms. Barriers placed by the center would have to take the form less of indirect financial impediments and more of institutional and administrative means such as restrictions on import licenses, but it is clear that equipping the engineering branches with NCMTs has been a priority development program.

As a final point, the existence of investment stringencies in the latter 1970s and early 1980s will not explain the exceedingly long period between the introduction, in 1966, and significant uptake of the new technology. Diffusion has been slow in a relative sense, judging by international experience, and not only by the concrete standard of the KGM-OMFB program. During the time in question, western economies also experienced at least three periods of economic stagnation affecting the rate of capital formation. Further, even in relatively slow periods overall investment in Hungary has been higher than is usual in the West. This draws attention to the contrast between the general level of investment in Hungary and the low rate of NCMT adoption and reinforces the validity of comparing the Hungarian experience with the diffusion process in West European countries.

The conclusion drawn from the discussion above is that investment constraints play a role in the diffusion process but are not by themselves sufficient explanation in the simple sense that a shortage of funds has caused the acquisition of NC equipment to be slowed. Rather, investment cycles may exacerbate the effect that the system's other elements have on the enterprise decision to adopt NC technology. The data suggest that when forced to make decisions in this respect, there are factors in Hungary pertaining to the performance of NCMTs or to other institutional elements that serve to make the traditional technology an acceptable, or even attractive, alternative.

Secondary sources, combined with enterprise interviews and the data obtained through the questionnaires returned by the sample firms give clearer insight into the more fundamental causes of the disappointing acceptance of NCMTs. However, before turning to these explanations it would be well to examine objective factors that recommend the adoption of this technology to the individual enterprise in Hungary.

Incentives for Adopting NC Technology

The most striking difference between the incentives noted in the literature on diffusion in the West and the Hungarian perceptions of the benefits of NC technology is that explicit cost saving, as formally calculated, was not a prime motivation for acquiring NC equipment in Hungary. Indeed, the interviews conducted within enterprises, with domestic NCMT suppliers, and with members of institutes suggested that, in the words of a manager of a machine tool park, "costs do not really enter into the calculation" (I 50). This is due in part to the difficulty the typical enterprise experiences in accurately conducting cost accounting at the level of individual activities within the plant, a theme to be returned to below, but also to the relatively small role wages play in the total cost structure of the enterprise. In fact, until the early 1970s, there was doubt in some circles as to whether NC technology was even applicable in Hungary because of this apparent cost structure (83-11NP). Rather, the advantages most often cited for the installation of NCMTs were:

1. an easing of potential labor bottlenecks by decreasing the enterprise's manpower requirements;
2. a greater ability to satisfy market demands than the traditional technology allows—an output-oriented goal achieved by reducing time required for reconfiguration of the tool and by reducing the need for transportation between work stations;

3. a capacity for introducing qualitative improvements into the output mix and for machining to more precise tolerances those goods currently produced.

After these three desiderata raised by all interviewees, several suggested that a decrease in warehousing problems and a reduction in the need for special tools and preparations were also important. These perceived advantages carry within them the sense of addressing implicit opportunity costs, but Hungarian enterprise officials indicated that the accounting procedures to which they adhere do not allow them to render the potential advantages explicit in cost calculations.

One additional reason was cited in several instances and provides another example of differences between the Hungarian and the western experience (although this dimension had not been dealt with specifically in the Gebhardt and Hatzold study.) This was that NCMTs were "fashionable"; they were emblematic of modernity and were perhaps installed in several instances where the necessary capacity to utilize the machinery in an appropriate or efficient manner was not available. As such, their main purpose might have been to serve as signals to prospective western partners that the enterprise should be viewed as a worthy candidate for cooperative production agreements. This point will be addressed in a wider context below.

For these reasons, many enterprises view NCMTs favorably although it is the case that installing such equipment increases production costs as they are formally calculated in Hungarian enterprises. The actual rate of adoption, however, has been slow. A study conducted by the Ministry for Machine-Building and Metallurgy that examined 90 enterprises in the machine industry in the first half of the 1970s, indicated that 31 of these firms did not have NCMTs nor planned to install any by 1980 even though outside analysts felt that they could have been employed economically in at least two-thirds of the cases (83–10NP). This raises the question of why, on balance, an enterprise may choose to forego NCMT adoption and continue to produce with the traditional technology.

Institutional Factors Affecting NCMT Adoption

One source of difficulty has been the mechanism for western equipment import. During the course of the five year plan from 1976 through 1980, the conception was that 20–25 percent of NCMTs emplaced were to come from domestic production, 45–50 percent from other CMEA countries, and only 30 percent from western sources. In the event, this did not prove possible. Since it is the case that Hungary does not produce equipment that fulfills the full range of necessary NC functions, imports, preferably from other members of the CMEA, would be necessary. CMEA sources are preferred because it is easier to obtain import permits, there are no customs duties attached to machinery or parts, there is no need to apply for an allocation of hard currency, and there is most often a large differential in price for machines of the same type.[8] However, many CMEA models are unreliable in use and there are severe problems in obtaining service and parts.[9] A technical director of a large enterprise indicated that while it might take four or five months to receive a replacement part for a Western machine, the first three months being devoted to the process of obtaining the necessary permits, it may take two to three years to obtain a similar part for an East European machine (I 52). It was also pointed out that Hungarian and other CMEA machines are not modified quickly with changes in the technology, in part because many models are produced under license. As a result, more reliance has had to be placed upon the West as a supplier of NCMTs of the most contemporary design. This may be seen in Tables 6 and 7 which disaggregate the gross NCMT stock by machine type and area of origin.

In the period 1976–1980, only 21 percent of installed NCMTs were

Table 6. Origin of Hungarian Gross NCMT Stock by Type (percentages)[a]

Machine tool type	By Number of NCMTs[b]				By Value of NCMTs[b]			
	H	E	W	Total	H	E	W	Total
Metalcutting								
Turning	66.6	35.4	26.4	47.4	48.6	45.0	25.5	35.2
Drill-/Boring	0.7	13.0	10.0	6.0	0.8	9.3	5.5	4.4
Milling	14.8	42.9	13.5	19.2	24.0	38.7	10.6	18.1
Machining Ctr	8.4	3.7	11.6	8.7	18.3	4.4	28.1	22.3
Spec. Milling	0	0	0.3	0.1	0	0	7.1	4.0
Other	9.3	3.7	20.3	12.1	8.3	1.6	19.2	13.7
Non-metalcutting	0.2	1.3	18.0	6.5	na	1.0	4.1	2.4
Total	100.0	100.0	100.1	100.0	100.0	100.0	100.1	100.0

[a] Percentages may not total 100.0 due to rounding errors
[b] H = Hungarian   E = Other CMEA   W = Western
Source: SPE data

Table 7. Composition of Hungarian Gross NCMT Stocks by Origin (percentages)[a]

Machine tool type	By Number of NCMTs[b]				By Value of NCMTs[b]			
	H	E	W	Total	H	E	W	Total
Metalcutting								
Turning	67.8	13.2	19.0	100.0	45.6	13.8	40.6	100.0
Drill-/Boring	5.5	38.2	56.4	100.1	6.3	23.0	70.7	100.0
Milling	37.1	39.4	23.4	99.9	43.9	23.2	32.9	100.0
Machining Ctr	46.8	7.6	45.6	100.0	27.1	2.1	70.7	99.9
Spec. Milling	0	0	100.0	100.0	0	0	100.0	100.0
Other	37.3	5.5	57.3	100.1	20.1	1.3	78.6	100.0
Non-metalcutting	1.7	3.4	94.9	100.0	na	4.1	95.9	100.0
Total	48.4	17.7	34.0	100.1	33.1	10.8	56.1	100.0

[a] Percentages may not total 100.0 due to rounding errors
[b] H = Hungarian   E = Other CMEA   W = Western
Source: SPE data

actually obtained from other CMEA countries. In the same period, 46 percent of all NCMTs in use in productive enterprises came from the West. In value terms these represented two-thirds of all NCMT investments. Nor have more recent restrictions on hard currency outlays affected these proportions. During 1980–1983, when controls were the most stringent and the CMEA machines made the more attractive thereby, only 11.3 percent of the number of NCMTs installed came from the CMEA, 7.3 percent by value. The number of western machines was affected, being but 29.2 percent of all units emplaced, but their value claimed a share, 56 percent, not much reduced from that of the earlier period. Considering the role that these imports have been forced to play in equipping Hungary with NC technology, the checks to their acquisition posed by the system must represent an important impediment.

The problem of supplying the spare parts required to keep NCMTs operational, irrespective of origin, has also been a difficulty. Costs and the need to obtain the necessary permits have restricted the effectiveness of NCMTs of western origin.[10] At the same time, the users of Hungarian and CMEA-produced machines have not been free from such problems. The well-known difficulties of obtaining spare parts in CMEA trade leads to a condition where a considerable investment must often be made in warehousing spares so that the expensive NCMT will not stand idle. Increased expense for spares offsets the advantage conferred by NC technology of reducing the necessary stocks of processed parts.

The cost of installing NCMTs is great. Besides the basic costs for the machine itself, the first adoption of the technology by an individual enterprise imposes a large burden in the form of expenses for training, programming, and the purchase of higher quality tools and spares. In Hungary this means, in effect, that there will be a marked predisposition for the larger enterprises to acquire NC machines at an earlier date than the small and medium-sized enterprises. This is due to the easier access to financial resources enjoyed by large enterprises, in large part due to effectively softer budget constraints. Thus, the enterprises that were the early adopters of the technology were not of the type considered to be the most innovative and flexible in Hungary (Becsky, 1982). Whereas the Gebhardt and Hatzold study indicated that in 1969, 54 percent of the Swedish, one-third of the British, and smaller proportions of the NC-utilizing sample firms in other countries had fewer than 500 employees, in Hungary few enterprises of less than 1000 employees had adopted the technology by 1984. Among the 50 firms in the Hungarian sample, the average size was 4355 employees. To provide a comparison, in 1983 the average size of an industrial enterprise was 1112 employees; within the machine-building branch of heavy industry the average was 1466 (*Statisztikai Evkonyv*, 1983). This suggests that the larger average size of Hungarian enterprises is not a sole cause of this effect. Only one firm had fewer than 500 employees. It appears that for the smaller firms, financial considerations and indirect administrative barriers have greatly outweighed flexibility and propensity for experimentation on the part of management as factors in NC acquisition.

On the other hand, among the enterprises that do presently use NCMTs, the interviews suggest that the cost of the initial investment was less of an overpowering consideration in the case of NC technology than has been true of other technologies. The suggestion is that there is a threshold of size, or influence, which is much the same thing in Hungary, beyond which the rule that "to him who hath much, much shall be given," comes into force. In addition, according to the questionnaire data there appears to have been greater exceptionality in the application of the general rules on enterprise investment financing than has been the case for other diffusion processes. Although on average the sample data suggest that the general rule of 30 percent cost contribution from enterprise Development Funds was adhered to in the acquisition of NCMTs, several firms responded that they were able to finance the entire cost of first acquisition through bank credits.

Finally, it must be emphasized that as much as the financial threshold weighs as a consideration in the decision to invest in NCMTs, there is also a threshold to be crossed in developing the necessary support to sustain the equipment after installation. Numerical control technology requires a high degree of internal organization, a point returned to in detail below, continuous supply of materials especially cutting tools of exceptional quality, expensive special support units, trained operators, three, or at least two, operating shifts, and adequate maintenance service (Nagy, 1981). It would be atypical for such an organization to already exist within an enterprise in Hungary (I36). The technical literature attributes a good part of the problem of achieving the expected results from NC technology to a continued lack of programming experts and a general operational background of an insufficiently high level on the part of most NC-utilizing enterprises (*Nepszava,* 1980). However, this problem of input shortages was anticipated by the architects of the nation's NC adoption process and led directly to the establishment of the SPE and other bodies charged with the responsibility for increasing the spread of technical information among firms. Enterprise officials contacted for interviews generally expressed satisfaction with these background arrangements. Further, the task of developing expertise has been aided by the advent of CNC technology in the mid-1970s. The self-contained nature of these devices, coupled with the generally user-friendly aspect of the hard-wired circuitry, reduced the demands for technical expertise related to hardware peripherals that had restricted the diffusion of NC machinery. The fact remains, however, that the difficulties in integrating the NCMTs into the enterprise's production process remain quite large. It suggests that the problem is not so much one of inadequate inputs as one of failing to organize their efficient use.

III. FACTORS MITIGATING EFFECTIVE USE OF NCMTS

The considerations of problems internal to the enterprise suggests that the diffusion of NC technology in Hungary has been slow and the achieved results disappointing not so much by reason of the actual number of units installed, although this has been the case, but more in terms of the practical effect of those units. That is, the embodied potential of the technology has been emplaced but the technology itself has not been fully elicited. The introduction of a new technology into an existing production process may raise a fundamental problem. The new technology must be integrated with productive capital of an older vintage. The problem becomes acute when, as in the case of NCMTs, the new capital performs at a higher rate than the old. The question is whether the performance of the new NCMTs will be brought down to the level of the traditional machine tool park, or whether the production process will be reorganized in such a fashion as to increase the performance of the traditional machine tools in concert with the possibilities of the new technology. The following section offers an interpretation suggesting that this problem may be especially pronounced in Hungary to the extent of seriously affecting the process of diffusion.

Behaviorally oriented models of diffusion focus upon the observation that the complete technical and economic parameters of an innovation are not fully calculable ex ante by potential adopters (see, for example, Davies, 1979). In such models, as time passes and more information becomes available, the potential benefits versus the possible risks of employing an innovation in a given setting are more clearly seen and this reduces the mean waiting time before adoption by individual enterprises. If such information is not forthcoming, or if the balance of net benefit does not appear more favorable as more is known, a reduction in mean waiting time before adoption should not be expected. This insight can be expanded by recognizing that, similarly, if the emplaced technology does not accord to expectations after adoption by an individual enterprise, or if its net benefit is not readily observable, the balance of decision affecting further commitment to the same technology may be adversely affected. That is, the persistence of uncertainty, depending upon its cause, may affect either inter-firm or intra-firm diffusion.

The balance of this section considers the proposition that many of the institutional factors affecting the environment for diffusion and innovation in Hungarian industrial enterprises operate with especially strong force to attenuate the effectiveness of NC technology in use. This affects the rate of diffusion of NCMTs or, what is of greater moment, the spread of the potentially realizable technology in application embodied in the NCMTs, through a process similar to the one sketched above. These factors may collectively constitute a fundamentally important influence on this diffusion process in Hungary.

The literature on NC technology indicates that due to the high cost of the equipment, its technical complexity, and its ability to perform at accelerated rates, it possesses characteristics that set it off qualitatively from the traditional technology. In the experience of western production managers, there is a qualitative difference between a NCMT park and the traditional one in that the former must be operated by a team that will reach beyond the shop floor. The danger lies in treating the NC equipment as an individual unit under the control of its operator rather than as the necessary object of a team effort, especially in the critical areas of machine selection and acquisition of peripheral support (Gettleman, 1980). In the area of production,

> NC machines can cause financial disaster if management fails to adjust its thinking to exploit the advantages of quick set-up, short machining time, and flexibility. To keep NC tools busy, jobs must be planned in advance and background preparation . . . fully developed before the machine becomes free. . . . Conversion of any manufacturing operation from conventional machining to numerical control is more than a change of equipment, it is a change of system and its concomitant philosophy (Tombari, 1978).

In practical terms, this means that in the majority of cases the NCMT cannot merely be substituted for the machine it replaces. It must be recognized that all work must be reoriented to the capacities of the NC equipment and that a new pattern of production must be erected with the NCMT as the focus. The changes required are so great that, "the first step in NC planning should be the appointment of an NC coordinator" to harmonize the various functions which must be included in the firm's NC task force (Tombari, 1978; p. 117). Not to do so will have a negative impact upon the cost structure of production and place a firm at a competitive disadvantage compared to those enterprises that do explore the internal logic of the technology and restructure the firm's production design in that light.

In view of this distinction, the introduction of NCMTs into a Hungarian industrial enterprise serves as an excellent test for difficulties that may serve to render institutions insufficiently sensitive to the need for accommodating change. These may combine to make the environment within the enterprise prejudicial to the opportunities for extracting the maximum advantage from the NCMTs put in place. The western literature makes it clear that such problems often become apparent in market-type economies as well. The difference lies in the degree to which organizations in either setting are forced to confront the problem. There may be a difference, as well, in the degree to which they are able to deal effectively with the need for organizational change.

One of the problems hindering the wider application of NC technology is the apparent lack of sufficient means to calculate the economic net benefit of NC utilization using the accounting procedures generally practiced in Hungarian industry (83–10NP, 83–11NP). In fact, one of the tasks set for the OMFB was to develop new accounting systems to trace more accurately the costs of NCMTs and, moreover, to make more readily apparent the secondary benefits that their use has for other aspects of production. An examination of enterprises conducted by the Industrial Research Group of the Academy of Sciences found that the present system does not allow the enterprise itself to assess what each operation or activity costs if each is completed using a different technology (Javorka, 1978; p. 93). To be sure, in the West it is often difficult to determine ex ante, or even ex post, what the profitability of a new process technology might be (Nabseth and Ray, 1974; p. 302). But in Hungary, the view expressed by technical managers is that the problem is rendered more awkward by the inability on the part of most firms to generate data on costs attributable to discrete activities (I50). In the behavioral, information-based model of diffusion this deprives the enterprise of the means to bring into sharper focus the calculation of net benefit. This point was frequently raised in enterprise interviews; it was stated by those managers pressing for the introduction of NCMTs that they did so in spite of the fact that such an adoption would invariably increase the costs of production as calculated by the standard means (I50, I54). That they were willing to do so was because they had been led by western experience to anticipate certain qualitative benefits from NCMT use.[11] A direct calculation of the ancillary benefits effected through the installation of NC machinery (reduced waste, better organization of machining steps, reduced stock requirements. etc.,) perhaps the most profound in terms of overall transformation of the work place, are the most difficult to detect ex ante in Hungary (I51).

There are several reasons for this. The first is that in the past the cost of machinery was not critical to the operating enterprise due to the existence of a generally soft budget constraint in the area of capital investment. This is a legacy of a system wherein decisions over capital acquisition were in large part made by bodies outside of the enterprise's structure. This served to reduce the enterprise's accountability. It remains true today that most firms have no means to collect and analyze the data required to assess the performance of individual production stations within the total cost structure.

The second reason is that the system of accounting was intended not so much for the use of an independent productive entity needing to track costs and efficiencies, but rather as a means to inform higher authority of the enterprise's activities with respect to those variables impinging upon centrally formulated aggregate targets (Javorka, 1978). The system was designed to provide the information required by the external institutions charged with hierarchic oversight. Since 1968, and even following the reform of certain accounting procedures in 1981, enterprises have largely failed to make use of even the limited flexibility granted them for improving local decisionmaking in this area (Csikos-Nagy, 1983). The old procedures remain largely intact. This vestige of the system of central planning makes it difficult for most enterprises to fully achieve their new status as the units for primary production decisions. The system is perpetuated by mandatory detailed accounting reports to the center, by accounting guidelines provided by the ministries, and by inertia.[12] The already difficult decision of whether to employ new technology is rendered more uncertain by the difficulty of assessing the effect either upon discrete aspects of the firm's activities or on their totality.

This problem is exacerbated in the instance of NCMTs. Wage policies maintain the price for labor at levels well below what the market clearing wage would most likely be if it reflected existing labor scarcity. Therefore, calculations of net benefit indicate that the installation of NCMTs will be quite costly because only the direct costs for labor, which are not consequential, enter into the assessment and not the potentially substantial opportunity costs of production that is unrealized due to severe labor bottlenecks. One of the original architects of the Hungarian NCMT national adoption plan stated the problem concisely: ''I know that NC machines are more economical, but how can I prove this to [enterprise] economists?'' (I54). For this reason, most discussions over the feasibility of installing NCMTs are in qualitative rather than quantitative terms. This creates a barrier of information within the context of the behavioral model. In the setting of Hungary, it also conceivably creates an additional problem for enterprise managers. They cannot be assured beforehand that the net benefit to be achieved by so sizable an investment in new technology will be expressible in the idiom of their formal (and informal) performance criteria, or otherwise made apparent to those whom they feel to some degree answerable. This problem extends beyond the consideration of NCMT diffusion. During the greatest part of the period from 1968, due to the presence of risks not easily offset by calculable benefits, the prospect of political/social rewards have perhaps provided more of an impulse for innovation in industry than have calculations of economic benefits (I49). The occasion of favorable mention in the news media or in local party circles has been a more compelling inducement in many cases than the prospect of increased competitiveness.

The problem of accounting remains a general one and affects the decision governing the employment of new technological means in many venues. However, the problem of non-adaptive intra-enterprise structure plays a pivotal role in explaining the diffusion of NCMTs in particular. Early in this investigation, the researcher was struck by the surprise expressed by several Hungarian students of innovation that the study of NCMTs would be of interest. In their view, the NC equipment was a "machine" innovation, that is, a modification of existing technology, and not a true process innovation in itself. This view is in marked contrast to the western experience as expressed in the technical literature and raises questions of how it can be perpetuated and of the extent to which it might affect the use of the technology in enterprises. The discussion to follow suggests that in the majority of cases this philosophy underlies the use of installed NC equipment. It accords with the existing form of enterprise organization in Hungary and protects the local interests intimately bound to it. The consequence is that the effectiveness of the installed machinery is reduced. This ultimately acts to retard more general diffusion in accordance with the behavioral model: the perception of potential net benefit does not increase with time, or increases only slowly.

The task force approach to the acquisition, use, and product planning of NCMTs prescribed as being essential by the literature is one for which most Hungarian enterprises are ill prepared. Functions are divided among departments of varying relative strengths so that questions of long-range development, ancillary support, changes in product profile, and sustainability of operations are dealt with sequentially rather than simultaneously. It is exceptional to have the technical department, to say nothing of the low-caste marketing section, provide primary input to purchasing decisions. These are usually performed exclusively by the enterprise economics department (I50). An example of the result may be seen in the instance of a machine park, considered to be "progressive," in an enterprise employing more than 10,000 persons. The equipment included four CNC machines and six NC machines. One operated in three shifts, two in two, while at least five still did not operate continuously a year after installation. Among the ten machines there were six separate control systems requiring the specialists to master six separate routines for programming, maintenance, and operation. The result was that it had not been possible to harmonize production; the enterprise could not continuously supply the equipment with work even though the enterprise was a large one (Gerencser, 1979).

This reveals that the decisions regarding NCMT investment taken by those within the enterprise who retain the prerogative for such decisionmaking do not treat the NC capital and its acquisition in a qualitatively different light from the purchase of traditional equipment. This in turn serves to bind those charged with the operation of NC equipment to employ the same philosophy in production. The fact that the utilization of NCMTs in a successful manner requires profound changes in organization (including the unification of the technical decisions in one department, a manufacturing program no longer set by managers but in large part determined by the scheduling required to operate the technology in an optimal manner, and the computerization and integration of separate work stations (I50)) is not recognized in their use.[13] In the words of a Hungarian critique of domestic NC utilization, the majority of NCMTs are installed only as "islands" within the production stream in that "the advantages expected from [NCMT] use are only relizable in fragments." (Gerencser).[14]

The argument is that practice has shown that modernization requires more than the installation of one or two new NCMTs. Rather, it is necessary to radically change the internal organization so that these new units can be used effectively.

> The utilization of the revealed possibilities of [NC] technology, however, requires the restructuring of internal enterprise relations of interest. . . . The possibility should exist not only in the 10–20 square meters [where the NCMTs operate] to reach the international level of sufficient technology.

The need for support extends beyond that part of the plant where the NC equipment is to operate.

In many cases, the adoption of NCMTs failed at the start since the technology was not felt to be right for an enterprise's production system (I55). This point is borne out by the Ministry study of potential NCMT adopters cited earlier. This, in effect, was to look at the basic problem the wrong way. Rather, as western experience illustrates, the need was to decide upon the long-run development strategy of the enterprise, decide upon the means to achieve it, and then rationalize the internal organization of the firm in light of these ends.

There are institutional factors preventing this from occurring in the average industrial enterprise. There is a fundamental resistance to the integration of intra-enterprise functions or the reorganization of the production scheme. This is a natural response for any large-scale organization unless it is forced to absorb the deleterious consequences resulting from a failure to adapt. In the Hungarian setting where enterprises have been more shielded from the environment than is usual in market economies, the signals that would be otherwise generated externally are either received only in an attenuated form or else may be safely ignored. If this is the case, it may not even be apparent to enterprise personnel that the fundamental relations of production within the enterprise are not conducive to supporting the utilization of NC technology. This is no more than to suggest that one of the benefits that a need to compete confers is that a substantial amount of information is gained through indirect means. It sheds light on the way in which the internal operation of the enterprise accords with industry standards. This source of information is for practical purposes denied to those enterprises insulated by institutional arrangements from direct competition with domestic manufacturers or imports. There may only exist a vague dissatisfaction that the actual results are less than the firm has been led to expect. This affects that firm's decision to introduce subsequent NCMT installations, and may dissuade potential first time adopters with whom the enterprise is in communication who are gathering information on the prospects of NCMT utilization.

A recent Hungarian case study of a large industrial user of NCMTs provides corroboration for these inferences. In this plant

> the CNC machines and their operators were integrated with the traditional organization and technology. The equipment, which arrived singly or intermittantly, was put in the place of the old machines. . . . Experts were unprepared for the new technology. For years these machines have been used as traditional machine tools. . . . The CNC machine park operates within the traditional enterprise organization among traditional machines and in structural conditions which have stood for several decades. The machines and their operating units did not come up to expectations.

Finally,

> it was expected that the new technology would increase productivity, decrease production time, improve quality, reduce costs, save . . . labor, ensure the continuity of production and sales receipts, and improve technological work discipline. They considered the CNC technology a magic charm but the miracle failed to happen (Balazs, 1985).

Those enterprises employing NC equipment in a "rational fashion" have found that a few such machines will have a great effect on production (I54). In the experience of the researcher, these enterprises have also been exceptional by the nature of the environment in which they have operated. In the instance of one firm that appeared to have introduced substantial changes in its internal regime in order to focus upon the development of an efficient NCMT park, the firm produced overwhelmingly for hard currency export. The output required the manufacture or assembly of units of extraordinary size and complexity in a well-defined product market where the international practice has been to charge substantial penalties for relatively minor delays in delivery. The director of the NC installation was able to argue successfully that the entire procedure for the manufacture, storage, and assembly of component parts should be completely redrafted with the object of making the NC machining steps the center of the operation. Only the extreme pressure exerted upon the enterprise by the need to compete was able to overcome a predilection for merely inserting the NC equipment into an otherwise unmodified production regime.

The need for a more syncretic approach to the compartmentalized functions presently surrounding NC utilization is seen no more clearly than in decisions touching upon the output profile of the enterprise. Gerencser states that in deciding whether to adopt NCMTs in an enterprise, an assessment should be made of the expediency of changing products in as much as the old structure of manufacture is usually not economic when considering the use of newer technology.

> That is, the coordinated planning of output selection and technological change together gives a firm answer to the question: is this progressive machine really necessary? . . . Of course, the fundamental reason [for the slow diffusion of NCMTs] is that the present character of product assortment does not suggest the need for a great many more new machines. However, the modernization of the product assortment and the exploitation of the implicit possibilities of modern output types are impeded by the slow diffusion of the new technology.

Many of the institutional arrangements in which socialist enterprises operate, not the least being the manner in which bilateral trade is conducted within CMEA, serve to perpetuate existing product lines (see Laki, 1979). The preceding passage implies that there is necessarily a tight feed-back loop drawing the type of output produced and the nature of the technology employed to produce it into a unified framework for decisionmaking and planning. This passes beyond the previous discussion of the relatively weak input provided by the marketing sections of enterprises in the decision-making process of the enterprise. It points directly to the ever more necessary requirement for an integrated, long-range planning of output and the means of production when considering the utilization of new technology. The typical Hungarian enterprise is not well suited to this sort of planning. Neither does the system for economic regulation draw the attention of the enterprise's directorate to such a planning horizon. The installation of modern technology is necessary to maintain or advance the competitive standing of Hungarian industry as a whole. The cost and complexity of this technology suggest that the separation of production decisions from development decisions, existing de facto since 1968 due to the separation of these functions by administrative and financial means between the enterprises on one hand and the central authorities on the other, will detrimentally affect the effectiveness in use of that equipment. Further, it calls into serious question the ability of enterprises as the primary decision agents in this field to assess accurately the net benefit conferred by the adoption of such technology. In this sense, the difficulty experienced in Hungary in achieving the full benefit of use from NC technology may be symptomatic of a systemic dysfunction that may come increasingly to affect the nation as a consumer of more advanced industrial technologies.

Passing beyond considerations of the enterprise's ability to effectively use NC technology, there is a certain sense in which the stringencies implicitly placed by such equipment upon adopting firms may act as a direct threat to intra-firm interests. Innovation, even in the case of success, means a change in the existing order of manufacture and so inherently leads to conflict (Herceg, 1982; p. 10). In the case of NC, the changes in the existing structure may be profound. It may be that not only is the existing order incapable of adequately supporting such technology, but the need for change will also serve to add further to the balance of risk perceived by individual decision-makers over the introduction of such intrusive equipment in an environment where the fundamental incentives to undertake such risk are weak. One interviewee, when questioned about his plant's experience with the introduction of NCMTs, spoke of the "environmental" effects surrounding the introduction of "foreign," in this sense, non-traditional, technology into the work place. The workers accept with great reluctance the higher degree of work discipline enjoined upon them by the introduction of NC technology within the framework of the existing wage rules and feel that the large investments required will affect adversely their short term interests through a reduced Sharing Fund (Balazs, 1985).[15] The managers, for whom "enterprise innovation and development is not a profitable matter," may feel this as well. "When speaking of increasing the technical level in and of itself—that is just a lot of worry"

(I50). Numerical control technology may thus be viewed by some as a threat, a challenge to the existing structure and its managers. It may well find them both wanting. There may even be considerable resentment if, as is often the case, the NC park is established as an "island" not associated with the traditional metal-cutting stations so that the cost savings achieved by the NC unit come at the expense of paying work being transferred from other sections (Gerencser). There is, therefore, reason to believe that the introduction of NCMTs in the manner in which they appear to be adopted in the majority of Hungarian cases may serve to raise a party of opposition to their success within the enterprise itself. This will not help instill the collaborative spirit that the western experience suggests is essential for success in expressing the full benefit of the technology.

A final point, not considered in the western literature but that may have a bearing on the diffusion process in Hungary, is that NC technology may be adopted in settings where the objective situation would not appear to warrant it. This is by its nature a difficult matter to assess without access to the types of production data that are rarely available. This point will not be drawn too finely for the present purpose. However, there are indications that some enterprises may have adopted NC technology because of "fashion" and for the purpose of signalling to prospective western partners that the enterprise was modern and a fit collaborator in industrial cooperation (I52, I55). This echoes the "technological bias" noted by Berliner in his study of Soviet innovation (1976). This is a situation not likely to arise except in an environment where the economic parameters are difficult to assess properly and where the enterprise can rely upon soft budget constraints.

> Very often behind the purchase of just one or two NCMTs is the thought that,
> 'first we will see what this new technology is all about and how it is to be
> handled, and just afterwards we will begin something with it.'

In these instances there is no question but that the effective operationalization of the technology would be called into serious question.

IV. PRELIMINARY EVIDENCE FROM SAMPLE FIRMS

The following section is based upon data collected from the fifty enterprises (a 59 percent response rate) that returned a questionnaire on NCMT adoption.[16] Before proceeding, it would be best to indicate certain shortcomings of the study that mitigate the statistical inferences.

The first is due to the anonymity of the respondents. The variable of most interest is the lag time before NCMT adoption by an individual enterprise. This represents the number of years after the first Hungarian adoption that the individual enterprise waited before installing its own first NC machine. Certain enterprises were not formally in existence in 1966, the data used in this study as the first year of adoption of NCMTs in Hungary. This makes it problematic to assign an appropriate lag time since the specification of the model is that the lag is a measure of the time the enterprise waited before adopting NC technology. The problem is complicated by the fact that some of the respondents were in existence but members of trusts or other large organizations that were subsequently dismantled. It is difficult to say what body had authority over the adoption decision, the enterprise or the larger unit. Due to the anonymity of the survey, removing observations from the data set on these grounds would not be justified owing to a lack of positive indentification.

Another potential problem is that the questionnaire actually forwarded to enterprises differed from that originally submitted by the researcher in that certain questions were redrafted by others in the interest of brevity. This leads to the unfortunate consequence that for certain questions the response of "zero" is indistinguishable from a possible failure to respond. This effect is greatest for those questions requiring answers framed as percentages.

Finally, it is the case that some enterprises responded only in a limited fashion choosing not to respond to questions about the enterprise's production or the financing of NCMT investment.

The inferences resulting from the study allow only tentative conclusions. It may well be that more sophisticated techniques would lead to stronger findings. Keeping these major reservations in mind, there is still value in examining the initial results since enterprise data from East Europe is rare.

The sample firm data provide some indication of the criteria used by central authorities to aid the financing of NCMT investment. There is a weak positive correlation (.381) between the granting of non-Bank, state credits for financing the first purchase of NCMTs and the percentage of the enterprise's production that was produced in cooperation with other CMEA partners.[17] This would imply that the nature of the enterprise's connection with the bureaucratic planning apparatus was a consideration in receiving state aid for NCMT adoption. This appears to have dominated considerations of increased export competitiveness as a criterion for allocating such credits since no significant correlation is shown with state aid. No enterprises in the sample received this form of assistance after 1977. On the other hand, the percentage of costs for the first purchase of NCMTs accounted for by credits from the Bank shows the strongest significant correlation with the proportion of enterprise production that was exported to the non-ruble area (.289). Such credits have been granted throughout the period in question.

The most interesting finding in this connection is that there was no significant correlation between the level of credits granted either by the state or the Bank and the lag in the adoption of NCMTs. Neither was there a significant relationship between the total of credits from all sources and lag times. This would lend support to the proposition that financial considerations and the effects of the investment cycle have not been the dominant factor in the adoption of NCMTs by Hungarian enterprises.

It was generally true that there was no significant correlation between the observed lag times and those variables that might be termed "economic" characteristics of enterprises as opposed to "structural." The former include the percentage of output exported to the ruble area in the first year of adoption, the percentage exported to the dollar area, the percentage of production produced under co-production schemes with CMEA partners, as well as with Western partners, and the value of gross output the first year of NCMT introduction. In addition, as a simple test of whether the installation of NC equipment ameliorated the export competitiveness of adopting enterprises, the change in export percentages between the first year of adoption and 1982, the last full year before the survey was circulated, was measured against lag times. One of the reasons offered for adopting NC technology was to produce qualitatively superior goods at competitive prices for export. Indeed, this strategy has been a prime motive force driving West-East technology flows during the past two decades. In this case the presumed relationship assumes that a shorter lag time might lead to a more pronounced advantage in satisfying the demands of export markets and would therefore, in this instance, be the independent variable. In any case, no significant correlation was displayed between lags in NCMT adoption and changes either in overall export performance or individual export performance on the ruble and dollar markets. Such a lack of significance could well be an artifact of the particular year from which values were obtained. A complete time series would perhaps demonstrate a more pronounced trend.

On the other hand, a significant correlation was found between the lag in adoption and several structural variables. One of the strongest findings of the empirical literature on diffusion in general is the significance of firm size. This is reconfirmed by the Hungarian experience with NCMTs. The correlation between enterprise size as measured by the number of employees and the lag in NCMT adoption is -.311. It is not possible to compare this with the experience of other countries as no statistical studies based upon enterprise data are available. The interesting question of whether the general predisposition of large firms to adopt a given innovation more quickly than smaller ones may be offset in this case by the greater applicability of NC technology to smaller, component manufacturing production cannot be answered. In any case, in light of the previous discussion it is not surprising that the collected data confirm the hypothesis that, all else being equal, size is of singular advantage in acquiring this expensive new technology in Hungary.

It was not possible to obtain detailed information on the existing levels of capital stocks in individual enterprises nor on productivity as such. However, the data available allowed calculation of the gross value of output per employee in the first year of NC adoption. This showed a positive correlation with lag, .538, with significance at the level of better than .99, indicating that the firms that performed best with respect to this measure waited the longest before introducing the first NCMT. The crudeness of this variable makes it difficult to separate the factors contributing to this correlation. Strictly speaking, this measure can be interpreted as nothing more than the amount of additional output produced on average by a single employee.[18] It is by no means an unambiguous measure of productivity in individual enterprises if for no other reason than that the values of intermediate inputs have not been netted out. If, in fact, we were to assume for the purpose of argument a rough comparability between the value of inputs of a similar degree of fabrication for all firms in the survey, as well as a roughly similar technological base, the result would not be too surprising. It would indicate that upstream manufacturing firms utilizing inputs of smaller initial added value find more use in NC machinery than do firms that are mainly final assemblers and that use intermediate components of greater value. The former would adopt more quickly. This would accord with the conventional western wisdom on NC utilization.

On the other hand, gross output per employee probably comes closer to being a measure of net productivity in Hungary than would be the case in the typical western economy. Systemic tendencies within the industrial sphere tend to drive enterprises to more intense vertical integration than is usual in MTEs. It is quite likely that a Hungarian producer of manufactured goods assembled from components will actually add a great deal of the final value of the output. In this sense, the measure of gross output per capita becomes a bit more credible as a measure of productivity. This, in turn, provides a crude measure of the relative capital intensity and the efficiency of the enterprise before the advent of its NC park, if we permit heroic assumptions about the comparability of production functions between individual enterprises and branches—such a connection acquires greater credence in the aggregate. Under this assumption, several inferences could be drawn from the correlation with lag times.

The first of these is that enterprises exhibiting high values are geared rather more to long series production than to short batches and already possess a large capital stock designed to facilitate their production. It must be borne in mind, however, that all firms in the sample are, in fact, NC users. This first inference would be most readily explicable if the enterprise also engages in ancillary activities of a small batch nature, or if it has indeed inappropriately calculated the applicability of NC technology to its production.

The second inference to be drawn is that the more an enterprise is committed to a large capital stock, the less likely it is to adopt NC technology quickly. This would certainly accord with the hypothesis raised earlier that the rules on amortization of capital as they existed in the 1970s and early 1980s tended to lengthen the average age of production equipment. Connected with this is the possibility that the more an enterprise is wedded to a particular production schema, the more its organization will be committed to the status quo and the less likely to introduce fundamental changes therein.

Finally, there is the suggestion that NC technology may only recommend itself to an enterprise's managers as an expedient to address problems which have already been perceived by the management. There may be less need to consider the long term questions of production and output profile, and the role which NCMTs might play, when the current indications are that the existing technology is apparently capable of serving the most immediate needs of the enterprise, or exists in ample quantities and is in good repair. Only a lower level of output per capita may signal to enterprise management that sweeping changes in production should be considered.

Finally, the following regression was performed:

$$LAG = a + b1 \text{ EMPLOY} + (b2-b1) \text{ SIZE} + c \text{ CAPOUT} \quad \textbf{(Eq. 1)}$$

The variable LAG is the number of years between the first industrial use of NCMTs in Hungary and the first adoption of NC technology by a given firm. EMPLOY is a proxy for the size of the firm as measured by the number of employees, and CAPOUT is the gross value of output in the first year of NCMT use per worker. The variable SIZE is a dummy which takes on a value of zero if the firm installed its first NCMT before or during 1976, and the value of EMPLOY if the first adoption was at a later date. This form was chosen since there is reason to believe that the underlying parameters of the diffusion process may have shifted around the time that the KGM-OMFB program of direct aid lapsed in 1975 (a one year lag in installation is assumed) and the stricter investment environment commenced in the latter 1970s.

The results of the regression are found in Equation 2:

$$LAG = 10.64 - 3.45 \times 10^{-4} \text{ EMPLOY}$$
$$(.9426) \quad (8.52 \times 10^{-5})$$
$$\textbf{(Eq. 2)}$$
$$+ 4.36 \times 10^{-4} \text{ SIZE} + 6.78 \times 10^{-3} \text{ CAPOUT}$$
$$(1.18 \times 10^{-4}) \qquad (2.83 \times 10^{-3})$$

$$R \text{ SQUARED} = .5248$$

All estimated coefficients were significant at the .99 level. The results show a clear distinction between the two periods. In the initial period of the diffusion process, the larger firms tended to adopt more rapidly. After that, the balance shifted to smaller firms. A number of inferences may be drawn from this result. That the larger firms were at first the most likely adopters is consistent with the preceding discussion. The mechanism of the system favored such enterprises; they were better able to present and foster an application for funds under the central program, and the program itself tended to favor those firms best able to guarantee adequate spare part and service support. Also, due to their prominence, these firms probably obtained information on NC technology at an earlier date.

The fact that smaller firms appeared to be more likely adopters in the latter period may be due to several factors. The first is that the absence of a central program for which size would be a lobbying advantage, coupled with the shift to programs serving to increase the general level of information and support available to all potential adopters, allowed the characteristics of the technology which lend it best to small series production to dominate. This is difficult to substantiate in the absence of enterprise data from other countries. Second, in the absence of other mitigating factors, these results also support the contention that financial considerations did not dominate the adoption decision. All other things being equal, in a time of financial stringency budget considerations should become a binding constraint upon small enterprises before they affect larger ones. That the smaller firms adopted more readily during the period from 1977 to 1982 suggests that financial considerations were not paramount.

This result also reinforces the second and third reasons offered in the discussion of the explanatory power of the CAPOUT variable. The more an enterprise is wedded as an organization to an existing production schema and the more it is able to insulate itself from its environment, the less readily it adopts a potentially disruptive new technology. The previous discussion suggested that larger firms in Hungary would be more likely to find themselves in this position. Finally, to the limited extent that CAPOUT could be taken as a measure of efficiency, the result would indicate that smaller enterprises are less likely, or can less well afford, to remain content with their current success.

APPENDIX

A Note on Citation and Attribution

A great deal of information was gathered during the course of this research from over twenty interviews with individuals at all levels of the economic hierarchy. These included interviews with managers at five industrial users of NCMTs, with officials from the Computing Technology and Automation Research Institute of the Hungarian Academy of Sciences, the Machine Tool Programming Association (SPE), The Ministry of Industry, the National Committee for Technical Development, and with Hungarian students of industrial management. A standardized interview protocol was used in all formal interviews. The understanding under which these interviews were conducted was that there was to be no direct attribution of individual sources. This anonymity has been preserved in this work. However, in those places where citation would normally be expected in a scholarly work, the attribution is present in the form of coded references. The intention is to indicate that sources exist for these statements, as well as to make it easier to provide more detailed information to those interested in pursuing specific points in greater detail.

The Nature of the Sample Firms

Industrial users of NCMTs were identified by referring to the 1982–83 SPE listings. Questionnaires were submitted to the Institute of Economics of the Hungarian Academy of Sciences. After vetting and revision, the questions were forwarded to the 85 enterprises and answers were returned to the author on an anonymous basis. Fifty enterprises responded all or in part to the questions. A translation of the questions as submitted to the enterprises may be found below.

QUESTIONNAIRE

On the Diffusion of NC Machine Tools

1. Is your enterprise state or cooperative?
2. Does the enterprise belong to the machine-building industry? If so, to which sub-branch?
3. How many plants (factory units) are there within the enterprise?
4. When did the enterprise first install NC machine tools and in what quantity? Of these machines, how many were domestic? Other CMEA? Capitalist?
5. Was the enterprise independent [not a member of a trust] at the time of first adoption?
6. In the year in which NCMTs were first acquired, how many were employed in the enterprise? How many of these were manual workers?
7. What percentage of the cost for the first NCMTs was covered by bank credits? By state aid?
8. What was the value of the enterprise's output in the year in which NCMTs were first acquired? In 1982?
9. What percentage of the enterprise's output was exported to the ruble and the non-ruble markets in the first year of NCMT use? In 1982?
10. What percentage of the enterprise's output was produced in

cooperation with CMEA partners and with capitalist partners in the first year of NCMT use? In 1982?

11.   In the first year of NCMT use was there an R&D unit (department) within the enterprise? If yes, how many members did it have?

ACKNOWLEDGMENTS

The views expressed in this paper are those of the author and do not necessarily represent those of The RAND Corporation. The author thanks Gregory Grossman, Laura Tyson, Josef Brada and István Dobozi for helpful comments in revising this paper. All remaining errors are in spite of their best efforts.

NOTES

1.   Appendix 1 explains the system of references used in the case of information derived from interviews.

2.   Although an interesting story in itself, the present study will focus only on the diffusion of NC technology and not on the travails encountered in developing a domestic industry. Studies of the latter may be found in K. Nagy, 1981, 1982.

3.   Western countries have held similar state-financed programs with a like end in view. The United Kingdom underwrote the risk of adopting this new technology by guaranteeing to potential users that the machinery could be returned to the original supplier within two years for reimbursement of an agreed upon fraction of the purchase price (Gebhardt and Hatzold). As in Hungary, the formal assistance supplied by the state appears to have been less influential in the decision to adopt than the climate which it served to foster.

4.   Barash (1979, p. 4) offers the forecast of a NCMT stock representing a 15 percent share in West Germany, and 25 percent in the USSR, by the year 2000.

5.   These figures are derived by calculating the gross values of installed NCMTs only in those enterprises which have been successfully categorized by branch. This, then, implies the extremely conservative assumption that all NCMTs installed in enterprises for which branch affiliation was uncertain are considered to lie outside the machine industry.

6.   While it would be possible to deflate the series on general investment given available data, it would be difficult to develop price indices for so heterogeneous a set of commodities as machine tools that would give figures of sufficient reliability to make comparison in real terms meaningful. It is not clear that this would be superior to the assumption implicitly employed in the discussion that all investment goods exhibited roughly similar price trends during this period.

7.   No sufficiently disaggregated data has been available to evaluate the relative price trends between NC and traditional machine tools.

8.   The trade-weighted duty on convertible currency imports of machinery and

spare parts is 23 percent, and may be up to 50 percent on certain categories. In addition, from September 1982 through April 1984, there was a 20 percent surcharge on such imports.

9.   It may be inferred from the SPE listings that only those machines produced in East Germany and Czechoslovakia are of sufficient quality to complement Hungarian output.

10.   In fact, an early ministerial study of the feasibility of NCMT uptake suggested that the ability to provide an adequate supply of spare parts should be considered as a prime determinant of which enterprises should receive state aid for the acquisition of NC technology (83–10NP).

11.   Although the information generated by interviews is by no means conclusive, the impression is that there tends to be less emphasis placed upon the experience of other domestic users during the process of gathering information on potential economic net benefit. This may be attributable to the lack of comparability of economic performance which non-normativity in economic regulation generates.

12.   The need for certain accounting rigidities may also be explained by the problems of coordinating pricing and profitability guidelines for three different markets: hard currency export, domestic, and CMEA. It should be noted that changes in the methods of accounting and cost allocation are being considered for introduction in the latest round (1985) of reforms.

13.   As an example, a large enterprise employing an NC flame cutter does not use it to cut a wide assortment of pieces rapidly from a single metal sheet as it was designed to do. Rather, single pieces are cut only as needed to keep pace with the unchanged flow of production and the rest of the sheet stored and the machine left standing idle for great periods (Balazs, 1985).

14.   In what is to follow, all quotations are from this article unless otherwise noted.

15.   It might be noted in passing that the enterprise whose very competitive environment forced it to introduce the drastic changes necessary to utilize the NCMTs properly, was able to bend the letter of the wage regulations somewhat and introduce an internal system of remuneration that served to compensate for the increased discipline enjoined upon the NC cadre.

16.   Please refer to Appendix 1 for information on the data sample.

17.   Unless otherwise indicated in parentheses, all correlation coefficients are significant to the .95 level of confidence.

18.   A constant returns to scale production function of the form $Q = AK^aL^{1-a}$ can be stated in per capita terms as $Q/L = A(K/L)^a$. Plainly, the ratio Q/L can be influenced by differences in capital costs as well as by either neutral (A) or non-neutral (a) differences in technology (Brown, 1966).

REFERENCES

Amann, R., J. Cooper, and Davies (1977). *The Technological Level of Soviet Industry*. (New Haven: Yale University Press).

Balazs, Katalin (1985). *"Innovacio alkalmazas nelkul,"* Institute of Sociology, Budapest (mimeo).

Barash, M. M. (1979). "The Future of Numerical Controls". *Mechanical Engineering,* September.

Becsky, R. and A. Inzelt (1982). *Miert rugalmasak?*. (Budapest: Kossuth).
Csikoks-Nagy, Bela (1983). Interview in *Figyelo*, 3 November.
Davies, S. (1979). *The Diffusion of Process Innovations*. (Cambridge: Cambridge University Press).
Friss, Istvan (1969). *Reform of the Economic Mechanism in Hungary*. (Budapest: Akademiai Kiado).
Gebhardt, A. and O. Hatzold (1974). "Numerically Controlled Machine Tools," in Nabseth and Ray (1974).
Gettleman, K. and K. Schultz (1976). "Building the NC Team is a Management Job." *Modern Machine Shop,* December.
Gerencser, F. and A. Toth (1979). "A hatekonysag szigetei." *Figyelo*. 9 May.
Hajos, G. (1976). "A numerikus technika a hazai gepiparban." *Gazdasag* (X) 4, pp. 88–99.
Herceg, J. (1982). "Az innovacio felteteleink javitasaval kapcsolatos szabalyozasi feladatok." *Muszaki Elet,* 11 November.
Horvath, M. (1984). "Gepipar: a megujulas feltetelei." *Figyelo,* 15 March.
Javorka, E. (1978). *Muszaki fejlesztes—hatekonysag—arak*. (Budapest: Kossuth).
Laki, M. (1979). *Uj termekek bevezetese es a piaci alkalmazkodas*. (Budapest: Kozgazdasagi es Jogi Konyvkiado).
Nabseth, L. and G. F. Ray (1974). *The Diffusion of New Industrial Processes*. (Cambridge: Cambridge University Press).
Nagy, K. (1981). "A magyarorszagi NC-technika a kezdettol az integralt gyartorendszerig." (Budapest:MS).
Ray, G. F. (1984). "A magyar ipar szinvonala nehany mutatoszam tukreben." *Ipargazdasagi Szemle* (XV) 1–2, pp. 57–69.
SPE (1982–5). *Szerszamgep Programazasi Egyesules NC Nyilvantartas*. (Budapest).
Statisztikai Evkonyv. (Budapest: Kozponti Statisztikai Hivatal).
Tombari, H. A. (1978). "Factors to be Considered when Evaluating the Purchase and Use of Numerically Controlled Machine Tools." *Production and Inventory Management,* 3.

RESEARCH, DEVELOPMENT, INNOVATION AND TECHNOLOGY FLOWS IN SMALL COUNTRIES:
THE EXPERIENCE OF HUNGARY

Mihály Simai

The world market reflects world-wide power relations in technical and economic development. Some "innovative" countries, the United States, Japan, the Federal Republic of Germany, France and the United Kingdom, hold particularly strong positions in the arena of international economic relations. The R + D background of these countries and the capital power of their transnational corporations help to maintain their leading positions. In the strongly monopolistic markets for new technology, the conditions of selling and buying depend on the sophistication of the technology in question, its age, its economic and strategic importance, and on the state of the competition among its producers. The presence of the socialist countries or of some developing countries in the technology markets has not so far proved substantial enough to cause any significant change in the conditions of the international transfer of high technology. However, the changes in

the world economy have had a definite impact on the conditions of
international trade in technology of medium or lower sophistication,
and have wrought significant changes in the specific conditions of the
international market for military technology.

The trends prevailing in the 1970s and 1980s suggest that the
number of firms offering the newest and also the highest level of
technology for sale is increasing and competition among them is growing keener. This is the case particularly in the industries using technologies that are less than entirely new, a development very relevant to
Hungarian technology imports. This does not of necessity entail a
significant improvement of the conditions of technology imports overall, but it does give the importers some choice among sources, and
does improve their bargaining positions somewhat. On the other hand,
corporations in the United States, Japan and some other western countries have shown a tendency to export high-technology finished products rather than the technology proper wherever a production monopoly is particularly important in safeguarding competitive positions.

Strategic restrictions on Western technology exports to the socialist
countries may give rise to occasional worries, especially since these
restrictions, applied to every member state of the Warsaw Pact, appear
to be here to stay. Intensified cooperation among the CMEA member-
states might to some extent offset these restrictions. To that end,
however, it would be necessary to improve the mechanisms of the
CMEA, and to integrate better than heretofore the interests of the
research institutes and enterprises. If this cannot be achieved on a
broad front, then separate, special forms of cooperation using mechanisms permitting more flexible and rapid action should be envisaged in
the high-technology sphere.

I.   THE INNOVATION PROCESS AND ITS
FACTORS

Innovation is a multi-dimensional category characterising the introduction of new product or process technology, but it is not confined to the
field of technology. Social, institutional, marketing and other improvements are often connected with the introduction of new forms of
activity, and hence they are also called innovations. On the macroeconomic level and in greater historical perspective this concept is
often interchanged with the category of "modernization." This paper
uses the concept to describe and analyse technological change, both on

the micro and macro-economic level. The concept of innovation on a macro-economic level is broader but on the level of the firms it can also be used in broader and narrower senses. It can be restricted to describe the technical process by which modern technology is introduced but it can also be used in a broader form, which would include the whole decision-making process and the factors influencing it.

From the research on the problems of innovation in Hungary or abroad, it is evident that the nature of the innovation process, the problems involved, the influencing factors, the limitations, and the costs and benefits are not very well understood. The broader the concept we use the more will be the unknown "grey areas" especially in the socio-economic environment.

On the macroeconomic level innovation is considered as a process by which technology is conceived, developed and deployed on a large scale. Innovation is not identical with R + D or invention. These are of course important parts of the innovation process. The process includes the evolution of the whole technological system, from research through invention to design for manufacturing and marketing or operational application. The social support system that facilitates the deployment and large scale use of technology is also an indispensable part of the innovation process. The social support system in itself is a rather complex structure of markets, policies, institutions and attitudes. Since the development of science and technology takes place in an interrelated and increasingly interdependent international system, the innovation process of the different countries, while being determined by factors prevailing within their national frontiers is influenced by international factors. The trans-border transfer of knowledge, know-how, machinery and equipment, the role of the innovating countries and their firms in this process has created an interrelated international chain. The position of the 160 countries that exist at present on our globe is highly unequal in the innovation process. A handful of developed industrial countries concentrate a large part of the world R + D potential and they not only dominate the production but also determine the nature of the market for new technology and the main conditions of technology transfer. Inequalities in this field increase the gap between rich and poor countries at the same time that they are sources of competition and conflicts among the innovating countries. The fact that a large proportion of R + D expenditures is spent for military purposes ties a major part of the innovation process and of technology transfer to strategic considerations.

The microeconomic concept of innovation is determined basically by the fact that, besides the general environment in which the given firm is working, the issues are often specific to particular branches, product groups, products or projects. The general environment includes the degree of independence in which technological decisions are made and implemented by the managers of enterprises, the system of financing, the incentives to innovate and the different constrains, such as taxes, regulations, etc., in which the enterprises have to work.

There are some general determining factors in the process of innovation in any given country. Historical experience and present comparative studies show the importance of the following interrelated factors:

1. the level of industrial development, the structure of industry, the size of the market, the growth and nature of demand;
2. the general educational level of the population, availability of labor and especially of highly skilled labor within the population;
3. the accumulated expertise, the production experiences or production culture, the versatility and the creativity of the labor force;
4. the magnitude of R + D expenditures and productive investments and their structural distribution;
5. the size, experiences, attitudes and organization of the research sector, in particular, its relations to industries, and interrelations between industrial and academic research;
6. the structure of firms and the general attitude of managers towards new products and processes. The latter is shaped by traditions, incentives, and pressures that influence the emphasis on process or product innovation. The readiness and ability to take risks, including the availability of venture capital;
7. the attitude of the workers and the general public towards new products or processes, and social incentives to accept or adapt to new things;
8. the degree of openness of the given economy, the importance of international economic relations and the nature of these relations to the great technological centers of the world, as well as the character of the different channels in the transfer process;
9. the priorities of economic policy and within this of the technological policy of the government;

10. the nature of technological development in the given era. At this stage for example, due to the characteristics of the new technological revolution, the new technologies represent a greater qualitative jump in relation to the old ones. They require more specific expertise. It is more difficult to control their socio-economic implications. Due to high research and development costs their international transfer is more costly and its control process is more strict. The competition is also stronger.

It follows from the above mentioned factors that those countries which could develop the optimal combination of the above mentioned factors could enjoy greater advantages in the innovation process or could use imported technologies more efficiently. Very few countries are characterised today by these abilities.

In the mid-1980s, taking into account the specific nature of the new technology there are very few countries that have the ability to develop a broad range of innovations. The vast majority of the 160 existing countries are technologically dependent upon external suppliers, and there are about 20–30 countries that have important positions in certain sectors, while in other sectors they also depend on imports of technology. All this is, of course, undertaken by individual enterprises. There are great differences between the possibilities and the strengths of the most important firms from the point of view of innovation, since their innovative abilities vary across a spectrum of technological and economic possibilities. While the priorities and the technological policies of governments may influence these firms, within the limits created by the general socio-economic environment they have a range of options and alternative strategies.

The most important characteristics of smaller countries under the present circumstances compare adversly with those of the larger countries at similar levels of industrial development, due to the smaller domestic demand and more limited resources and research and engineering staff of the former. This does not exclude the possibility that with proper concentration some firms in smaller countries could achieve internationally leading position in certain sectors or pursue correspondingly offensive innovation strategies.

In the case of Hungary, the comparative analysis of relevant factors indicates that the market size in itself is not enough to explain successes or failures. Some of the problems in Hungary resemble those of the larger countries with the same economic and social system or on similar level of development. Other problems are more general and independent of country size or system characteristics.

At the present stage of technological development, when the new technical advances require large research establishment and R + D expenditures, even the more developed and larger countries have to rely increasingly on international sources of technology in many areas. In order to be competitive, they have to concentrate on those areas where their traditions are strong and their industries have the greatest possibilities. The pressure for specialization and international cooperation in the innovation process is increasing even in the larger countries. Not only such relatively small countries as the Netherlands, Belgium, Switzerland and Sweden rely on the sources new technology of the technological centres in the larger countries, beyond their own research facilities, but the larger countries are also increasingly forced to utilize international sources in different forms. Of course, some of these countries, through their transnational corporations, were always active technology importers and exporters.

II. THE RESEARCH ESTABLISHMENT IN HUNGARY

Among the 160 countries of the world, in 1981 Hungary was fortieth in GNP, thirty-sixth in per capita GDP and twenty-eigth in per capita industrial output. According to UNCESCO, for the late 1970s Hungary was seventeenth in the magnitude of human and financial resources devoted to R + D per million of population.

In the pre-Second World War period, Hungary's R + D capacity was small but in comparison to her size, economic development level and economic performance, it was not negligable. Some firms were able to compete in technology intensive sectors. The still-existing firm Tungsram, concentrated the best researchers in the field, developed new products, and became one of the leading international producers of light bulbs. Important progress also took place in research in optics. Individual researchers, working mostly in universities, contributed to the progress of science through basic research.

The research and development establishment in general corresponded to the needs and characteristics of the technology of the period. The predominant part of new products and processes introduced in Hungarian industry was of foreign origin, coming mostly from Germany, Switzerland, Great Britain, and other western countries. Although the volume of industrial output in GDP was rather small, the main new industries were on a high technological level and their performance in terms of productivity, organization, efficiency etc. was not much below that of the original supplier.

A major transformation took place in Hungary after World War II. Starting from the early 1950s Hungary was cut off from the main western industrial technological centers. This was due not only to the embargo connected with the Cold War, but also to Hungary's own policies and priorities. In an increasingly closed economic system pursuing a policy of rapid industrial transformation and following extensive industrialization policies, Hungary began introducing new products and processes, establishing new industrial branches, and opening up new markets. For the implementation of these policies a new institutional structure was formed. Under the circumstances of permanent scarcities and rapidly growing demand, the policy of industrialization became oriented toward expanded output and neglected quality and efficiency. The sources of technology imports were basically middle-level economies that, in most cases, lagged behind world standards by eight to ten years. The products of newly established research and development institutions were also on a lower level. They were either copies of models already on the market, or in case of original inventions, their development and commercial utilization was very slow. While these changes represented a major industrial and technological transformation within Hungary in comparison to the past, they built large industrial blocks into the Hungarian economy that were considerably behind the leading countries. With the exception of certain sectors, the lag that developed in technology has remained basically the same since that time, and efforts to reduce it proved to be, by and large, unsuccessful. In certain areas Hungary did manage to reduce the gap and reach the level of the leading countries or firms in the world economy, but these were isolated cases. There was some reduction in the gap as a result of the reform in planning and management in the 1960s, connected mostly with the increasing inflow of Western technology facilitated by new attitudes toward industrial cooperation, imports and international financing. The introduction of new products and processes became somewhat faster. This process slowed down during the 1970s, and the gap started increasing again.

It would be a mistake, despite this increasing gap, to consider the 1970s and the preceeding years only as a period of futile efforts or errors. Important changes took place in certain areas and valuable experiences were gained that will help Hungary in the coming decade, if they are properly utilized and if the international environment does not deteriorate to an extent that would undermine the present structure of international relations. The tasks are substantial and require comprehensive efforts as well in those areas where progress has been greater.

III. REORGANIZATION OF THE R + D SECTOR

Improving the performance and efficiency of the research sector is one of the most important future tasks in the area of innovation. Hungary has developed in the past decades an impressive research base with a system of academic, university and industrial research institutions working in almost all of the larger scientific areas. Between 1960 and 1980 the total staff of the R + D institutions increased by 140 percent to 83,300 and within this the actual researchers increased by 180 percent to 37,000. Fifty percent of them worked in research institutes, nineteen percent in university departments and thirty percent in other research centers. Until 1980 little or no change took place in these proportions. With the reoganization that took place in 1981 several research institutes were transformed into research firms thus, according to data provided by the Central Statistical Office of Hungary, these proportions were modified to 35 : 19 : 46. The aim of the reorganization was to force research institutions to better performance by changing their financing from a budgetary to a contract basis.

Beyond the numbers, the overall performance of research institutes was far from satisfactory. With the exception of a few outstanding achievements in the fields of agricultural hybrids, pharmaceuticals, instruments and logical toys, no important invention characterised their output. Only 6 to 8 percent of the total research work was concentrated on original ideas. The research sector was, and is, too diversified. International specialization is too low and cooperation is not strong enough. The internal organization of many institutes is out of date, there are few interdisciplinary teams, and the proportion of successfully completed projects is too small. In 1981 altogether about 2.4 percent of the new products introduced in industry came from the inventions of the research institutions. Basic research was also a diminishing proportion of total research. In 1980 about 12 to 14 percent of the total research effort was in the category of basic research, and in certain important fields it has reached such a low level that their future existence is endangered.

Important policy decisions and initiatives has been taken to improve the efficiency of the research sector, during the last decade and especially during the recent years:

a.   Steps were taken for the better selection of researchers and for the implementation of qualitative changes in the staff working in the institutions. The ongoing reform of the system of higher education and the changes in the qualifications of scientific workers are also considered important to this purpose.

b.   New plans have been formulated and measures have been taken for the better integration of R + D with production and marketing. Priority is given to research projects that serve product or process innovation in the new research enterprises. Special financing and venture funds are provided with similar aims.

c.   No increase is anticipated in the proportion of R + D expenditures in the institutes. These are considered sufficiently high since they represent about 53 percent of the total R + D expenditures. Although total R + D outlays are said to account for 3 percent of national income, there are doubts concerning the actual proportion since the 3 percent includes the direct costs of production of certain instruments, parts and components produced in special manufacturing units of the research institutes. It is considered necessary, however, to increase substantially the expenditure per researcher, which would provide better instruments, equipment, additional services, etc. This may also be achieved by a qualitative change brought about by reducing the number of scientific workers and leaving in the institutes those whose performance and qualities are better.

IV.   INTERNATIONAL COOPERATION AND ITS EFFICIENCY

Hungary, a country with middle level economy and industry, relies to a very great extent on the import of technology. It is impossible to calculate directly what proportion of the new products and processes introduced are of foreign origin. The proportion of new products introduced in industry in 1981 through licenses was about 8 percent, and the share of new products developed by the enterprises was 89 percent. It is evident that a large part of this 89 percent also had "foreign" content. The in-house development by the enterprises was seldom based on qualitatively original ideas. Both the commercial and the non-commercial channels of technology transfer were important in the case of in-house innovations. Even the research institutes are "cross fertilized'' in their projects by ideas of international origin. These, of course, are not unknown methods among western firms or institutions either, and in themselves they imply little about the level of efficiency of R + D in Hungary. The problems are connected more with the low level of imported technology in relation to the world standards. Difficulties in assimilation also reduce efficiency of technology transfer, and internal diffusion, especially in industry, is slow. Out of these factors comes the especially important task of improving efficiency and increasing the intensity of technology imports into industry, agriculture and services.

In the past decade, Hungary has used three main channels for commercial technology imports in the following order of importance: direct purchases of new machinery and equipment, licences and industrial cooperation. In the case of technology imports from the East the direct purchases were most important while in the case of western technology imports licences and industrial cooperation were most important. There is little doubt that there are several unfinished tasks in this field.

a.   It will be necessary to integrate technology imports into technological development policy and thus into the long-term development strategy of the country. The practice of the National Council of Technological Development must be changed in this respect to deal with longer-term policy issues. This would facilitate a better and more purposeful integration of imports and domestic research, especially research for adaptation and development of the imported technology in the most important industries.

b.   It will be necessary to integrate those branches of the Hungarian industry that have relatively good performance and growth potential with the main foreign technological centers through direct relations among firms, direct investment, cross licencing, joint development, cooperation in third markets, etc. Through these channels, the two-way flows of technology must be also better combined.

c.   Within the limits of existing possibilities, the forms of technology transfer that should be preferred are those:

•   that help the development of the imported technology, jointly or by the Hungarian research sector;
•   that have limited additional import requirements for materials,

parts or components, and for which supporting industries are available or could be rapidly developed;

- that help to increase exports;
- that facilitate the domestic diffusion of imported technology.

It is evident from the above that the most efficient forms are joint ventures and industrial cooperation projects that integrate the interests of the participating partners. Imported technology cannot by itself improve the performance of the economy. The Hungarian experience also proved that in order to be able to utilize the imported technology efficiently, the whole innovation process must be improved. Foreign technology cannot cure sick economies. It can, in fact, increase their problems due to the high price that must be paid for imports of technology.

V.   INNOVATION AND THE ENTERPRISES: STRATEGIES AND MOTIVATIONS

While the macroeconomic conditions are very important, the innovation process takes place at the level of the firm. The experiences of Hungary indicated clearly that both in the case of "native" technology or in technology imports, the firm is the unit determining the speed of introduction, the degree of efficiency and marketing. The strongest resistance against innovations is also concentrated on the level of the firm. This means that firms must be encouraged or must be put into a competitive environment in order to be forced to innovate. The previous system of central directives also attempted to give instructions and funds to the firms for innovation. It was not only the resistance of the firms that hampered the fulfillment of the technology plans, but also the system of scarcities, the automatic purchase of products by intermediary units or consumers, the absence of pressures to innovate and the disincentives to introduce new products or processes.[1] While the reform of planning and management in Hungary since 1968 changed the attitudes and the capabilities of the firms, these changes were insufficient and the autonomy of the firms for risktaking and enjoying the benefits or bearing the costs was insufficient. The pressure to innovate was also relatively weak in relation to the dangers and inconveniences usually characterizing the first stages of the process. This situation was aggravated by the difficulties caused by external

economic problems in the 1970s. In order to speed up the introduction
of new products and processes several measures must be undertaken:

  a.   Hungarian firms must be encouraged to think in terms of long-
term world market strategies. Some of the internationally known strategies have certain lessons for them. Since the mid 1970s, experts and
even politicians in Hungary have talked about introducing an offensive
strategy. An ''offensive'' innovation strategy is defined as one that is
designed to achieve a leading position or leadership in the given sector
or in a given market by the introduction of new products. While on the
national or regional CMEA market such a strategy is not impossible,
on the world market an enterprise selecting and pursuing such a strategy must either have a very strong independent R + D capacity of its
own or must have a special relationship with leading research and
technology actors in the world. A special relationship means some
form of direct integration through capital investments, contractual research, consultancy arrangements, personal links, etc. In practice,
only a small minority of the firms in a given sector is able and willing
to follow an offensive innovation strategy on a global scale and even
those are seldom able to pursue it consistently for an extended period.
They may be forced into ''consolidating the achieved position.'' The
great majority of firms follow strategies that could be characterised as
''defensive'' and sometimes as ''imitative.'' These strategies are
closer to the possibilities of Hungarian firms.

  The ''defensive'' innovator may also need relatively large R + D
expenditures but he does not wish to be the leader in developing new
products and thus incurring the heavy risks involved or he cannot be
the first. He wants to profit from the experience of early innovators and
their opening up of the market. He may have at the same time greater
strength in production process design and in marketing than the original ''offensive'' innovator. The defensive innovator does not seek to
produce a copy of or an imitation of the product. Rather he makes
technical improvements and tries to compete by establishing independent patents. If he buys licenses he uses them as a springboard. The
imitative or ''carbon copy'' strategy follows the leading firms, often
with a long lag. This strategy may offer certain advantages to the
imitators in closed or ''captive'' markets and to those with lower labor
costs. If they want to compete with the original innovators they must
have very low production costs, or high subsidies and other protective
measures.

  These strategies may be present simultaneously among the different firms in any country. Naturally the size of the country will influence both the degree and the forms of specialization, but obviously country size in itself is insufficient to explain innovative performance, government policies or managerial attitudes. While there are chances that a few Hungarian enterprises will be able to follow offensive strategies in a few products, the majority of these firms will be able to elaborate and follow a well conceived defensive strategy. Nevertheless, many firms will be confined to "carbon copy" strategy in the domestic or in the regional market. There are already certain good examples of the elaboration and implementation of such strategies. The Hungarian state farm, "Babolna" is implementing an "offensive" innovation strategy in some areas. The "Medicor" firm, producing medical instruments is effectively using "defensive" elements in its long term strategy. The "Ikarus" firm, producing buses, is a typical example of a defensive strategy.

b.   The elaboration and especially the implementation of these strategies is very closely connected with the possibilities and forms of financing innovations and the necessary investments. Innovations of enterprises are increasingly financed from their own Technology Development Funds (TDF), from different special credit sources from the Central TDF, and in certain cases and in diminishing proportions from the state budget. The role of the TDF, its formation and the conditions of its use have been changed substantially, with the aim of increasing the independence of the enterprises and of separating investment financing from the financing of innovation. In 1981 75 percent of the total R + D expenditures were financed from TDF sources and 25 percent came from others. Since 1980 special credit with 3 years maturity and in special cases for a longer term is also available for innovation projects. As a result of the reform measures, TDF, which is created on the basis of predetermined norms, remained mandatory only in engineering and chemical industries. From January 1, 1983 in the rest of the economy the enterprises themselves decide about the creation of such a fund, which is, up to a certain point, a part of their costs. It has been also determined which industries and enterprises have to contribute to the Central TDF. All enterprises can apply for additional money from the central authorities. Sixty percent of the central funds are distributed on the basis of special contracts between the Ministry and the enterprise. Until 1983 a large part of TDF remained unused and very few firms applied for innovation credits. This is due to the fact that while funds have been available for the enterprises in the last few years, the use of these funds is overregulated, and the transfer from one sub-item to another is even more difficult. There is not enough flexibility in this important field of financing. The new system of financing made improvements, in some areas, and as a result the profit interests in successful innovations as well as the risks of failures more directly influence profitability than before. It will be necessary to increase the freedom of enterprises to shift funds if sudden new opportunities emerge or if, in the process of the implementation of the given R + D project, requirements change. This is true also in all other cases of enterprise finance.

c.   The reorganization of the enterprises, their decentralization and deconcentration, the establishment of smaller more flexible firms, the encouragement of enterpreneurship are accompanied by measures that facilitate special relationships among firms to undertake innovations. The establishment of special banks with venture capital to finance the first part of the innovation process in smaller firms also creates better conditions for the innovation process. The results of these measures will be felt at a later stage. The success of the changing organizational forms from the point of view of improving the speed and efficiency of innovation will depend greatly on the different supporting measures in the field of financing, on the availability of international sources of knowledge, investment funds, etc.

d.   Improved marketing also represents an important factor in the innovation process. This must be understood in a broader sense; market research in connection with the availability and conditions of technology imports, the sales of Hungarian technology within the country and abroad, the establishment of joint ventures or Hungarian enterprises abroad for the sales of technology and for services.

e.   The "human factor" plays a key role in the innovation process at the level of the firm. Strong incentives must be created to overcome the reluctance of top managers and to stimulate engineers and workers. The personal involvement of the research workers in the innovation and marketing process of the enterprises could be also achieved with a different system of incentives. The proper distribution of highly skilled manpower, especially of engineers, between the R + D system and the production process must also be facilitated. This connects the human problems of innovation with the greater mobility of workers, engineers and managers. This would include also a better interchange of experts between industry, research institutes and universities. The international mobility of research workers and engineers must be also increased substantially.

VI. CONCLUSION

Hungary, as a result of her economic, social and technological transformation reached the higher stage of the middle level economic development by the 1980s. She could enter into the group of highly developed industrial countries during the coming 15–20 years provided certain specific conditions can be met. One of the most important tasks in this respect is the faster technological progress in industry, agriculture, and infrastructure. These cannot be achieved without introducing further reform measures, implementing far reaching institutional changes and without more intensive international relations with the main centers of science and technology in the world. Taking into account all her present economic problems, the situation of the world economy and of international politics, the transition will be more difficult than had been anticipated a few years ago. The efforts to improve the mechanism of the innovation process in the country are considered as vital instruments to overcome some of these difficulties.

NOTE

1.   New products are more important at this stage for export and because the rate of their introduction slowed down since the late 1970s.

PART III

HUNGARY AND THE WORLD ECONOMY

HOW EFFECTIVE IS THE CMEA?
AN INTERNATIONAL COMPARISON

Josef C. Brada and José A. Méndez

I. INTRODUCTION

Although Hungary's trade with the developed market economies is of
importance because it permits Hungary to acquire technology not
available from its partner countries in the Council for Mutual Economic Assistance (CMEA) and because trade with the West may impose some competitive pressures on Hungarian firms, it is trade with
CMEA that forms the foundation for Hungary's trade policy and for
the overall success of the Hungarian economy. Not only does the
volume of trade with CMEA encompass the majority of Hungary's
imports and exports (Table 1), but such trade is also vital to Hungary's
ability to develop new and dynamic industries (Brada 1984, forthcoming). Thus, whether or not Hungary's efforts at reform and restructuring will prove successful depends, to a large extent, on the environment within CMEA for the expansion of trade and for the promotion of
specialization and technological progress.

The ability of the CMEA to meet Hungary's foreign trade needs in
turn depends on its ability to generate the static and dynamic gains that
economists identify as the main benefits from regional integration. In

Table 1.   Hungarian Trade by Regions (%)

	Exports		Imports	
Year	CMEA	Developed Market Economies	CMEA	Developed Market Economies
1960	61.6	22.0	63.2	24.3
1970	66.9	27.2	62.5	27.1
1975	68.5	21.8	63.5	27.4
1980	51.5	35.1	47.3	40.2
1983	54.4	33.0	52.6	34.4

Sources: Vienna Institute for Comparative Economic Studies, *Comecon Foreign Trade Data, 1982.* (London: MacMillan, 1983) and Hungarian Central Statistical Office, *Hungary Today.* (Budapest: Statistical Publishing House, 1985).

the next section of the paper we examine the static gains from integration, in the form of increased intra-member trade, that CMEA generates. We conclude that, in terms of gross trade creation among members, the CMEA appears to be a relatively effective integration scheme. In Section III we examine CMEA's ability to generate dynamic gains from integration, and, again, we conclude that CMEA compares well on this score when judged against its objectives and against the performance of other integration schemes. Based on these findings we then examine the rationale for Hungary's participation within CMEA and the political economy of future intra-CMEA relations.

II.   STATIC GAINS FROM INTEGRATION: INCREASING TRADE AMONG INTEGRATING COUNTRIES[1]

Static gains from integration arise from the increase in intra-member trade that results from the lowering of barriers to trade among the integrating countries. The increased volume of trade lowers prices in importing countries and brings about a more rational allocation of resources. At the same time, there may be losses associated with integration if trade with efficient non-members is reduced in favor of trade with less-efficient members of the integration scheme. Thus, to judge the efficacy of CMEA as an integration scheme we need to reach an understanding both of the trade creation effects of CMEA integration and of the diversion of CMEA members' trade from non-member countries.

In this section, we first compare the ability of the CMEA to promote intra-member trade to that of integration schemes among developed and developing market economies. Then we examine, from the Hungarian standpoint, the impact that the CMEA's trade diversion may have on Hungary's share of the static gains from integration.

The Model

With the exception of Balassa's (1967) study of trade creation and diversion in the EEC, the common approach to quantifying the effects of integration on trade flows has been to utilize the so-called gravity equation. The gravity equation has proven popular for several reasons. First it provides an empirically tractable general equilibrium framework for modelling bilateral trade flows. Second it has a sound theoretical basis, Bergstrand (1985), and it has proved useful in a variety of applications; Geraci and Prewo (1977), Linnemann (1966), Poyhonen (1963) and Tinbergen (1962). In its basic form the model is written as:

$$\log X_{ij} = A + a_1 \log Y_i + a_2 \log Y_j + a_3 \log N_i + a_4 \log N_j + a_5 D_{ij} + \log e_{ij} \quad \textbf{(Eq. 1)}$$

where
- X_{ij} = value of exports from country i to country j
- A = constant
- Y_i, Y_j = income in the exporting and importing countries
- N_i, N_j = population in the exporting and importing countries
- D_{ij} = distance between countries i and j
- e_{ij} = lognormal error term.

The income and population variables represent the trading countries' endowments and tastes. Since greater productive capacity and income promote trade, a_1 and a_2 are expected to be positive. Large countries have more diversified production and thus satisfy a greater proportion of domestic demand while small countries tend to be more specialized and thus more dependent on trade, suggesting that a_3 should be negative (Leamer and Stern, 1970, pp. 152–3). The population of the importing country should have a positive effect on the volume of trade, since a larger population permits a greater division of labor and diversity of production enabling imports to compete with domestic goods at more stages of the production process. Moreover, a large market better compensates exporters for the cost of acquiring information and establishing a sales and distribution network. Thus a_4 should be positive.

The distance variable represents resistance to trade. This resistance has an economic element, consisting of transportation and information costs; a structural element reflecting differences in consumption patterns and resource endowments as, for example, between temperate and tropical countries; and a policy element including the effects of economic integration. Because the structural factors are ambiguous in their effect, with differences in endowments promoting trade but differences in consumption hindering it, we focus our attention on the other two factors by improving on the way that the effects of integration on resistance to trade are specified.

Researchers have used the gravity equation to measure the trade-augmenting effects of integration in two ways. The more common, used by Tinbergen (1962), Aitken (1973) and Hewett (1976), is to employ a set of dummy variables to measure the effect of integration on intra-member trade. Whenever two members of a preferential trading group trade with each other, the dummy is equal to 2; when trade is with or among non-members the dummy equals 1. The larger the value of the coefficient of the dummy variable, the greater the volume of intra-member trade relative to "normal" or non-preferential trade and the more effective the integration scheme. An alternative approach, employed by Pelzman (1977), is to choose a pre-integration period on the basis of which Equation 1 is estimated. The parameter estimates are then employed to project expected intra-member trade during the post-integration period. The excess of actual intra-member trade over the expected volume of trade is attributed to the effect of integration. While either approach is acceptable when one or a few integration schemes, made up of countries at similar levels of development, of similar size and with the same economic system, are analyzed, both methods break down when we turn to the more heterogeneous sample of countries required to compare the effects of integration among developed and developing market countries and among the members of the CMEA.

The effect of integration on intra-member trade is influenced by three sets of factors. The first of these is the environment, which we take to mean the physical and economic characteristics of the integrating countries and their economic relations with the rest of the world. For example, countries close to each other should experience, ceteris paribus, a greater post-integration stimulus to mutual trade than would two integrating countries that are far from each other. A second influence on the effectiveness of integration is the economic system of the integrating countries. The literature on the trade behavior of the planned economies suggests that such economies will trade less, ceteris paribus, than comparable market economies. Finally, there is the element of policy; some integration schemes lower barriers against intra-member trade to a greater degree than do others and thus are more effective in increasing intra-member exchanges. When we deal with a homogenous group of countries, we can assume that the integration dummies or the difference between actual and predicted trade flows do not reflect systemic differences; nor do we expect that environmental factors change sharply over time or differ appreciably between integration schemes. Thus the coefficients of the integration dummies or the differences between expected and actual post-integration trade can safely be attributed to the policy variable, economic integration. However, with a more heterogeneous sample, estimates of the effect of integration will become tainted at best and swamped at worst by the differences in system and environment that exist among the various integration schemes.

In order to overcome these difficulties, we modify the gravity equation to take into account environmental effects on the effectiveness of integration. The two environmental variables we model are distance among integrating countries and their level of development. The hypothesis that distance among integrating countries will influence the amount by which intra-member trade increases is based on many of the same arguments employed to include distance as a trade resistance variable. For example, if countries A, B and C agree to reduce trade barriers among themselves, and A and B are close to each other but both are distant from C then the degree of integration and consequently the increase in trade should be greater between A and B than between A and C or B and C. In part this will occur because for some bulky or highly perishable products trade between A and B might become feasible while remaining uneconomic between A and C. The larger distance between A and C will also place businesses in C at a disadvantage vis-à-vis those in B in assessing and reacting to market opportunities in country A, since they will have less precise information about A and less direct acquaintance with the culture and economy of country A. Thus they will be less successful in penetrating A's markets. Finally, countries close to each other are likely to have greater cultural similarities and also relatively similar climates, leading to similar patterns of consumption and production, that, in turn, lead to greater opportunities for exchanges of products (Linder, 1961). Consequently, an integration scheme with relatively small distances among members should stimulate intra-member trade more, ceteris paribus, than one consisting of countries located far from each other.

The level of development should also have a positive impact on the effects of integration largely because less developed countries have a structural bias against trade and thus benefit less from integration. Their production is concentrated in subsistence agriculture and in services, neither of which enter into international trade. The bulk of their trade is thus with countries of differing levels of development and consists of exchanges of agricultural products and raw materials for manufacturers. Developed countries' production, concentrated in manufactures, permits both complementary trade (manufactures for raw materials) as well as a large measure of intra-industry exchanges of manufactured goods.

To measure these environmental influences on trade flows we respecify Equation 1 as:

$$\log X_{ij} = A + a_1 \log Y_i + a_2 \log Y_j + a_3 \log N_i + \\ a_4 \log N_j + a_5 \log D_{ij} + b \log Q_{ij} + c_1 P_{ij} \\ \log(Y_i/N_i)(Y_j/N_j) + c_2 P_{ij} \log D_{ij} \\ + \log e_{ij} \qquad \textbf{(Eq. 2)}$$

where $Q_{ij} = 2$ and $P_{ij} = 1$ if countries i and j belong to the same preference area and $= 1$ and 0 respectively when countries i and j belong to different or no preference areas. The coefficient c_1 measures the effect of per capita incomes on the effectiveness of integration. If the coefficient is positive, then the effect of integration on inter-member trade increases with the level of development of the integrating countries, reflecting the higher proportion of tradables in their output. The coefficient c_2 measures the effect of distance on the trade augmenting power of a customs union. The greater the distance among members, the smaller, ceteris paribus, is the augmentation of their trade with each other.

Empirical Results

Data was collected for the trade of the member countries of the European Economic Community (EEC), European Free Trade Area (EFTA), Central American Common Market (CAM), Latin American Free Trade Area (LAFTA), and the Andean Pact with each other and with 18 developed and developing countries belonging to no integration scheme.[2] Trade flows of the CMEA countries were not employed in estimating the parameters of Equation 2 since, due to systemic differences between them and the other countries in the sample, the trade of the CMEA was not expected to follow the regime implied by parameters estimated on the basis of the trade of market economies. Because the observations could not be pooled over time, it was necessary to estimate parameters for Equation 2 for each year and these parameter estimates are presented in Table 2. The coefficients for income and population have the expected signs, and these as well as a_5, the coefficient for distance, are similar to those reported by Aitken and Hewett, whose samples were restricted to industrialized countries. With the exception of the constant term the coefficients are relatively stable over time.

Estimates of the values of the coefficients measuring integration effects are reported from 1960 onward, since that year marks the founding of EFTA and LAFTA as well as the first year of operation of the EEC. The estimates of b, the parameter of the coefficient for the integration dummy, Q_{ij}, are not significant in the early years of integration. This is to be expected since it is likely to require some time before traders can take advantage of the opportunities offered by reductions in barriers to intra-member trade. With the passage of time, the magnitude and significance of b increase, reflecting the gradual increase in intra-member trade as the effects of integration make themselves felt. The value of b reaches its peak in 1969, and then declines until 1972 when an upward trend in its value asserts itself. The post-1968 decline may reflect the delayed effects of the Kennedy Round tariff cuts which should have reduced the tendency of integration to promote inter-member trade at the expense of trade with outsiders.

The coefficient for per capita incomes of integrating countries, c_1, is generally positive and significant. This means that, ceteris paribus, integration among high per capita income, or developed, countries causes a greater increase in inter-member trade than does integration among low-income countries. The value of c_1 falls over time and after 1973 is not significantly different from zero. This we attribute to the effects of the worldwide increase in the prices of fuels and raw materials, since this increase then caused complementary trade in such goods among countries of different income levels to be weighted more heavily in total trade than competitive trade flows among developed countries. Finally, c_2, the coefficient of the distance dummy is negative. This indicates that the effects of integration on trade are dimin-

Table 2. Parameter Estimates for Equation 2 (Coefficients of Independent Variable)

Year	Constant	D_{ij}	Y_i	Y_j	N_i	N_j	Q_{ij}	$P_{ij}\frac{Y_i}{N_i}\frac{Y_j}{N_j}$	$P_{ij}D_{ij}$	R^2	F	Obs.
1960	−1.028	−0.252 (−3.08)	1.035 (9.53)	0.251 (5.54)	−0.249 (−1.79)	0.451 (6.18)	1.501 (0.26)	0.344 (1.64)	−0.698 (−2.71)	.506	70.64	561
1961	−1.000	−0.224 (3.42)	1.031 (13.43)	0.212 (5.62)	−0.253 (−2.50)	0.475 (8.44)	3.301 (1.05)	0.328 (2.84)	−0.860 (−5.55)	.591	134.75	756
1962	−1.187	−0.265 (−3.89)	1.039 (13.81)	0.230 (5.98)	−0.223 (−2.28)	0.529 (9.03)	1.916 (0.68)	0.286 (2.75)	−0.629 (−4.33)	.607	144.50	757
1963	−1.578	−0.183 (−2.73)	1.033 (14.11)	0.224 (6.08)	−0.290 (−30.2)	0.492 (8.86)	3.668 (1.40)	0.247 (2.56)	−0.701 (−5.18)	.600	145.78	788
1964	−0.324	−0.296 (−4.18)	0.964 (13.35)	0.231 (5.86)	−0.230 (−2.46)	0.479 (8.16)	2.614 (0.94)	0.268 (2.72)	−0.631 (−4.35)	.562	130.20	821
1965	0.757	−0.274 (−30.3)	0.995 (10.57)	0.220 (4.79)	−0.242 (−1.99)	0.524 (7.57)	6.628 (2.09)	0.119 (1.00)	−0.718 (−4.42)	.533	91.63	652
1966	0.048	−0.364 (−5.34)	1.066 (14.66)	0.188 (4.99)	−0.402 (−4.18)	0.494 (8.79)	5.093 (1.95)	0.140 (1.51)	−0.630 (−4.76)	.593	149.87	833
1967	−0.648	−0.365 (−4.95)	1.165 (14.94)	0.178 (4.29)	−0.461 (−4.52)	0.462 (7.60)	6.106 (2.24)	0.102 (1.08)	−0.642 (−4.55)	.601	148.76	798
1968	−1.592	−0.370 (−5.03)	1.175 (14.47)	0.196 (4.48)	−0.214 (−1.84)	0.525 (8.21)	10.680 (3.92)	−0.011 (−0.12)	−0.858 (−5.78)	.700	192.10	668

Year											
1969	-1.122	-0.458 (-6.30)	1.231 (16.05)	0.188 (4.45)	-0.406 (-3.99)	0.584 (9.35)	7.713 (2.83)	0.081 (0.86)	-0.754 (-5.44)	.640	184.27	837
1970	0.974	-0.543 (-8.09)	1.092 (15.80)	0.157 (3.94)	-0.291 (-3.05)	0.574 (9.57)	3.772 (1.85)	0.194 (2.13)	-0.619 (-4.40)	.651	199.69	864
1971	1.245	-0.539 (-8.56)	1.035 (16.53)	0.154 (4.12)	-0.221 (-2.54)	0.577 (10.31)	2.650 (1.04)	0.208 (2.59)	-0.536 (-4.09)	.682	226.93	858
1972	1.622	-0.573 (-8.12)	1.051 (15.60)	0.140 (3.53)	-0.276 (-2.88)	0.619 (10.36)	3.031 (1.14)	0.190 (2.34)	-0.565 (-4.08)	.683	217.33	818
1973	2.711	-0.581 (-8.64)	0.972 (15.92)	0.136 (3.59)	-0.089 (-1.02)	0.477 (8.41)	4.679 (1.87)	0.104 (1.85)	-0.630 (-4.91)	.693	215.31	774
1974	2.980	-0.550 (-8.56)	0.942 (16.51)	0.129 (3.64)	-0.080 (-0.98)	0.460 (8.70)	4.214 (1.78)	0.079 (1.13)	-0.504 (-4.11)	.707	233.79	785
1975	2.202	-0.548 (-7.56)	1.084 (16.31)	0.111 (2.82)	-0.238 (-2.62)	0.485 (8.29)	4.195 (1.54)	0.042 (0.52)	-0.418 (-3.02)	.674	202.75	795
1976	1.606	-0.472 (-7.39)	1.034 (17.98)	0.146 (4.15)	-0.185 (2.42)	0.442 (8.57)	4.831 (1.97)	0.058 (0.83)	-0.525 (-4.25)	.706	234.58	789
1977	0.584	-0.421 (-6.08)	1.093 (17.95)	0.162 (4.07)	-0.210 (-2.55)	0.390 (6.86)	5.348 (1.97)	0.047 (0.61)	-0.553 (-4.03)	.669	199.79	800

Numbers in parenthesis are t-values.

179

ished as the distance between integrating countries is increased. The absolute value of c_2 declines over time, although the coefficient remains statistically significant. This implies that some of the obstacles to integration among countries more distant from each other, caused, for example, by a lack of knowledge regarding trading opportunities, are dissipated over time as traders gain more information.

The ratio of post- to pre-integration trade is given by $2 \exp (b + c_1 (Y^*/N^*)^2 + c_2 D^*)$ where Y^* and N^* are the average income and population of the integrating countries and D^* the average distance among them. This number represents the amount of intra-union trade creation expected in a customs union among countries of a given level of per capita incomes and inter-member distance assuming that the policies adopted to promote integration were of the same effectiveness as that of the average of those adopted by the five integration schemes in our sample. Table 3 presents the total value of $b + c_1 (Y^*/N^*) + c_2 D^*$ as well as of its components for each integration scheme for each year of its existence.

Overall the differences between the six integration schemes reported in column 2 are relatively small, indicating that differences in per capita incomes explain little of the difference in the ability of integration schemes to stimulate intra-member trade. They also decline with time, in large part because of the decreasing value of c_1. Rather, the principal environmental source of such differences is, as the data in column 3 suggest, the difference in average inter-member distance, which varies from 306 miles for CACM to 9,173 miles for LAFTA. As a result CACM, although made up of the least-developed countries in our sample, is expected to increase intra-member by a factor somewhat greater than is the EFTA. LAFTA, on the other hand, is expected to have a relatively minor impact on intra-member trade largely because of the great distances among members. In terms of environmental factors promoting intra-member trade, the CMEA compares favorably with the EEC and EFTA. While per capita incomes are somewhat lower in CMEA (Column 2), inter-member distances within CMEA are less than those in EFTA although somewhat greater than those in the EEC (Column 3). Thus, for example, the EEC was expected to raise intra-member trade by a factor of $2^{2.25} = 4.8$ in 1962, 8.6 in 1970 and 6.6 in 1977. The EFTA was expected to raise inter-member trade by $2^{1.66} = 3.2$ in 1962, 5.5 in 1970 and 4.6 in 1977. For the CMEA, the comparable figures are 3.0 for 1962, 5.5 for 1970 and 5.2 for 1977. Thus in terms of level of development and distance among members the CMEA clearly has the potential to raise intra-member

Table 3. Environmental Effects on the Ability of Integration to Augment Inter-member Trade

Year	b (1)	c_1 $(Y^*/N^*)^2$ (2)	$c_3 D^*$ (3)	Total Effect (4)
		ANDREAN PACT		
1970	3.77	2.35	−4.61	1.51
1971	2.65	2.54	−2.60	2.59
1972	3.03	2.34	−4.22	1.15
1973	4.68	1.41	−4.68	1.41
1974	4.21	1.06	−3.79	1.48
1975	4.20	0.57	−3.14	1.63
1976	4.83	0.79	−3.95	1.67
1977	5.35	0.65	−4.05	1.95
		CACM		
1961	3.30	3.57	−4.50	2.37
1962	1.92	3.15	−3.39	1.69
1963	3.67	2.79	−4.01	2.45
1964	2.61	3.05	−3.62	2.04
1965	6.63	1.36	−4.11	3.88
1966	5.09	1.62	−3.61	3.10
1967	6.11	1.19	−3.67	3.63
1968	10.68	−0.13	−4.91	5.65
1969	7.71	0.95	−4.32	4.34
1970	3.77	2.31	−3.58	2.50
1971	2.65	2.51	−3.10	1.76
1972	3.03	2.32	−3.27	2.08
1973	4.68	1.30	−3.65	2.33
1974	4.21	1.01	−2.92	2.30
1975	4.20	0.55	−2.42	2.33
1976	4.83	0.78	−3.04	2.57
1977	5.35	0.65	−3.20	2.80
		CMEA		
1962	1.92	3.89	−4.22	1.59
1963	3.67	3.38	−4.71	2.34
1964	2.61	3.70	−4.24	2.07
1965	6.63	1.66	−4.82	3.47
1966	5.09	1.97	−4.23	2.83
1967	6.11	1.45	−4.31	3.25
1968	10.68	−0.16	−5.76	4.76
1969	7.71	1.77	−5.06	3.82
1970	3.77	2.85	−4.15	2.47
1971	2.65	3.09	−3.60	2.14
1972	3.03	2.85	−3.79	2.09
1973	4.68	1.58	−4.23	2.03
1974	4.21	1.22	−3.39	2.04

(*continued*)

Table 3. Continued

Year	b (1)	c_1 $(Y^*/N^*)^2$ (2)	c_3D^* (3)	Total Effect (4)
		CMEA		
1975	4.20	0.66	−2.81	2.05
1976	4.83	0.92	−3.53	2.22
1977	5.35	0.75	−3.72	2.38
		EEC		
1960	1.50	4.77	−4.27	2.00
1961	3.30	4.64	−5.15	2.79
1962	1.92	4.09	−3.76	2.25
1963	3.67	3.58	−4.20	3.05
1964	2.61	3.94	−3.78	2.77
1965	6.63	1.77	−4.34	4.06
1966	5.09	2.10	−3.77	3.42
1967	6.11	1.54	−3.84	3.81
1968	10.68	−0.17	−5.14	5.37
1969	7.71	1.25	−4.51	4.45
1970	3.77	3.05	−3.71	3.11
1971	2.65	3.34	−3.21	2.78
1972	3.03	3.09	−3.38	2.74
1973	4.68	1.74	−3.95	2.47
1974	4.21	1.35	−3.17	2.39
1975	4.20	0.72	−2.63	2.29
1976	4.83	1.01	−3.30	2.54
1977	5.35	0.84	−3.47	2.72
		EFTA		
1960	1.50	4.84	−4.96	1.38
1961	3.30	4.73	−6.05	1.98
1962	1.92	4.17	−4.43	1.66
1963	3.67	3.63	−4.93	2.37
1964	2.61	3.98	−4.45	2.14
1965	6.63	1.76	−5.12	3.27
1966	5.09	2.12	−4.44	2.77
1967	6.11	1.55	−4.53	3.13
1968	10.68	−0.17	−6.05	4.46
1969	7.71	−1.26	−5.32	3.65
1970	3.77	3.06	−4.37	2.46
1971	2.65	3.35	−3.78	2.22
1972	3.03	3.10	−3.98	2.15
1973	4.68	1.74	−4.56	1.86
1974	4.21	1.36	−3.65	1.92
1975	4.20	0.73	−3.03	1.90
1976	4.83	1.02	−3.80	2.05
1977	5.35	0.84	−4.00	2.19

(*continued*)

Table 3.   Continued

Year	b (1)	c_1 $(Y^*/N^*)^2$ (2)	c_3D^* (3)	Total Effect (4)
		LAFTA		
1960	1.50	4.04	−5.72	−0.18
1961	3.30	3.88	−7.02	0.16
1962	1.92	3.34	−5.14	0.12
1963	3.67	2.92	−5.72	0.87
1964	2.61	3.21	−5.15	1.67
1965	6.63	1.44	−5.87	2.20
1966	5.09	1.73	−5.15	1.67
1967	6.11	1.24	−5.24	2.11
1968	10.68	−0.14	−6.95	3.59
1969	7.71	1.02	−6.18	2.55
1970	3.77	2.46	−5.08	1.15
1971	2.65	2.66	−4.39	0.92
1972	3.03	2.48	−4.63	0.88
1973	4.68	1.46	−5.13	1.01
1974	4.21	1.11	−4.10	1.22
1975	4.20	0.57	−3.40	1.37
1976	4.83	0.79	−4.27	1.35
1977	5.35	0.65	−4.50	1.50

trade to levels observed in the EEC and EFTA if the CMEA integration mechanism were as effective as those of the other two integration schemes.

Having thus demonstrated the importance of environmental factors for the effectiveness of regional integration schemes, we turn to an analysis of the policies by which integration has been promoted. Among the six integration schemes in our sample there are important differences in integration policies. Among these differences are the type of integration scheme, such as a free trade area or a common market; the extent to which non-trade barriers are lowered among members and the height of tariffs imposed on imports from nonmembers; and the economic system of the integrating countries. Our procedure in comparing the effectiveness of integration policies followed by the six integration schemes in our sample is to determine whether the actual increase in intra-member trade is greater than that predicted in Table 3. Since increases in trade predicted by Table 3 reflect environmental differences between integration schemes but assume identical integration policies for all schemes, any difference between predicted and actual increase in intra-member trade thus reflects

differences in the effectiveness of the policies adopted by each integration scheme. The ratio of actual to expected pre-integration trade for
the i-th integration scheme can be expressed as:

$$2^{b(i)} = \frac{\text{actual post-integration trade}}{\text{expected pre-integration trade}} \qquad \textbf{(Eq. 3)}$$

$$b(i) = (b + \pi(i)) + c_1 (Y^*/N^*)^2 + c_2 D^* \qquad \textbf{(Eq. 4)}$$

where $\pi(i)$ measures the difference between the effectiveness of the i-
th integration scheme's policies and the effectiveness of the average
integration policy. The results are reported in Table 4, for selected
years only to save space.

For four integration schemes, CMEA, the EEC, LAFTA and the
Andean Pact, the $\pi(i)$s are negative indicating integration policies of
less than average effectiveness. As may be seen from column 4, CMEA
and the EEC achieved increases in trade that were equal to roughly 60
percent of the potential gains that could have been achieved with
policies of "average" effectiveness given the characteristics of the
integrating countries. LAFTA and the Andean Pact also implemented
integration policies of less than average effectiveness. Although the
$\pi(i)$s for these two schemes fluctuate more than those for CMEA and
EEC, they bracket them, suggesting that integration policies in Latin
America were about as effective as those in the two European schemes
and that the differences in trade creation between the two European and
the two Latin American schemes evident in column 1 reflect largely
environmental factors. The EFTA and CACM, on the other hand,
appear to have implemented policies above average effectiveness, with
those of CACM appearing to be more effective than those of EFTA.

In sum, then, we can conclude that CMEA integration has generated
as much of an increase in inter-member trade as have customs unions
among developed market economies when environmental factors are
taken into account. Despite this evident success, CMEA integration
has been criticized by Bergson (1980), Desai (1985) and Holzman
(1976, 1985) as an unsuccessful customs union, one that is, to use
Holzman's words ". . . a losing proposition in economic terms"
(1976, p. 59). The basis for this argument is the low level of trade of
CMEA countries with non-members, which to CMEA critics reflects
trade diversion within CMEA.

This diversion of trade towards higher cost producers within CMEA
and away from low cost producers in non-member countries can, however, impose losses only on those CMEA members whose terms of

Table 4. Effects of Policy on Intra-member Trade Flows in Regional Integration

Integration Scheme	Year	$b(i)$ (1)	$b+c_1(Y^*/N^*)+c_2D^*$ (2)	$\pi(i)$ (3)	$2^{\pi(i)}$ (4)
Andean Pact	1970	1.01	1.51	−0.50	0.71
	1973	−0.27	1.41	−1.68	0.31
	1976	0.91	1.67	−0.76	0.59
CACM	1970	4.00	2.50	1.50	2.83
	1973	3.07	2.33	0.74	1.67
	1976	3.13	2.57	0.56	1.47
CMEA	1970	1.62	2.47	−0.85	0.55
	1973	1.36	2.03	−0.67	0.63
	1976	1.46	2.22	−0.76	0.59
EEC	1970	2.35	3.11	−0.76	0.59
	1973	1.73	2.47	−0.74	0.60
	1976	1.77	2.54	−0.77	0.59
EFTA	1907	2.50	2.46	0.04	1.03
	1973	2.34	1.86	0.48	1.39
	1976	1.91	2.05	−0.14	0.91
LAFTA	1970	0.63	1.15	−0.52	0.70
	1973	−0.34	1.01	−1.35	0.39
	1976	0.53	1.35	−0.82	0.57

trade are worse than they would be if their trade was cleared at world market prices (WMPs) and on those non-member countries that could have supplied goods at lower prices. Within the CMEA, it is evident that machinery and consumer manufactures have been the categories of commodities where the majority of the diversion from non-CMEA suppliers to CMEA producers has taken place. The supply of fuels and raw materials has come largely from the Soviet Union, but at relatively, and often absolutely, lower than world market prices. Consequently, it is the Soviet Union that suffers from trade diversion; the more developed CMEA members, including Hungary, do not suffer from trade diversion within CMEA. In fact, they may benefit in the sense that trade diversion has enabled them to shift resources to industry, where labor productivity and factor productivity growth are both higher than in agriculture and services.[3] Consequently, from Hungary's standpoint, it is unlikely that trade diversion within CMEA is a serious source of static losses from integration, and, as a result it is likely to enjoy static gains from integration that reflect the relative success of the CMEA in promoting inter-member trade.

III.   DYNAMIC GAINS FROM INTEGRATION[4]

In addition to the static gains from trade described above, economic integration is alleged to be the source of dynamic gains that have a long-run effect on the growth of the integrating countries. The increase in growth results from two conceptually different effects. The first of these is an increase in the rate of growth of factor inputs, particularly that of capital. The second effect is an increase in technological progress, usually measured as the growth of total factor productivity.

In market economies integration increases the volume of investment and thus the growth of the capital stock by increasing the return and lowering the risk to investors. The creation of a large multinational market reduces the risk attributed to individual investment project in a national market in two ways. First, the greater heterogeneity of the multinational market should be more likely to provide a sufficiently large group of consumers with particular needs to make the investment successful while a similar investment constrained to a national market might fail due to the lack of sufficient demand. Second, to the extent that the member countries have asynchronous business cycles or seasonal buying patterns the opportunity to operate plants at rates closer to capacity or to reduce the inventory-to-sales ratio exists. Firms within the union should also be able to realize greater profits from lower production costs caused by economies of scale and the mobility of capital and labor, and, even if factors are not free to move within the integration scheme, free trade will permit firms to relocate production facilities so as to take advantage of factor-price differentials among members. The risk of inter-member trade will also fall relative to other foreign trade because the risk of changes in tariff and nontariff barriers among members is much less than in trade with nonmembers. Finally, the risk to investors may be reduced through the establishment of a regional capital market that, because of its size and international scope, would be less subject to the imperfections that characterize small, national capital markets.

Of course, in the process of integration there will be both losers and winners. Some firms will be successful and capture a large share of the expanded market and subsequently increase their volume of investment. At the same time other firms, shorn of the protection of tariffs, will prove unable to compete and begin to disinvest. To the extent that firms able to compete within the entire region have some excess capacity before integration, they may view it prudent to serve the new demand at first by operating existing plants more intensively. Only some years after the formation of the trading bloc when the potential of the area-wide market has proven itself will they begin to increase their investment outlays. In contrast, some inefficient firms may begin to reduce investment outlays before integration takes place in anticipation of losing their market to more efficient producers in the integrating countries while other firms will begin to suffer losses from competition after integration and may thus be forced to curtail their capital outlays. As a result, investment in the integrating countries may actually decline in the first few years following integration and then increase gradually to levels exceeding, ceteris paribus, those of the pre-integration period.

While the above mechanisms may well apply to market economies, they are clearly not relevant to the member countries of CMEA. In the latter, the volume of investment is set by the state with little regard to the risk-return calculus. Moreover, the difficulty in CMEA countries has been to rein in the growth of investment rather than to stimulate it. Indeed, one of the objectives of the CMEA is to reduce the level of investment in member countries by promoting specialization and by eliminating the need for investments by one member country that needlessly duplicate capacity being constructed by other members. Consequently with regard to the growth of inputs, the dynamic effects of CMEA must be reviewed in a way opposite from that employed for market economies.

Even if integration were not to lead to higher rates of growth of inputs, the growth rate of output could be increased because integration promoted a higher level of "disembodied" technological progress among member countries. One source of such progress would be economies of scale, since a larger market would permit the use of more specialized equipment and labor. Firms could also become more specialized and thus lower their production costs. As sectors of the economy begin to benefit from economies of scale, their increased demand for inputs or lower output prices stimulate production in other sectors, creating further economies of scale. Thus what began as a static effect for one industry cumulates into a dynamic, economy-wide process. To the extent that a larger market leads to an increase in firm size, the quality of management would also increase.

Regional economic integration also eliminates the protection of monopolistic and oligopolistic industries. After integration, the firms in these industries will have to intensify their efforts to survive and prosper and thus they must become more dynamic and innovative. The ability of firms to innovate through increased research and development outlays will also be improved through integration. First, firms will have a larger market over which to amortize their research outlays. Second, larger firms in any case spend more on research than do small ones. Finally, research and development activities themselves are thought to benefit from economies of scale, so that the increase in research outlays ought to yield particularly favorable results.

Economic integration also provides greater scope to entrepreneurship. Since one of the functions of the entrepreneur is to facilitate the transfer of resources from declining industries to those where factor productivity is high and increasing rapidly, the greater the supply of entrepreneurial talent, the more rapidly such resource transfers occur and the more rapidly the economy grows. With regard to this second set of dynamic effects, the objectives of CME members and market economies are identical. CMEA integration, specialization and scientific cooperation are all seen as important stimuli to the technological progress of member countries.

The Model

Because there are two separate effects of integration to be measured, a system of simultaneous equations was employed. The system consists of an investment function with terms to capture the effects of integration on investment behavior and of a production function that permits integration to influence the rate of technological progress. The two equations are linked by the relationship between investment and the growth of the capital stock. Dynamic effects of integration are estimated by means of these equations for the CMEA and, for purposes of comparison, for the EEC, EFTA, LAFTA, CACM, and the East African Common Market (EACM).[5]

In all countries, investment was modelled by means of an accelerator model. In the case of developing countries the role of inflows of foreign capital was thought to be sufficiently important to warrent the inclusion of this variable in Equation 5. Thus for developing countries:

$$INV_{i,t} = a_0 + a_1 RY_{i,t} + a_2 FY_{i,t} + a_3 CU_{i,t} + a_4 CUDT_{i,t} + e_{i,t} \quad \textbf{(Eq. 5a)}$$

and for developed countries:

$$INV_{i,t} = a_0 + a_1 RY_{i,t} + a_3 CU_{i,t} + a_4 CUDT_{i,t} + e_{i,t} \quad \textbf{(Eq. 5b)}$$

where

$INV_{i,t}$ = (real gross domestic capital formation/real gross domestic product) in country i in year t,

$RY_{i,t}$ = growth of real gross domestic product in country i in year t,

$FY_{i,t}$ = (real foreign capital inflow/real gross domestic product) in country i in year t,

$CU_{i,t}$ = 0 if country i was not a member of the integration scheme in year t,

= 1 othersise,

$CUDT_{i,t}$ = $(CU_{i,t}/(t-1950))$,

$e_{i,t}$ = error term.

The dummy variable $CU_{i,t}$ measures the permanent or long-term of integration on capital formation. However, as mentioned above, integration may have some transitory effects on the volume of investment as well, either by depressing it below its long-term level at the onset of integration or by temporarily raising it above its long-term level. This transitory effect is measured by $CUDT_{i,t}$ a variable that decreases over time. A significant value for a_3 indicates that integration has long-term impact on the level of capital formation in the integrating countries, while a significant value for a_4 indicates that the short-term impact of integration on capital formation was different from the long-term effect.

Output growth in both developed and developing countries was modelled as depending on the growth of labor and capital inputs, on disembodied technological progress, and on the effect of integration on productivity growth.

Thus:

$$RY_{i,t} = b_1 RK_{i,t} = b_2 RL_{i,t} + b_3 CU_{i,t} + b_4 T + u_{i,t} \quad \textbf{(Eq. 6)}$$

where

RK = rate of growth of capital stock in country i in year t,

RL = rate of growth of population in country i in year t,

$$T = (t - 1950),$$

$u_{i,t}$ = error term.

The system is closed by an equation linking investment to the growth of capital stock by:

$$RK_{i,t} = (Y_{i,t} \bullet INV_{i,t}/K_{i,t-1}) - K_{i,t-1} \qquad \textbf{(Eq. 7)}$$

where

$Y_{i,t}$ = real gross domestic product of country in year t,

$K_{i,t}$ = real capital stock of country i in year t.

Empirical Results

Data for the period 1951–77 were collected for the members all integration schemes. Equations 5, 6, and 7 were estimated for each integration scheme by pooling observations across member countries and over years.

Parameter estimates for Eq. 5 are reported in Table 5. With the exception of LAFTA, the R^2s are reasonable for pooled cross-section data, and the parameter estimates are generally significant. As expected, estimates of a_1 are positive and significant as are those for a_2 in the case of the CACM and EACM, indicating that capital formation is

Table 5. Parameter Estimates for Equation 5

Integration Scheme	a_0	RY a_1	FY a_2	CU a_3	CUDT a_4	R^2	Number of Observations
CACM	0.121	0.398	0.494	0.038	−0.523	0.426	130
	(19.97)	(5.43)	(5.95)	(2.92)	(−2.38)		
LAFTA	0.162	0.110	0.094	0.032	−0.407	0.093	277
	(29.78)	(4.04)	(1.32)	(2.79)	(−2.19)		
EACM	0.143	0.162	0.348	0.048	−0.441	0.570	60
	(26.11)	(4.04)	(6.32)	(2.39)	(−1.03)		
EEC	0.191	0.260	—	0.028	0.197	0.383	208
	(47.78)	(4.79)		(3.76)	(1.69)		
EFTA	0.191	0.416	—	0.039	0.026	0.206	182
	(22.60)	(3.64)		(2.82)	(0.12)		
CMEA	0.442	0.944	—	−0.281	1.049	0.162	179
	(10.99)	(2.02)		(−2.68)	(0.51)		

t-ratios in parentheses.

related both to the growth of output and to inflows of foreign capital. The dynamic effects of integration are captured by a_3 and a_4. With the exception of the CMEA, estimates of a_3 are positive and significant. Thus integration raised the proportion of output devoted to capital formation both in the case of developing and developed market country schemes. Also encouraging is the fact that the estimates of a_3 are rather tightly grouped, ranging from 0.028 to 0.048. Among market economies, integration thus appears to have a positive long-term impact on the rate of growth of capital in integrating countries. The estimate of a_3 for CMEA is negative and significant, while that of a_4 is not significantly different from zero. This indicates that CMEA integration measures begun in the early 1960s did in fact serve to reduce the volume of investment by promoting specialization and by coordinating the investment efforts of member countries.

The effects of increased levels of capital formation on output as well as the effects of integration on technological progress are determined by means of Eq. 6, for which parameter estimates are reported in Table 6. The rate of growth of the capital stock is significant for all market-economy integration schemes. The rate of growth of the population is not significant save for the EFTA. For the developing country schemes, where labor is in surplus, such a conclusion is not surprising; nor is the negative b_2 for the EACM where workers may have been redundant.

Table 6. Parameter Estimates for Equation 6

Integration Scheme	RK b_1	RL b_2	CU b_3	TIME b_4
CACM	1.553 (4.78)	0.092 (0.22)	0.021 (2.14)	−0.001 (−1.59)
LAFTA	0.955 (1.68)	0.561 (0.71)	0.030 (1.36)	−0.001 (−0.44)
EACM	1.913 (2.10)	−1.213 (−0.94)	−0.016 (−0.44)	−0.001 (−0.26)
EEC	1.094 (4.06)	0.142 (0.17)	0.003 (0.45)	−0.001 (−2.66)
EFTA	0.980 (4.72)	0.377 (4.23)	0.008 (1.45)	−0.001 (−4.05)
CMEA	0.273 (0.86)	0.256 (0.51)	0.037 (2.48)	−0.002 (1.66)

t-ratios in parentheses
R^2 not reported due to constraint $b_0 = 0.0$

The coefficient for the integration dummy, b_3, is significant only in the case of the CACM and the CMEA. In no other integration scheme is there any evidence that technological progress increased following integration. Thus, with regard to fostering technological progress, CMEA appears to have been considerably more successful than its generally more favorably regarded counterparts among developed and developing market economies.

Measuring the Gains from Integration

Having thus demonstrated that economic integration does produce some dynamic gains for the integrating countries, we next turn to determining whether such gains are of sufficient magnitude to make economic integration an important mechanism for promoting growth. To do this we compare the GDP that the member countries could have achieved either at the time the integration scheme was terminated or in 1977, the last year of our sample, with and without the dynamic benefits of integration. GDP in the terminal year without integration was computed by means of dynamic simulation of Eqs. 5–7 from the

Table 7.   Increase in Terminal-Year Gross Domestic Product Due to Dynamic Effects of Integration (as percentage of terminal year GDP without integration)

Integration Scheme		*(1)* Increase in GDP Due to Higher Investment Level	*(2)* Increase in GDP Due to Higher Rate of Technological Progress	Total = 1 + 2
CACM	1961–77[a]	1.2	3.1	4.3
LAFTA	1960–77[b]	1.1	NS	1.1
EACM	1967–72	3.0	NS	3.0
EEC	1959–77[c]	1.1	NS	1.1
EFTA	1960–77[d]	0.9	NS	0.9
CMEA	1964–77	−0.4	5.0	4.6

Notes: NS = Technological progress coefficient not significant.
   [a]Except Honduras 1961–69; Nicaragua, 1962–; Costa Rica, 1963–.
   [b]Except Colombia and Ecuador, 1961–; Venezuela, 1965–; Bolivia, 1967–.
   [c]Except Denmark and United Kingdom, 1973–.
   [d]Except Denmark and United Kingdom, 1960–72.

first year of the sample to the terminal year with $CU_{i,t} = 0$ for all years and all countries. Thus the terminal year GDPs for all member countries reflect no dynamic effects of integration. The terminal year GDP with dynamic effects of integration was also calculated by means of Eqs. 5–7, but this time with $CU_{i,t} = 1$ for those years in which each individual country belonged to the integration scheme. Only those values of a_3, a_4, and b_3 that were significantly different from zero were employed in these calculations.

The results are reported in Table 7. Although terminal-year GDP was calculated on a country-by-country basis, for brevity we sum the results for each integration scheme. As may be seen, the CMEA achieves the greatest gain from the increase in technological progress as well as the greatest total gain from integration because the gains from technology are sufficiently large to offset the negative effect of slower capital growth, the latter being, in any case, intentional.

III. CONCLUSIONS

Our comparative examination of the CMEA leads us to conclude that CMEA integration has been considerably more successful than its critics have been willing to grant. When compared with integration schemes among market economies, the CMEA does well in terms of inter-member trade expansion and outperforms western integration schemes in the provision of dynamic gains in the form of an increase in factor productivity growth of its members' economies. Hungary's participation in CMEA would thus appear to be based on a perception of these advantages and to offer the Hungarian economy the opportunity to develop new products and new industries that will find a stable and profitable outlet on the CMEA market.

ACKNOWLEDGMENT

Brada wishes to acknowledge financial support from the National Council for Soviet and East European Research for the research underlying this paper.

NOTES

1. This section substantially extends results first reported in Brada and Mendez (1985).

2. The countries in the sample with dates they joined (and left) a particular integration scheme are:

- CACM: Guatemala (1961), El Salvador (1961), Honduras (1961/1970), Nicaragua (1962), Costa Rica (1963).

- LAFTA: Mexico (1960), Argentina (1960), Brazil (1960), Paraguay (1960), Uruguay (1960), Bolivia* (1967), Chile* (1960), Colombia* (1961), Ecuador* (1961), Peru* (1960), Venezuela* (1965).

- Andean Pact: The members of LAFTA marketd by an asterisk joined the Andean Pact in 1970, save Venezuela which joined in 1974.

- CMEA: Bulgaria, Czechoslovakia, East Germany, Hungary, Poland, Romania, USSR. The CMEA was officially formed in 1949 although serious integration measures were not instituted until the early 1960s.

- EEC: Belgium-Luxembourg (1959), France (1959), Italy (1959), Netherlands (1959), Federal Republic of Germany (1959), Denmark (1973), United Kingdom (1973).

- EFTA: Austria (1960), Denmark (1960/1973), Norway (1960), Portugal (1960), Sweden (1960), Switzerland (1960), United Kingdom (1960/1973).

- Non-members: Algeria, Egypt, Zaire, Nigeria, South Africa, Iraq, Iran, Saudi Arabia, Hong Kong, Singapore, Japan, Canada, Panama, United States, Greece, Spain, Turkey, Ireland.

3.   The costs of this trade diversion have been estimated by Marrese and Vanous (1983), although their interpretation does not follow the customs union approach. See, however, Brada (1985).

4.   This section reports, in greater detail for the CMEA, the results of Brada and Mendez (1988).

5.   The member countries of EACM and the years they joined and left the union are: Kenya (1967/1972*), Uganda (1967/1972*), Tanzania (1967/1972*). (* = defacto, not de jure). For the other integration schemes, see footnote 2.

REFERENCES

Aitken, Norman D., "The Effect of the EEC and EFTA on European Trade: A Temporal Cross-Section Analysis." *American Economic Review*, Vol. LXIII, No. 5 (December 1973), pp. 881–892.

Balassa, Bela, "Trade Creation and Trade Diversion in the EEC." *Economic Journal*, Vol. 77 (March 1967), pp. 1–21.

Bergson, Abram, "The Geometry of Comecon Trade," *European Economic Review*, Vol. 14, No. 3, (1980), pp. 291–306.

Bergstrand, Jeffrey H., "The Gravity Equation in International Trade: Some Microeconomic Foundations and Empirical Evidence." *Review of Economics and Statistics*, Vol. 67, No. 3 (August, 1985) pp. 474–481.

Brada, Josef C., "Industrial Policy in Hungary: Lessons for America." *Cato Journal*, Vol. 4, No. 2, (Fall, 1984), pp. 485–505.

Brada, Josef C., "Soviet Subsidization of Eastern Europe: the Primacy of Economics over Politics?" *Journal of Comparative Economics*, Vol. 9, No. 1, (March, 1985), pp. 80–92.

Brada, Josef C., "Industrial Policy in Eastern Europe." In J. C. Brada, E. A. Hewett and T. A. Wolf (eds.), *Economic Adjustment and Reform in Eastern Europe and the Soviet Union* (forthcoming).

Brada, Josef C. and José A. Méndez, "Economic Integration Among Developed, Developing and Centrally Planned Economies: A Comparative Analysis." *Review of Economics and Statistics*, Vol. 67, No. 4 (November, 1985), pp. 549–556.

Brada, Josef C. and José A. Méndez, "An Estimate of the Dynamic Effects of Economic Integration." *Review of Economics and Statistics* Vol. 70, No. 1 (February, 1988).

Desai, Padma, "Is the Soviet Union Subsidizing Eastern Europe?" *European Economic Review*, Vol. 29, No. 4, (December, 1985).

Geraci, Vincent J. and Wilfried Prewo, "Bilateral Trade Flows and Transport Costs." *Review of Economics and Statistics*, Vol. 59, No. 1 (February 1977), pp. 67–74.

Hewett, Edward A., "A Gravity Model of CMEA Trade." in Josef C. Brada, (ed.), *Quantitative and Analytical Studies in East-West Economic Relations*, (Bloomington: International Development Research Center, 1976).

Holzman, Franklyn D. *International Trade Under Communism*. (New York: Basic Books, 1976).

Holzman, Franklyn D. "Comecon: A Trade-Destroying Customs Union?" *Journal of Comparative Economics*, Vol. 9, No. 4, (December, 1985), pp. 410–423.

Leamer, Edward A. and Robert M. Stern, *Quantitative International Economics*, (Boston: Allyn and Bacon, 1970).

Linder, Stefan B., *An Essay on Trade and Transformation*, (New York: John Wiley and Sons, 1961).

Linnemann, Hans, *An Econometric Study of International Trade Flows* (Amsterdam: North-Holland Publishing Co., 1966).

Marrese, Michael and Jan Vanous, *Soviet Subsidization of Trade with Eastern Europe: A Soviet Perspective*, (Berkeley: University of California Institute of International Studies, 1983).

Pelzman, Joseph, "Trade Creation and Trade Diversion in the Council for Mutual Economic Assistance: 1954–70." *American Economic Review*, Vol. LXVII, No. 4 (September 1977), pp. 713–722.

Poyhonen, P., "A Tentative Model of the Volume of Trade Between Countries," *Weltwirtschaftliches Archiv*, Band 90, Heft 1 (1963), pp. 93–100.

Tinbergen, Jan, *Shaping the World Economy: Suggestions for an International Economic Policy*, (New York: The Twentieth Century Fund, 1962).

WORLD ECONOMIC GROWTH AND EAST-WEST ECONOMIC COOPERATION IN THE 1980s

Béla Kádár

The new epoch in international economic and political evolution that unfolded in the 1970s changed the external conditions for the growth of some countries as well as trends in international economic coopera-tion, including East-West economic cooperation. East-West economic relations were influenced as well by worldwide changes in domestic and foreign and military policies as well as by changes in economic and social values, in power relations and in Soviet-American relations. This paper sketches the basic trends that can be observed so far in East-West relations in the 1980s, and then those elements in the world economic situation that are judged to be most important in their influ-ence on East-West cooperation.

I. THE EVOLUTION OF EAST-WEST ECONOMIC RELATIONS

The international economic and political processes that unfolded in the past decade had, in total, a long run unfavorable influence on the growth of economic relations between the European CMEA countries and the OECD countries. With strong fluctuations from country to country and from year to year, as a general trend the expansion of East-West relations evident in the first half of the 1970s came to a standstill. In the second half of the decade, the volume of the exports of the CMEA countries to the OECD countries still rose on the average by 6 percent per year, and their imports by 7 percent, but in the average of the years 1980–83 the volume of their exports stagnated and that of their imports rose by only 2.2 percent. In value, the imports of the CMEA countries fell between 1981 and 1984 by an average 2.4 percent annually, while their exports rose by 3.4 percent. Within the upswing of world trade in 1984, the value of the trade of the OECD countries rose by approximately 8 percent, while East-West trade stagnated, falling by 0.5 percent. At the beginning of the 1980s trade between the two groups of countries expanded at a slower pace than the world average. In the first half of the 1970s, East-West relations represented about 3 percent of world trade, in 1980–82 2.4 percent, and in 1983 already as little as 2.2 percent. Of course, this order of magnitude cannot influence world economic processes, but also owing to reasons of the order of magnitude it reacts sensitively to world economic changes. Between 1977 and 1984 the share of the CMEA countries in the exports of the OECD countries fell from 5.2 percent to 4 percent, and in their imports from 3.6 percent to 3.5 percent, including intra-German trade. However, within the falling relative importance of total East-West trade, the importance of the Soviet market has remained unchanged on the export side and has been increasing on the import side, while the share of the small CMEA countries dropped from 2.8 percent to 1.8 percent in western exports and from 2 percent to 1.5 percent in western imports. With the exception of the German Democratic Republic the loss of markets has been considerable for all small CMEA countries, but especially large for Poland and Romania.

In the long run, the purchases of the CMEA countries expanded faster in East-West trade than their sales. However, the emerging tensions caused by their indebtedness induced the CMEA countries to restrict imports vigorously. The effect of this policy on their external balance has made itself felt since 1982 and its success has caused surprise internationally. The balance of trade between the two groups of countries showed, in the period 1975–79, an accumulated CMEA deficit of 31 billion dollars, in 1980–81 the deficit diminished to 2.7 billion dollars, and then in 1982 the CMEA countries achieved a surplus of 1 billion dollars, in 1983 of 2.3 billion and in 1984 of 7.8 billion dollars.

East-West financial cooperation has changed radically in its trend since the beginning of the 1980s and has contracted in volume. Calculated at current exchange rates, within relations between the banks, in the average of the years 1976–1978 5.6 billion dollars annually, and in the average of the years 1979–1981 2.9 million dollars of net external financial resources flowed to the European CMEA countries, making trade deficits and the servicing of past debts possible. Owing to the tensions that have accumulated in the international monetary system, to the sharpening of the foreign exchange problems of some CMEA countries, and to the appearance of the endeavours of some western countries or financial institutions to introduce a credit embargo, the sum of new credits granted to the CMEA countries diminished and, in 1982, amounted to 0.7 billion dollars, and in the first half of 1983 only 0.2 billion dollars. Some growth occured in the second half of 1983, 0.8 billion dollars, and the stock of new credits granted in 1984 also amounted to approximately 1 billion dollars. The extent of the withdrawal of western deposits that had been placed in CMEA banks was also considerable. Thus, instead of external resources flowing to the CMEA countries in 1982 approximately 6.6 billion, in 1983 4.2 billion, and in the first half of 1984, 3.0 billion dollars worth of financial resources flowed out of the CMEA countries of East-West financial transfers. As may be seen, at the beginning of the 1980s a decade long stage in East-West economic cooperation in which the CMEA countries were able to draw on substantial external financial resources and thus break the link between the volume of imports and exports came to an end.

A basic feature of the product pattern of East-West trade is that it does not resemble the structure of trade among industrialized countries but instead resembles trade between industrially developed and developing countries. Based on the level of development that the CMEA countries have already reached and on international comparisons, the share of industrial products in CMEA exports is low and has remained essentially unchanged. Although in the small CMEA countries the share of industrial products has risen since the beginning of the 1970s from 54 percent to 58 percent, in the case of the Soviet Union it has fallen from 26 percent to 12 percent. The share of primary energy in Soviet exports amounted to 43 percent in the average of the years 1971–76, 59 percent in the average of the years 1976–80, and in 1982, 78 percent.

One-fifth of the industrial exports of the CMEA countries consists of metallurgical products, one-quarter of chemicals, and more than one-quarter of the products of light industry. These are material-intensive

products that are sensitive to cyclical fluctuations as well as to competition from the newly industrializing countries. In the industrial markets of the OECD countries the market shares of the CMEA countries
improved in the period from 1970 to 1982 in fertilizers, plastics, ships,
metallurgical products, textiles and clothing. Over the same period a
trend of their being crowded out could be experienced in the OECD
market for business machinery, electrical machinery, instruments, and
machine-tools.

On the import side, in the average of the years 1971–80 the share of
machinery and equipment, the import categories that affect domestic
economic, structural and technical progress, as well as competitiveness, amounted to 33 percent, but in the average of 1981–83 it
dropped under 27 percent in Soviet imports and to 28 percent in the
imports of the other European CMEA countries. The share of chemicals fluctuated in Soviet imports around 9 percent in the course of the
past decade, but in the small CMEA countries it rose from 14 percent
to 18 percent despite the large-scale expansion of their own production
that occurred in the past decade. In the imports from the West of the
small CMEA countries the share of raw materials and primary energy
remained unchanged at 9 percent in the past decade, while the share of
the so-called material-intensive industrial products accounted for 26
percent in the average of the 1970s and for 21 percent in the average of
the years 1980–83. The share of food products rose in the imports
from the West of the Soviet Union from 15 percent to 20 percent, and
in the small CMEA countries from 11 percent to 15 percent.

The country by country structure of the external economic relations
of the various countries and country groups is shaped by a great
number of geographic, political and institutional factors in addition to
economic and technical ones. From the geographic-historic side, East-
West relations are determined by the geographic situation of the European CMEA countries and by their historic embeddedness in the European division of labor. The share of Western Europe in total East-West
trade was 87 percent in 1970 and 84 percent in the average of the years
1982–83. The weight of the United States and Canada in total trade
rose from 6.0 percent to 8.0 percent, and in 1984 to 9.4 percent, that of
Japan from 7.3 percent to 7.5 percent. As may be seen, the Eurocentric
nature of East-West relations has remained unchanged in the longer
term, especially on the import side. On the export side, the share of the
overseas OECD countries accounted for 28 percent in 1982 and 24
percent in 1983.

Trade with the countries of the Common Market, which strives for the regional regulation of the economic and external economic processes, is of great importance from the aspect of the system of control and of economic policy. The policies of the Common Market have an especially great influence on the evolution of the exports of the CMEA countries, because, due partly to its expansion and partly to the effect of other processes, the share of the Common Market in CMEA exports to the West accounted for 45 percent in 1970, and in 1983, 65 percent. In the exports of the CMEA countries, and consequently in the developement of East-West relations, the nature of relations with the organization and member countries of West European regional integration schemes has become decisive in the 1980s.

During the period of detente the share of the two leading world trade powers, the Federal Republic of Germany and the United States, grew rapidly in western deliveries. It was generally the large companies of the leading world trade powers that had the complex skills necessary for the solution of the novel problems occurring in trade between capitalist and socialist countries. They also had a more extensive organizational background and technological transfer capacity, as well as the potential for "sitting out" the longer time needed for transactions to be implemented and returns to materialize from participation in the envestment projects of the CMEA countries. Thus the share of the United States in western deliveries was 6 percent in 1970, 15 percent in 1979, 10 percent in 1980, the year of Carter's embargo; the share of the Federal Republic in the same years was 21 percent, 23 percent and 25 percent respectively.

The deterioration of the international atmosphere after 1979 and the slowing down of the large restructuring investments by the CMEA countries, which had created a great demand for technology and capital, limited also the growth of the role of the leading OECD countries as suppliers. In the average of the years 1981–83 the share of the United States in western exports dropped to 9 percent, that of the Federal Republic of Germany to 22 percent, while Japan's amounted to 12 percent. Thus 43 percent of CMEA imports still originated from these three leading OECD countries, which, from the buyers' side, is a politically sensitive factor, since it strengthens the political considerations in the choice of partners, and respectively concentrates the promotional inputs primarily on the CMEA countries that are more important from the political aspect.

The higher than normal share in East-West trade of the leading CMEA countries also helps to explain the predominant role played by large corporations in this trade. On the basis of their global strategy, these transnational corporations press primarily for cooperation with the Soviet Union, since here the size of the market and the international prestige achieved by their market presence counteract the problems of cooperation between companies of countries belonging to different social systems.

The preponderance and strategy of the big companies also contributes to the fact that most CMEA countries conduct a more intensive industrial cooperation on the export side too with the leading OECD countries. So for instance, in 1981, 20 percent of the total western exports of the CMEA went to the Federal Republic of Germany, 5 percent to the United States and 4 percent to Japan. At the same time, 25 percent of the industrial exports of the small CMEA countries went to the Federal Republic of Germany, excluding intra-German trade, 11 percent to the United States. Among the different CMEA countries, the industrial market share of the Federal Republic was nearly 40 percent in the case of Hungary, more than 30 percent for Poland, 27 percent for Bulgaria, 25 percent for Romania, and the share of the United States 25 percent in the case of Romania, 14 percent for Poland and 7 percent in the case of Hungary.

A similar political sensitivity and rapidly growing concentration can be experienced also on the CMEA side. In the course of the past decade the terms of trade shifted to the benefit of the Soviet Union, which today accounts for the bulk of East-West trade. In 1970 the share of the Soviet Union in the western exports of the CMEA was 37 percent, and in the average of the years 1982–83 it amounted to 60 percent.

These changes in the pattern of East-West trade have led to a loosening up of the uniformity of the substance of the problems involved, leading to a process of differentiation. On the western side, the interests and opportunities for manoeuver of the leading trade powers and of the small neutral countries increasingly differ. The East-West commercial and financial position of the Soviet Union resembles less and less that of the other CMEA countries. The changes in the international terms of trade had an extremely favorable effect on Soviet trade. According to calculations of the United Nations Economic Commission for Europe, in the period of 1975–83 the Soviet terms of trade improved by 40 percent in East-West relations. Owing to its huge purchasing power and the strategic importance of its energy exports, the Soviet Union represents an attractive trading partner, and in the short run it is less vulnerable to various economic policy pressures. On the other hand, the relative positions of the smaller Central European

CMEA countries, which earlier represented the backbone of East-West relations, have deteriorated continously since the mid-1970s due to unfavorable price changes, indebtedness, and the vulnerability and low growth of their export supply.

The regression that could be observed in East-West relations at the beginning of the 1980s is undoubtedly connected with the slowdown of the rate of economic growth. In the developed OECD countries the gross domestic product rose in the 1970s at an average annual rate of 3.3 percent, it stagnated between 1980 and 1983. In the small CMEA countries, net material product grew in the 1970s by an average annual 5.9 percent, and stagnated in 1980–83. In the Soviet Union too, the growth rate dropped from 5 percent to 3 percent. It is difficult to explain why the world economic boom which started in the United States at the end of 1982 cannot be felt more forcefully in East-West relations. Today it is already widely recognized that by the mid-1970s the quarter-century old process of world economic growth had arrived at a breaking point. The past decade and the second half of the 1980s may be considered the first stage of adjustment to the changed conditions of the new scientific-industrial revolution, the outlines of which are becoming more and more clear. Consequently, changes in growth rates are far from being the most significant factor for changes in the world economy and the structure of economic growth. East-West cooperation must also adjust to the new world economic environment, and its development thus far, as well as its expected evolution, are difficult to analyze without examining development patterns on an international scale.

II. THE CHANGING SOCIAL-POLITICAL-ECONOMIC CONDITIONS OF WORLD ECONOMIC DEVELOPMENT

Demographic Projections

The demographic trends that can be expected in the second half of the 1980s fall in line with the main patterns characterizing the last quarter of the century, including the reduction of the growth rate of the population, the lengthening of the average life span, the strengthening of the regional unevenness of population growth, the increasing proportion of mankind living in the less developed countries. In the period between 1980–90 the share of the world population living in the

OECD countries will fall from 17 percent to 15 percent, and that in the Soviet Union and the East European countries from 9 percent to 8 percent.

The demographic trends that can be expected in the 1980s in the OECD, and to a lesser extent in the CMEA countries, affect the conditions of economic growth from several aspects:

a.   In the wake of the lengthening of the life span and of the considerable extension of social security in the 1970s, the share of the economically inactive population, and in connection with this the indirectly distributed share of national incomes, increases.

b.   Owing to the diminution of the birth rates, which began already in the 1960s, in the second half of the 1980s the increase in the number of new households will slow down in some developed countries and stagnate in others. Demand for traditional industrial products and certain services will decline to levels dependent on the rate of replacement or on the increase in value caused by qualitative improvement. Within the population of the more developed countries, in contrast to the preceding quarter century, the share of the younger age-groups will diminish as will their, in certain cases decisive, role on consumer markets.

The Framework of Social and Domestic Policy

One of the historic trends of the third quarter of our century was the increase of state intervention in the economy, the continuous strengthening of the role of governments, and consequently the rising political sensitivity of the economy. This decade is characterized by a reverse trend, the strengthening of the economic sensitivity of the political sphere. The increased economic sensitivity of the political sphere. The increased economic sensitivity of the political sphere is connected with the fact that the situations of instability appear in the economic sphere very rapidly and in the most transparent form. Owing to the post-war spread of the consumer society and to consumption becoming a social value, the social consciousness reacts much more forcefully and directly to changes in the economic situation than it did earlier. The progress of mass communication and manipulatory techniques has also contributed to the sphere of social and economic control having to deal to a greater extent and more frequently with the problems caused by changes in the socio-psychic atmosphere. The source of the socio-psychic problems is the growing pressures of structural change and technical progress, changes in occupation, domicile and living conditions, the widening range of confrontation with the enhanced requirements of the sharper competitive climate and with the increasing number of individual and company failures. In the second half of the 1980s, the social capacity for tolerance and the appraisal of the socio-psychic environment of the economy represent strategic tasks of enhanced importance.

Today the rearrangement of the earlier relationship between the political and the economic sphere may be seen in the rehabilitation of economic laws and the broadening of the elbow-room of the economy. In the 1980s, in contrast to the experiences of the preceding quarter century, the political sphere is guided by a higher degree of pragmatism and by the requirements for practical policies suitable for easing social-economic tensions. In the party dimension of the power relations of domestic politics in the western world the 1980s are generally characterized by the social democratic parties losing ground or becoming weaker from the second half of the 1970s and by the maintenance of the governmental positions of the parties of the center right. Although the domestic political evolution of the smaller OECD countries continue to be varied, in the leading countries such as the United States, Britain, the Federal Republic of Germany, and Japan, the present conservative cycle is likely to last to the end of the 1980s.

In spite of this shift in domestic politics, its extent has not brought about many firm majority governments and thus the elements urging consensus have survived, and the differences between the programs of the political forces opposing each other will not grow in the near future. The parties of the center-right are compelled to acknowledge the ''limits to the restrictions'' of the welfare state in the United States, Great Britain, and the Federal Republic of Germany and the social-democratic parties the needs of adjustment in Sweden, Spain, France, etc.

The economic policy environment is generally characterized in most countries of the world as battling with the legacy of the imbalances which came about in the 1970s. The consequences of the accumulated state debts compel the maintenance of restrictive budgetary policies, and the reduction of welfare and other nonessential expenditures. Power relations between the state and the private sector have shifted accordingly. Within the narrowing of the means available to the state, the continuation of the rearrangement of objectives that began at the end of the 1970s is expected to continue. The pace and direction of the rearrangement of objectives are influenced from the side of domestic policy by the circumstance that the endeavors at consolidating the developed capitalist society and economy unfold, unlike in the 1970s, not within the framework of reform capitalism of the social democratic type but by means of programs inspired by the neo-conservative forces of the center-right. Within economic policy, welfare policy commitments become weaker, and priorities aiming at the improvement of performance become stronger. In development policy, parallel to the whittling down of the, as yet decisive, subsidies granted to the declining branches, the stimulation of progressive economic activities by direct and indirect means becomes stronger. Within the regulative mechanisms and instruments of economic policy, new proportions within the mix of budgetary and monetary policies are developed, which, cleansed of the extremes of the beginning of the 1980s, reflect greater reliance on monetary policy.

Among the CMEA countries, the Soviet Union is characterized by endeavors at rationalization aimed at improving the present model of economic control. The unfording of more comprehensive economic reforms aimed at increasing the sensitivity of the economy to the market or to costs may be expected in Bulgaria and in Poland. However, these changes have not yet made their influence felt either on the domestic economy or on the conditions for international and regional cooperation in the East European region.

The Characteristics of the System of International Relations

The basic medium-term driving force in the system of international relations is the relationship between the Soviet Union and the United States. Adequate resources are not available for a substantial medium-term modification of military power relations between the two world powers, and therefore military, as well as domestic and economic interests and movements, point towards the moderation of confrontation and conflict.

The cooling down process that began in the mid-1970s and was followed at the end of the decade by the sharpening of tensions are being replaced by a slow normalization of political relations between the two world powers. On the planes of ideology and political rhetoric, as well as in the conflicts over developing countries and in the Central and South European region tensions of a lower intensity are reconcilable through selective normalization. The most likely medium-term course of Soviet-American relations excludes not only the outbreak of a direct military conflict, but also the lasting and broader limitation of economic cooperation.

A subtle difference from the earlier decade is represented by the changing role of the Far-Eastern countries in the system of international relations, which means, in the case of China, the strengthening of the external economic elements in politics, and in the case of Japan the tendency to close the gap between its strong economic and passive foreign policy roles.

In contrast to the regional block approach of the third quarter of the century, elements of country by country selectivity are becoming stronger, and these influence in different ways the autonomy of the various countries in East-West relations. The international situation that appears likely in the 1980s raises the importance of foreign policy autonomy in international relations and of cooperation with those countries that have greater foreign policy autonomy in pursuit of developing relations.

The economic policy environment of the system of international relations is influenced considerably by the fact that, unlike in the domestic economy, the consequences of external economic imbalances, of slower growth and of falling income are a further strengthening in most countries of the external economic presence of the state, the interweaving of the economic and political elements of external economic relations, and increased importance of economic diplomacy for growth and trade. A strengthening of protectionism in the world economy is inseparable from the shock effects, and the moderate boom since the end of the 1970s has been sufficient only for the blunting of growing protectionist tendencies. Owing to the export constraints of the countries representing a decisive share in world trade, the curbing and reversal of protectionist tendencies may be expected only from a more vigorous and lasting upswing. In the world economic environment that can be expected, the few countries that are able to expand considerably their import capacities are going to open their markets to exporters according to the yardstick of economic diplomacy. At the same time, in a period of fragile world economic growth and uncertainties regarding the division of labor, the various forms of bilateralism and of direct exchange will become stronger in the relations between governments and between companies.

From the aspect of the evolution of the international environment also of great importance is that, despite some scientific and political assumptions that had spread at the beginning of the 1970s, the growing importance in the world economy of transnational corporations has not become exhausted, especially not in the technology, intensive branches of, nor have these corporations become controllable by the instruments of economic policy. In connection with the increasing budgetary constraints in the nation states and the narrowing of the scope of governmental economic policies, the governmental endeavors aiming at the improvement of the external economic position are compelled to rely to a greater extent on cooperation with transnational corporations. External economic policy, economic diplomacy, and international regional cooperation on a governmental level will gradually integrate the factors of cooperation with the sphere of transnational corporations. On the markets of an increasing number of oligopolized products and product groups, such as pharmaceuticals, cosmetics, aluminum, vehicles, and electronics, and the majority of engineering products, the creation of a worldwide marketing organization represent a precondition for competitiveness the importance of which is on the increase all the time.

In the remainder of the 1980s it is not yet justifiable to count on the transformation and further development of the international institutional system to mitigate international tensions. In the OECD countries, and possibly in the CMEA countries, endeavors aiming at the harmonization of economic policies may gather strength in the form of high-level consultations, policy coordination and summit meetings. The number of developing and CMEA countries participating in the international economic institutions, GATT, IMF, the World Bank, may increase, but the adjustment to the world economic processes will unfold fundamentally within the framework not of international or regional but of national economic decisions.

The transformation of the structure of the world economy gathered speed in the 1970s and entered a new stage. In the post-war quarter century the share of industry continuously grew in the combined production of the OECD countries at the expense of agriculture. This process came to an end in the first half of the 1970s, the share of industry peaked, and then began to decline, the process of re-structuring being the most vigorous within industry. After the traditional branches of light industry, from the beginning of the 1970s vehicle manufacture, metallurgy, heavy chemical industry also entered the rank of branches that were beginning to decline, and at the same time growth remained rapid in most branches of the electrical industry and in the light chemical industry even in the years of the recession. So, for instance, between 1973 and 1984, within the 19 percent growth of manufacturing output, output fell by 8.5 percent in the textile industry, by 7 percent in the clothing, tanning and shoe industries, by 4 percent in the timber and furniture industries, by 19 percent in the metallurgical industry, while it grew by 22 percent in the food industry and in the chemical industry, and by 64 percent in the electronics industry. The electronics industry output expanded at an average annual rate exceeding 10 percent also at the beginning of the 1980s.

These growth characteristics of the OECD countries, which influence development trends in the world economy to a decisive extent, reflect in a condensed way the world-wide rearrangement of supply and demand conditions. Since the mid-1970s the reduction of the natural resource requirement of economic growth has gathered speed. The higher relative prices of energy and raw materials and problems of the security of supply have stimulated specific savings more forcefully than before. The accelerated structural changes, the stagnation and regression in the material- and energy-intensive heavy chemical, metallurgical, construction and vehicle industries, and the extremely low material- and energy requirements of the new growth-carrying branches of the 1980s, microelectronics, computer engineering, fine chemicals also limit the earlier role of natural resources in growth.

Beyond the fall in the growth of demand for natural resources and materials, in the countries that are on a higher level of economic development, a market saturation came about on the markets of traditional light industry and consumer goods and also of some durable products of the engineering industry. On the market of these products the growth demand is modest in the longer term, and is linked primarily to the requirements of replacement. At the same time there is a very lively demand in the markets of technical novelties, in the electronic and control engineering industries, and of products and services of higher quality that satisfy the desire for more leisure time and a higher level of enjoyment.

The developments of the past decade drew attention to the fact that changes in the conditions of world market supply played a much larger role than the changes in the demand structure; although the latter were undoubtedly important they unfolded more evenly. In the wake of the acceleration of industrialization in the developing countries, the geographic migration of comparative advantage in basic manufactures, and the lack of co-ordination in post-war world economic growth, parallel capacities on a worldwide scale and an international oversupply of a structural nature came about in the markets of most light industry, metallurgical, and heavy chemical products, as well as in transport vehicles. This oversupply caused a large-scale under-employment of capacities, sharp international competition, an unfavourable relative price dynamic and profitability, and in the countries protecting their declining branches with protectionist measures it increased the social costs of growth. Parallel to this, increasing supply constraints were experienced in the flow of the most modern technologies.

Consequently, the long run and cyclical disturbances in the East-West industrial division of labor manifest themselves primarily in a given product structure, owing to changes in international supply and demand. In recent years, the increasing deterioration of the export positions of the CMEA countries is linked most directly to the increased restrictions on agricultural exports which had been imposed earlier by West European agrarian protectionism and by the fact that the overwhelming part of East European industrial exports consist of products considered "market sensitive" by western structural and trade policies. The general economic, industrial and import policies of the OECD countries strive increasingly for the elimination and moderation of the structural crisis phenomena that unfold in an increasing number of industrial branches. Accordingly, in addition to the continuing liberalization in the second half of the 1970s of the conventional trade policy by means of the Tokyo-round of GATT, a sectoral protectionism of a new type, often independent of the atmosphere of general trade policy, has become stronger in most OECD countries, even within the Common Market. The various barriers to market entry, customs tariffs, non-tariff barriers, measures restricting competition from imports, bilateral voluntary export-restricting agreements, etc. are widening. Consequently, the fluctuations, loss of dynamism, unfavorable price trends manifest on the CMEA export side are linked primarily to the extraordinary and lasting sensitivity of the structural characteristics of the CMEA supply and the OECD demand, and not to the universal phenomena of the business cycle.

From the aspect of East-West cooperation both the changes in the product structure of supply and demand in the world economy and the structural rearrangement that can be observed in the geographic pattern of economic growth are an unfavorable phenomena. The shifting of the dynamism of world economic growth towards the Pacific region is fed by various driving forces. The shifts in economic dynamism towards the Pacific coasts and the Southwestern states in North America and towards Siberia in the Soviet Union represent a long-term historic process. In this region the movements of four leading powers, the United States, the Soviet Union, Japan and China, meet geographically, and these upgrade the importance of the region politically and dissolve the earlier links to the European region in the system of international relations.

Within these global movements, different from the third quarter of the century, in the past decade and especially since the beginning of the 1980s the growth of Western Europe has been slower than the average of the OECD countries. In the average of the 1970s GDP rose by 2.8 percent annually in Western Europe, by 2.9 percent in the United States, and by 4.5 percent in Japan. From the long-term standpoint it is even more unfortunate that in the 1970s the main source of West European economic expansion was provided by the extension of government services. The average annual growth of manufacturing output was 2.5 percent in Western Europe, 2.8 percent in the United States, and 6.1 percent in Japan. Within this, in the key sector of industry, the electrical industry, as against a 4.4 percent growth rate in Western Europe, the United States reached a growth rate of 8 percent and Japan 11 percent.

Owing to the trends mentioned, to the slow pace of European adjustment to the world economic changes and to rigidities in the institutional system, in the 1980s economic dynamism shifted much more unequivocally towards the overseas OECD countries. In the first half of the 1980s the growth rate of western Europe reached only 1.4 percent as against 3.2 percent in the United States and 4 percent in Japan. In the United States and Japan economic growth relies to a much larger extent than in the other OECD countries on the technology-intensive sectors that require extremely low raw material and energy imports, as well as on productive and financial services. The low level of the real capital costs increases the international economic power of the two leading OECD countries, and arises from the dominant international financial position of the United States and the rapid growth of Japanese capital exports and of the savings of the Japanese economy. The domestic economic growth of these two countries is also more resistant to the high cost of capital, since the level of profitability of the new pulling sectors of growth is much higher than the level of the capital costs.

Consequently, the economic dynamism of the 1980s and the trends of technical-structural development are shaped primarily by the processes that unfold in the North American region and in Japan. These regions provide today one-third of the foreign trade of the OECD countries, about 60 percent of their production, and 60–80 percent of their direct long-term capital exports as well as of their exports of modern technologies.

The process can also be seen in terms of products. In the conventional material and energy-intensive semi-finished products, as well as in the labor-intensive branches of light industry and in engineering branches producing the technologically less sophisticated traditional consumer durables, comparative advantage continuously shifts towards the developing, mainly Far Eastern, countries. At the same time, concentration is taking place on the market for modern technologies. The future-oriented sectors are increasingly concentrated in the United States and Japan; the technical gap between Western and Eastern Europe and these two countries has grown steadily for a decade.

The shift unfolding in the foci of world economic growth, the weakening of the earlier Eurocentric or Atlanticentric system of world economic relations, and the effect of the new growth center developing in the Pacific region are not reflected in the essentially unchanged Eurocentric East-West economic relations because Europe accounts for five-sixths of trade. Thus the migration of the growth centers creates generally more difficult environmental conditions for East-West cooperation than existed earlier. The shift in the focus of world economic growth makes the situation of the smaller landlocked Central European countries especially difficult, because the ability of the small countries and economic units to interact with more distant economies is limited and cooperation with the dynamic overseas countries raises additional logistical problems.

From the aspect of the lasting trends of East-West relations the changes that can be observed in the different sources of economic growth and in the relative importance of their driving forces are especially significant.

The overwhelming majority of the theories and economic policies developed in the 1970s assumed, based on the experience of the oil price explosion, that the challenge to growth would come from the scarcity of natural resources. In the wake of the oil price explosion and the reappraisal of the aspects of the security of supply, energy exports became of decisive importance in the Soviet Union and their importance grew also in the western trade of several smaller CMEA countries. By the beginning of the 1980s it had become clear that the radical world market price changes of the preceding decade represented, on the one hand, the correction of the incorrect management of natural resources in the third quarter of the century, and on the other, in the case of primary energy, the redistribution of rents between consumers and producers. Most economic phenomena indicate that the process of correction came to an end at the beginning of the 1980s, and the relative positions of energy exporters have since ceased to improve.

The material-intensive exports of the CMEA countries are restricted by the existence of the high under-employment of capacities in the western heavy chemical and metallurgical industries, and by the general fall in material-intensiveness. East-West agricultural cooperation is influenced unfavourably from the export side by the oversupply in relation to the effective international demand of the 1980s and by the relative erosion of prices. The driving force for the changes was represented by the extension of the scope of the Common Market's agricultural policies, both geographically and in terms of effective control. The system of regulation governing agricultural imports in 1962 covered only one-half of the farm production of the EEC, in 1970 already 87 percent, and in 1980 more than 90 percent. In the wake of the vigorous stimulation of production and the entry of new agricultural producers, in the case of most large-volume farm products, excepting tropical products and fodder of high protein content, the level of self-sufficiency reached and even surpassed 100 percent. From the aspect of the farm product exporting CMEA countries this development has in itself a market-restrictive effect, and, beyond the expansion of the West European agricultural potential, the South American countries have been compelled to force their exports on world markets and thus to contribute to the oversupply that has come about on the market for temperate-zone products.

The sales conditions for the labor-intensive light industry exports of the small CMEA countries are affected unfavorably by the processes influencing the market value, role and bargaining power of labor that began at the end of the 1970s and fully unfolded in the 1980s. In the third quarter of the century the demand for manpower and the relative level of manpower costs still increased on a worldwide scale. From this aspect a change was brought about by the acceleration of labor-saving technical progress, the fall in the share of the traditional labor-intensive branches, the indirect additional manpower supply through the industrial exports of the developing countries, the gaining ground of an investment policy that gave priority of the technical standard of the place of work over the creation of employment, the weakening in the political bargaining power of the organs politically representing labor, especially the trade unions and the center-left parties. In the 1970s the oversupply of manpower affected primarily unskilled labor. In the 1980s the worldwide oversupply spread also to the market for trained and even graduate manpower. The last-mentioned process is accelerated not only by the appearance of the consequences of the tertiary education and training programs started in earlier decades, but also by the growth of microelectronics and their job-liquidating nature. As a result of the different processes influencing the labor market, mainly in the West European countries the proportion of the unemployed is not likely to drop even if the business cycle improves.

As a result, the earlier advantages of specialization based on the abundant supply of low or medium-skilled labor are eroding. Parallel to this, the comparative advantages of the companies and countries disposing of a highly and specially trained labor force that keep down their specific wages costs through international cooperation are upgraded.

The role of technical development in growth is influenced by contradictory trends. On the one hand, the lower dynamic of world economic growth, the greater uncertainty, and the stricter budgetary constraints influence unfavourably the inputs devoted to research and development and especially to investments that bring a return in the longer term or the returns of which are uncertain. At the same time, the international pressures for restructuring and adjustment, the sharpening of market competition, the strategic revaluation of technologies, the growing spillover into the civilian sectors of the technical achievements of armaments enhance the pace of technical development and its role in growth.

In the 1980s the most important front of technical development was represented by the electronic revolution. The wide diffusion of microelectronics has modified the structure of employment, costs, organization and control forms that are optimal at present. In the second half of the 1980s, microelectronics will make it possible for modern technologies to be applied economically in small plants. In this connection the reduction in the concentration of production and the decentralization of economic activities will modify the role of the smaller economic organizations and national economies in the industrial division of labor. The development of energetics and of biotechnology will exercise an effect on the organizational system and on economic control, speed up the velocity of information gathering, decision-preparing, decision-making and the management process. The research-development-production cycle will become shorter in the area of microelectronics, and the peculiar income ratios, the high risks and rates of profit in this sector will influence the business cycle and structural processes to a greater extent as this sector becomes a larger part of the economy.

Among the international interconnections of technical development of great importance are the market conditions for acquiring modern technologies. These have become more difficult since the mid-1970s because the positions of the technology exporters have become stronger. This is a result of the long-term growth of the specific research and development costs of modern economic activities, of strengthening oligopolization in the market of modern technologies, and the increasing intertwining of capital and technology flows. The acquisition and efficient transfer of modern technologies occur to an increasing extent within firms or through the close interweaving between them. In the international environment of the second half of the 1980s, the openness of capital and technology transfers in the capital and technology exporting countries maintained by economic-political means on the one hand and by the rationalization of management of imported capital and technology and their harmonization with the external economic options on the other, will become more important. Adjustment to these environmental changes has been made more difficult by the political atmosphere of East-West relations by particularities in the system of control in the CMEA countries.

One of the most vigorous changes in the international evaluation of the various growth factors has been experienced since the end of the 1970s in the sphere of financial resources. The main elements of the worldwide oversupply of capital and low or even negative interest rates in the 1970s were characterized by the sudden wealth of the OPEC countries which had a limited capacity for absorbing capital, by the weakened political bargaining strength of the owners of capital in the 1970s, and by the reduced level of investment. The sudden increase in capital costs at the beginning of the 1980s was brought about by processes that started in the United States. Contributing factors were the spread of balance of payment tensions, the reduction and then disappearance of capital over-supply by the OPEC countries and the recovery of investment in the wake of the consequences of sharpening competition.

In the 1980s, financing represents a very hard and costly limit to growth. The average interest rate calculated on the basis of the European currency basket was 6.2 percent in 1978, 8.5 percent in 1979, 11.1 in 1980, 13.9 percent in 1981, 11 percent in 1982, and 8.4 percent in 1983. Due to the vigorous fall in the rate of inflation, by the beginning of the 1980s a level of real interest had come about that is rather rare in economic history.

A high level of interest always differentiates between companies or countries and enhances the importance of the ability to generate income and ensures the success only of units of above average profitability. Unlike the 1970s, the developments in the credit—and capital markets increase in East-West relations the costs of the maintenance of the "Loentieff paradox", by which is meant the maintenance in CMEA exports of a product structure which is much more capital-intensive than are CMEA imports. The elimination of this pattern will impose limits on capital-intensive projects and on imports relying on external financing, and generally will force the taking into consideration of the consequences of the capital-intensity of growth and of trade.

III.   SOME CONCLUDING COMMENTS

The trends in East-West economic cooperation of the first half of the 1980s, the undoubted deterioration in the intensity and quality of cooperation, the developments in politics and economic policy, the economic confrontation that centered earlier on food products, later on loans and then on the flow of technology, led numerous analysts to make pessimistic forecasts concerning the future of East-West cooperation. Opinions stressing the political sensitivity of East-West relations, and views building on this and suggesting isolation, have become especially numerous.

The over-emphasis on the political sensitivity of East-West economic cooperation can, on both sides, be the source of errors in economic policy that may have grave consequences. The actual economic flows accompanying the deterioration of the political conditions, especially Soviet-western relations lead to perhaps the most surprising political conclusion of the first third of the 1980s, that is the modest extent to which the sharpening of the elements of confrontation between the great powers has influenced economic processes.

The changes that have occurred so far in the conditions of East-West economic relations and the expected medium-term outlook warn that it would be wrong to explain the modification in the favourable trend of cooperation in the 1970s and the difficulties of the present and of the near future by cyclical or political reasons. The business cycle between 1980 and 1982 belongs to the province of the past. And the heaviest costs of the deterioration of the political situation are not caused by what happened but by what did not happen: the early quantitative growth of the 1970s did not change to a qualitative stage of closer division of labor involving industrial-technical-financial cooperation, since these closer forms of cooperation demand an atmosphere of mutual political trust. It is primarily from this aspect that the medium-term future of East-West economic relations, too, can be considered politically sensitive, since the intensification of modern forms of economic cooperation does not merely demand the toleration of relations but requires a positive assistance from the political sphere.

However, the new expansive stage of relations between the two groups of countries requires new approaches not only in the political sphere, but primarily in the economic sphere. The existing limits to cooperation are increasingly of a structural nature, caused by lasting changes in the system of conditions of economic growth and of East-West cooperation. Accordingly, energies for establishing new contracts may be set free first of all by fast, complex and mutual adjustment to the requirements of the changed situation. The acceleration of mutual adjustment and its harmonization are historic tasks of key importance not only from the aspect of the dynamization and rationalization of East-West economic cooperation but also the improvement of the international atmosphere and the reversal of the beginning of the economic decline of Europe.

The recognition of the objective and structural nature of the unfavorable trends that have developed in East-West economic relations and the elaboration and implementation of developmental strategies adjusted to world economic changes will have a beneficial influence on the export abilities and world economic positions of the CMEA countries, and thus also on the outlook for East-West cooperation. However, the success of these endeavors assumes and demands a much more constructive "economic policy receptivity" by the OECD countries than exists at present, as well as the stimulation of a more intensive flow of goods, technologies and financial resources.

The unfolding and growing visibility of Western Europe's decline may give rise to and strengthen interests and movements wishing to counteract and stop the weakening of the European position, of Europe's losing ground in the world economy, by the intensification and greater efficiency of all-European, East-West cooperation. In the second half of the decade these movements may create new driving forces in East-West relations and may improve the regional conditions for cooperation.

ECONOMIC RELATIONS BETWEEN HUNGARY AND THE UNITED STATES

Péter Lőrincze

Before World War I economic relations between Hungary and the United States were at an understandably low level. Hungary, then a part of the Austro-Hungarian Empire, had its own centuries-old traditional relations in Europe. While the total exports of the United States in 1912 amounted to 2.204 billion dollars, the Austro-Hungarian Empire took out of this only goods in the value of 22.4 million dollars, its share thus being 0.01 percent. Concerning imports, the data reveals a similar picture. In 1912 the United States imported goods from abroad in the value of 1.653 billion dollars but only 0.01 percent of it came from the Austro-Hungarian Empire in the value of 16.7 million dollars.[1]

These figures might seem modest, but in reality they are really enormous when we look at the trade statistics of the post-war period. In 1925 United States exports to Hungary amounted to only 819,000 dollars, and imports were at the level of 719,000 dollars.[2] All this was not greatly altered after 1925 when a "Friendship, Trade and Consular Agreement" was signed between the two countries in which they mutually provided each other with most favored nation (MFN) status. Ten years later Hungary's exports to the United States reached the level of 3 million dollars but United States exports to Hungary remained still at the extremely low level of 351,000 dollars.[3] During the World War II and, of course, afterward economic relations became very restricted. The United States Government revoked Hungary's MFN-status and as a consequence the United States and Hungary had to face prohibitive tariffs at each other's markets.

From the beginning of the 1960s economic relations with West European countries expanded and trade increased rapidly. Hungarian exports to the United States were not more than 10 million dollars in 1970, while the amount of our total exports at that time in convertible currency reached about 700–800 million dollars. Our imports from the United States were larger, 26 million dollars, but even this was strikingly low level. It was the starting point of trade, however, from which the dynamic development of the past one and a half decades began.

As one can see from Table 1, during the 1970s both Hungarian exports and imports increased rapidly. However, while Hungarian exports surpassed the 100 million dollar mark only in 1979, United States sales to Hungary already had achieved this level in 1974. This increase in Hungarian imports can be explained to a large extent by the continuous purchases of feed for animals from the United States. In fact, quite often during the 1970s around 40 percent of the total Hungarian imports from the United States in a given year represented soymeal. In addition, we have to be mindful of the fact that during the 1970s an ambitious agricultural development program also took place and as a result of this Hungarian purchases of agricultural machinery and breeding stock from the United States grew substantially. The lack of MFN treatment was not an obstacle to United States exports as the higher tariffs imposed on goods of United States origin were offset by their competitiveness.

At the same time, only some Hungarian products could be exported to the United States in major quantities. It is worth mentioning that many of the goods exported presently to the United States in high volume were even then on the export list. For example, Hungary exported rear axles, pharmaceutical raw materials, incandescent bulbs, inflatable rubber camping mattresses and canned ham and bacon in this early period.

The fact that trade between the two countries could not be based on MFN treatment, although the Hungarian side pursued the matter persistently, became an obstacle in the path of the development of bilat-

Table 1. Hungarian-American
Trade, 1970–1984
(in million US dollars)

Year	Exports	Imports
1970	10.4	25.9
1974	27.2	116.1
1975	37.5	123.2
1976	53.7	104.0
1977	56.4	136.0
1978	80.9	156.1
1979	111.24	147.2
1980	122.3	241.0
1981	145.9	231.3
1982	146.8	195.5
1983	189.4	224.7
1984	247.6	201.1

Source: Hungarian Ministry of Foreign Trade
Note: Hungarian and U.S. trade statistics very often differ. Apart from the necessary difference in timing of recording the transactions, the main reason for this is that the United States customs statistics often do not record the Hungarian destination but only the European port to which the shipment first goes. From here on this paper will utilize Hungarian data for these trade flows.

eral exchanges. Quite probably this was one reason why the share of machines in Hungarian exports to the United States stagnated around a mere 1 percent until the end of the 1970s. It was only in 1978 that this matter was resolved in a form compatible with the generally accepted norms of international trade. By then the financial issues outstanding between the two countries, including the claims for United States citizens' losses stemming from nationalization in Hungary, were resolved successfully and the international situation as well as the reputation of our country improved in such a fashion as to make any further delay in granting MFN status impossible. The trade agreement concluded and brought into force in 1978 normalized trade relations between the two countries.

Its effect can be demonstrated by a simple calculation. In the first half of 1979 Hungary exported to the United States goods worth 45.2 million dollars. Lacking MFN, the tariff burden would have been 11.6 million dollars but under the post-1978 conditions the actual burden was only 2.6 million dollars. In other words, this "saving" of 9 million dollars provided a hypothetical chance for Hungarian exporters to raise their prices by that amount. Consequently, the immediate result of the normalization of trade relations was a chance for Hungarian companies to boost their export earnings. In theory the magnitude of this was equal to the difference in customs tariffs, in practice, however, the emerging profit was often shared with the importing American partner. The benefit of the greater price competitiveness of Hungarian goods is reflected in the trade statistics. Between 1978 and 1979 Hungarian exports grew by 30 million dollars and a major share of this increase was due to more competitive prices. It is also worth noticing that the share of machinery in our exports, which was 6.3 percent in 1978 when the effect of MFN treatment came into force, jumped to 15.6 percent in 1979 when the first 15 buses appeared on our delivery list. In the late 1970s Hungarian exports increased quickly and their value doubled between 1980 and 1984.

The value of the United States exports to Hungary in the late 1970s remained over 200 million dollars, with the exception of one year, but the earlier pace of growth decelerated. This was due to a number of reasons. After 1978 a policy was implemented in Hungary to decelerate the growth of the economy in order to restore our external balance. Domestic demand was restricted primarily in the field of investments so as to protect as much as possible the existing standard of living. Under such conditions, of course, agricultural investments had to be

Table 2. Structure of Hungarian Exports
to Developed Market Economy Countries
and to the United States in 1984
(In percent)

Product group	Developed market economy countries	United States
Energy sources	6.7	0.0
Materials and semi-finished products	41.4	32.0
Machinery	5.9	21.9
Consumer products	17.4	29.0
Agriculture and food industry	28.6	17.1
Total	100.0	100.0

Source: Hungarian Ministry of Foreign Trade

reduced. Furthermore, by the end of the 1970s several agricultural programs involving major investments were already completed. Moreover, in 1980 a reform of wholesale prices was initiated in Hungary that linked domestic prices directly to those of the world market. As a result of this step a major increase occured in the prices of chemicals and this in turn induced agricultural enterprises to economize on their use of agricultural chemicals and fertilizers. Finally, we should not forget the fact that, in some cases, Hungary purchased commodities, for instance soymeal, elsewhere as the alternative source proved to be more competitive.

During the 1980s, Hungary's exchange rates followed the upward progress of the dollar. While on January 1st, 1980 a Hungarian exporter was given, and the importer had to pay, 34 forints for a dollar, in 1984 the exchange rate fluctuated around 50 forints. Naturally, the revaluation of the dollar also helped our exports to the United States and acted as a brake on our imports.

In the 1980s the role of agriculture as a major consumer of imports from the United States has been taken over by the telecommunication and instrumentation industries. In these areas, however, the restrictions on exports from the American side are more significant than in the agricultural sector. As a result, Hungary achieved a surplus in trade with the United States in 1984. It is worthwhile, however, to remember that the accumulated surplus of the United States versus Hungary reached some 568 million dollars between 1975 and 1984 and that our exports in this period only covered two-thirds of our purchases.

By the mid-1980s the development of Hungarian-American relations reached a point at which the United States is our ninth most important partner in exports and the tenth largest in imports. Among the developed market economy countries the role of the United States is much greater; in exports she is our fourth, in imports she is our third most important partner. In Hungarian exports the share of the United States is 2.9 and in imports 2.4 percent. Among developed market economies the United States share is 8.1 percent in exports and 6.9 percent in imports.

When evaluating the development of economic relations one must also consider the fact that there are some 80 cooperation agreements in force between the companies of the two countries. In a wider sense these mean some form of a permanent business relationship in production, sales or research. Defining the notion in a more restricted sense, some 14 cooperation agreements can be reckoned with. Examples include the import of tractors in return for agricultural machine parts; the production of Levi's jeans in Hungary, and a cooperation in which we are developing and manufacturing Cummins Diesel's horizontal motors.

I. CHARACTERISTICS OF TRADE WITH THE UNITED STATES

When comparing United States-Hungarian trade with Hungarian trade with other developed market economies in quite a few aspects, we observe that, for Hungarian companies, the American market has some important advantages over Western Europe although the latter is considered to be a close and traditional market for us. These advantages are primarily the conditions of access to the market and the trade policy treatment of our products. For example, there are no discriminatory quantitative restrictions against our goods as there are among the countries of the Common Market. The United States not only refrains from adopting anything similar to the concept of the well-known "Common Agricultural Policy" of the EEC but quite often the Hungarian and American governments have criticized the CAP, raising identical arguments on international fora. From the practical point of view the greatest difference between the United States and Western European markets can be found in the area of tariffs. Only some 15–20 percent of West European imports fall under the tariffs of the MFN status. Trade inside the Common Market is, of course, customs-free and trade between the EEC and EFTA countries is either customs-free or preferential. There are also agreements in force with Mediterranean countries providing for various preferences in the EEC market and we should not forget the Lome Agreement between the Common Market and the ACP countries, as well as the other preferences provided by West European countries of the Third World, such as the General System of Preferences (GSP). As a result, from the point of customs treatment, Hungary falls, in Western Europe, into the same category as the United States, Japan, Canada and the Far Eastern countries. For all these the existing tariff structure represents a permanent obstacle to their access to the West European market. In the trade policy of the United States on the other hand the principle of the most favoured nation status is employed generally; only developing countries enjoy an even more favoured treatment than this in the GSP. Therefore ever since 1978 Hungary has been in a position to seek out customers on an equal footing with most of her competitors. It is worthwhile mentioning that the U.S. Trade and Tariff Act of 1984 contains the idea of concluding free trade agreements for the first time and with this the possibility of letting some imports now dutiable at MFN rates enter the United States duty free. This favourable possibility should be emphasized even if, on the other hand, specific limitations were to cover the importation of some of the products and if the political tendency of United States policy were to provide gradually for a greater role for non-tariff barriers. Currently quantitative restrictions are in force from among our exports on cheese, sugar and beef and Hungary has undertaken voluntary restrictions in seven categories of textile products and in steel. Summing up, favorable access to the market "compensates" Hungarian companies for such disadvantages as the lack of traditions in our economic relations, the great geographical distance, the different system of weights and measures and the relatively high costs of promotion and marketing when entering the market.

Concerning the future of our conditions of access to the American market, Hungarian policy makers do have concerns about several issues. Hungary, of course, will never have such a weight in the foreign economic relations of the United States as to encourage either the Administration or the Congress to pursue an entirely "separate" trade policy towards Hungary. Events, however, in trade with other countries might generate such reactions and protectionist measures that then would afflict Hungary as well. It might happen for some products that the domestic producers could succeed in convincing the Administration to employ protectionist measures, and while Hungarian products would not be the main targets here either, they could hardly avoid being hit by the effects of the measures employed.

Having shown that Hungarian goods have access to the West European and the United States markets under different conditions, it remains to show how this factor influences the structure of Hungarian exports.

Comparing these two sets of numbers, the first difference is that Hungary does not export energy sources to the United States. This and the lesser role of the category of materials and semi-finished products is a consequence of the great geographical distance. The transportation costs would absorb any profits in the case of a number of products and it would be quite an uphill task to compete with local or more closely located suppliers. While we sold major quantities of so-called bulk chemical products such as benzene, members of the polypropylene family, PVC powder and chemical fertilizers to Western Europe, these products are almost entirely missing from our exports to the United States. The most striking difference, however, is to be found in the category of machinery. In 1984, the United States was the most important foreign market for our machinery from among the developed market economy countries, taking one-third or our total machinery exports designed for this group of countries. This ratio was only one-fourth in the case of the Federal Republic of Germany which is geographically closer to us, can be considered a traditional partner, and buys in general 160 percent more from Hungary than does the United States. It is also an auspicious sign that the share of consumer products in our exports to the United States also exceeds the average share of this product group in the total exports to developed market economy countries. The fact that the share of agricultural and food products is greater in our exports to the developed market economy countries than to the United States is quite comprehensible since the United States is a net exporter in this category and only some 5 percent of its total imports consist of agricultural products. We also cannot neglect the fact that domestic agricultural production is quite often protected by various regulations and market orders. Naturally, the so-called traditional suppliers enjoy some kind of access to the market even in this case. Hungarian companies, however, are not in a position of having earned the role of a traditional supplier in any commodity as this market opened up to Hungary only in 1978. The above factors probably explain the fact that we have hardly any agricultural exports to the United States. Our sales in the food industry sector are concentrated on only some goods such as canned ham, canned shoulder, bacon, wine, salami and juice concentrate. After having investigated the export side it is also useful to take a look at the distribution of imports.

It is obvious why we do not buy energy sources from the United States, but it needs to be explained why the category of materials and semi-finished products has such a large weight in Hungarian imports, since earlier in the case of Hungarian exports, this was exactly the category where the limiting effects of geographical remoteness and freight costs were mentioned. Our imports in this category consist partly of raw oxhides of which the United States is one of the most important suppliers in the world. Taking the quality factor into account, it is understandable that Hungarian industry covers a good part of its demand from this source. We also import pharmaceutical base materials because freight costs are obviously less than in the case of bulk chemicals. Anyway, in this field it is less the price and more the reputation, reliability and quality of the product that play a decisive role. Moreover, Hungarian companies also supply pharmaceutical base materials and finished products to the United States in the value of about 10 million dollars, so that a close two-way relationship and a bilateral cooperation are in existence. Further, we buy different chemical agents such as raw materials for the fertilizer industry.

Machinery represent about one-fourth of our entire imports from the United States and this is essentially bigger than the weight of this product group in our total imports from developed market economy countries. This is explained by the ability of the United States to offer truly advanced technologies in several branches. The most active purchasers from our side are the telecommunications, instrumentation and electrotechnical industries and our sizable export of machinery also influences our purchases of machinery. (There exist several cooperation agreements between companies of the two countries, for example in the vehicle industry where in Hungary several products such as machinery are manufactured under American license and the production in Hungary naturally calls for the continuous delivery of parts and components from the United States.)

Our agricultural imports have traditionally consisted of soy meal and by-products of the vegetable oil industry. We are regular importers also of protein fodders and here the position of the United States in world trade makes it necessary for Hungary to have, if the conditions

Table 3.   Structure of Hungarian Imports
from Developed Market Economy Countries
and from the United States in 1984
(In percent)

Product group	Developed market economy countries	United States
Energy resources	0.8	0.0
Materials and semi-finished products	69.0	52.0
Machinery	15.3	24.7
Consumer products	11.9	4.9
Agriculture and food industry	7.0	18.4
Total	100.0	100.0

Source: Hungarian Ministry of Foreign Trade

of trade are competitive, a major part of her demand supplied from there.

The role of the United States in Hungarian machinery and equipment purchases could be even higher since it is hardly up to the economic potential of the United States at its present level. However, regulations in the United States concerning the exports of sophisticated technology hinder American industry's ability to win business away from its competitors in Western Europe. One effect of these hindrances is that the customers will gradually stop requesting bids from the United States even in those cases when the product in question is not covered by the embargo. This is because, if the delivery of spare parts were to come under restrictions later on, the machine itself would become useless. Consequently Hungarian firms find it more useful to start buying there where the probability of future restrictions is smaller. The importance of export licenses, from the point of view of American sales, is enhanced by the fact that, according to forecasts in the second half of the 1980s, one of the most rapidly growing items on our import list will be precisely the advanced technologies of electronics, telecommunications and products of the instrumentation industry.

When we talk about how an administrative measure can cause uncertainties in business relations, we should not forget the effect caused by the annual extension of MFN status to Hungary. The period of validity for the trade agreement of 1978 was three years, but MFN treatment for Hungary reviewed by Congress annually. So far there has never been any doubt that the MFN status would be prolonged for Hungary, but this procedure introduces an element of uncertainty into inter-company relations. It is especially true for those American firms that do not know this situation well and remember only that Hungarian companies are provided MFN status for one year at a time. Thus customs tariffs charged on Hungarian exports might suddenly be increased manifold as a result of the loss of MFN status. It should be emphasized here again that this is not a practical possibility at present. Still this will surely restrain some firms from establishing long-term relations with Hungarian companies and from concluding contracts stipulating obligations for more than one year. Business interests, international practice, and sound common sense all call for the abolition of extending MFN status annually and extending it for at least the period of the validity of the agreement. In other words, for a minimum period of three years.

II. PRACTICAL CONSEQUENCES OF BEING A LATECOMER

Trade between Hungary and the United States started under normal conditions only in 1978. That means that contrary to the tendency of a revival in our trade with Western Europe following the Cold War period, there is a delay of approximately one and a half decades in our trade with the United States. Quite interestingly, this has both negative effects and some positive consequences as well.

The lack of long trade relations in the area of agricultural products coming under market orders, specifically cheese and sugar, meant that Hungary could not become one of the traditional suppliers and thus we could not enjoy privileges deriving from these regulations. The fact that it is only for less than a decade that we have been present on the United States' market under normal conditions also adversely affected the exports of other products. It is quite probable, because our products were competitive otherwise, that we could have conquered more of the United States market had access to the market been available for 17 instead of 7 years. The difference becomes particularly important if we take into account that, from the products exported by us to the United States and considered to be sensitive, like steel and textiles, the authorities intend to restrict imports around the levels currently achieved. Our levels of course would be higher had we exported for 17 years under the conditions of MFN treatment. Thus in quite a number of cases our companies are forced to discuss possible restrictive measures with the American party knowing that the level of Hungarian exports has not yet reached its proper market share in the United States.

But this "overture" of 1978 also has some positive aspects. It was a Hungarian economy on the level of development of 1978 which came into contact with the American market. In other words, a Hungarian industry that has had three decades to develop after World War II and that was modernized by major investments during the 1970s. This industry was already capable of fulfilling these American demands that were higher than the average of the world market. Of course, we were forced to take this attitude by high freight costs too. In case of mass commodities the cost of transportation could have taken away the entire profits quite easily. Because of the conjunction of market demands and delivery possibilities, our industry succeeded in achieving fair results in quite a number of fields.

For example, we deliver hardly any agricultural products for the

United States market. Instead, our agricultural exports take the form of goods of the processed food industry. It is not an exaggeration to say that American sales educated our meat industry. We have learned to manufacture meat products on a level that is appropriate for American standards and this achievement helped to expand our exports into other regions as well. Special meat processing plants were established just to produce for the American market and our canned meat, ham, bacon and salami thus no longer reached the customer as a mass product, rather they are marketed under individual brand names. Obviously it also benefited our industry to become accustomed to the higher demands of the American market as regards packaging and labelling. Thus we consider the achievements of our food industry's exports on this market as a successful example of how to enter a demanding market not with primary agricultural commodities but with processed food industry products. One could cite similar examples from other branches as well. Instead of aluminum ingots we sell semi-finished products on this market and even doubled our sales in 1984 as compared to the previous year. Our ladies' shoes also achieved a measure of renown. Our light bulbs try to compete successfully with firms like Sylvania and Westinghouse. Our buses, manufactured in cooperation with local firms, are rolling on the street of Portland, Oregon and Santa Clara and San Mateo, California. American tourists might also see our buses in Canada. We deliver rear axles and running gear for products manufactured by companies like Steiger, International Harvester, Eaton and General Motors. John Deere buys parts for agricultural machinery from us. Our wines reach American consumers through the intermediate hands of Coca Cola and Pepsi Cola. In the pharmaceutical industry our contacts are firms like Johnson and Johnson and Pfizer; in the chemical industry we cooperate among others with Eli Lilly, Dow Chemical and Occidental Petroleum. In summary we can point out that the firms we trade with have a reputation and the majority of our partners are listed on Fortune's 500. As a consequence, most of our export goods could also have achieved some recognition for themselves. As far as the structure of our exports is concerned, it is as we have seen earlier, expressly favourable.

All the above suggest that a great proportion of bilateral trade is based on multi-year, stable business relations. This is equally true for shoes as well as for rear axles, or wine exports or meat preserves for that matter. This is a positive factor, because it helps to stabilize trade turnover and provides a certain measure of safety for both sides. Our exports, however, are also concentrated from another point; there are relatively few articles involved but the individual values are remarkable. This is well demonstrated by Table 4.

As can be seen, in 1984 seven product groups provided for 70 percent of our total exports. This level of concentration also exists from the point of view of the number of American companies participating in these trade flows and the number of supplying Hungarian companies is likewise limited. If we make comparisons we find that the level of concentration of our exports to the United States is much greater than in our deliveries to the Federal Republic of Germany, Hungary's largest Western trading partner. In theory the result of this should be a certain amount of vulnerability in our exports since there are relatively few items with a large weight in the trade flow and if the deliveries of one of them should fall for any reason this will be registered by a steep drop in our total exports. So the task emerges for us to reduce the level of concentration in our exports by introducing new articles and by establishing business relations with new firms.

I would like to add that this concentration exists in a regional sense as well. For easily comprehensible reasons our products are far better known on the East Coast and in the Midwest than they are on the West Coast or in the Sunbelt. It is also desirable for our companies to work on altering this situation. What is characteristic of our exports is likewise typical, to a certain extent, of our imports. In our purchases soy meal for instance, can be considered a stable item. Our animal hus-

Table 4. Exports of Some Hungarian
Products for the United States in 1984

Product	Value (in million dollars)
Canned meat and meat products	33.3
Aluminum semi-finished products	18.2
Incandescent bulbs	17.3
Pharmaceutical products	10.9
Ladies' shoes	5.9
Ready-made clothing	30.2
Components and parts for the machinery industry, rear axles, running gears	59.1
Total	174.9

Source: Hungarian Ministry of Foreign Trade

bandry is forced to buy protein fodders abroad continuously and if they are competitive in price and in other business conditions, American suppliers can permanently rely on the Hungarian market. Also stable are those purchases of parts and subcomponents that are then assembled by our company RABA into various agricultural machines manufactured under license. It is worthwhile mentioning in this context that American agricultural machines played a rather important role in the mechanization of our agriculture and helped us boost our corn production per hectare to over 10 metric tons. American chemical fertilizers and pesticides have also helped us to achieve the present level of development in our agriculture which can be considered as high by international standards. Several basic pharmaceutical chemicals supplied to us by American firms are incorporated into the production of Hungarian companies. Concerning products of the electrotechnical and telecommunication industries such as laboratory equipment, components, semi-conductors, instruments, etc., the importation of these products is closely correlated with our efforts to increase the role of electronics in the Hungarian economy and to introduce robotics and computerized technologies. Here again American firms may quite well rely for a long term on our market in correlation with their competitiveness. In the final analysis, the above product groups accounted for almost 60 percent of our imports in 1984. As we can see the degree of concentration is fairly large in this respect, too, involving all of its advantages and hindrances.

III. FUTURE PROSPECTS FOR THE ECONOMIC RELATIONS BETWEEN HUNGARY AND THE UNITED STATES

Quite obviously, on the Hungarian side the prime objective will be to maintain the already existing beneficial commodity structure of trade and to increase our machinery exports. We have already created the prerequisites for increasing our sales in medical equipment and to supply more of our numerically controlled (NC) and compueter-NC machine tools to the United States. Hungarian firms, however, must do their homework to achieve all this. There is a need, for instance, for them to consider in their development plans all the technical requirements that are different from the European ones and to accept the different practices in marketing and after-sales service. Quite probably in some cases Hungarian companies will even have to establish spare-parts depots in the United States, and they might have their own individual sales networks as well.

It is to be expected that the existing cooperation agreements in sales and production will be developed further with American partners. I have primarily in mind the vehicle industry, in the case of engines and rear axles, where it has happened and hopefully will happen again that the American and Hungarian partners develop an end-product or a component jointly. A similar cooperation is developing in the delivery of meat products, where new products are marketed according to guidelines concerning the tastes of the American buyer supplied by American partners. There are major possibilities for Hungarian and American companies to cooperate on third markets, primarily in the vehicle industry. Our enterprises think that United States firms also have fair chances on the Hungarian market primarily in the machine-tool industry, in electronics and instrumentation, in machinery for agriculture and the food industry, as well as in research and development plus exploitation of hydrocarbons.

In Hungary there is at present one American company in the service sector, IBM, and four mixed Hungarian-American joint ventures operating in the areas of instrumentation, plastics processing and chemical industries. Quite probably the direct equity investment of American firms will increase in Hungary. This is supported by the fact that the relevant Hungarian legal regulations are liberal, permitting the repatriation of profits and, based on a special license, a majority share for the foreign partner. The potential investor will quite obviously consider the proximity of Hungary to significant international markets, the internal stability of the country, her international reputation, the highly skilled labor force and its relatively inexpensive character as compared to the United States. There are also special factors that provide incentives to an American company to invest eventually in a producing company in Hungary. Namely, both Hungary and the United States pay "only" the MFN tariffs in Western Europe, so from this aspect the conditions of getting to the market will not deteriorate for the American firm. On the contrary, they will improve as, compared to overseas production, the enterprise can save intercontinental freight charges and operate with lower wages.

Three Hungarian companies have subsidiaries in the United States; in the pharmaceutical industry, surgical instruments and the textile industry, and four have established joint ventures in the rubber industry, marketing of shoes and gloves, leather confection, light bulb manufacturing and the exploitation of a coal mining process. It can be stated with a fair probability that the number of these ventures will also increase as our companies will want to get closer to the American customer, to obtain market information independently and maybe also to have a product now delivered from Hungary to the United States assembled or manufactured on the spot instead.

In the future, services will play an increasingly important role in our imports. In this regard one might consider legal services, consulting not only as regards the effective law of the United States but in relation to a third country as well. Here I would certainly include insurance and financial services too. As the market share of our exports increases, we will have to influence the market with targeted promotional campaigns requiring, of course, the purchasing of services. Today only a few Hungarian companies worry about taxation in the United States but the dimensions of this problem may also increase. This will be particularly important if we intend to increase significantly our presence on the market by establishing Hungarian firms in the United States that will be able to operate like any "native" American company.

In terms of Hungarian market demand it is possible for economic relations to develop dynamically in the forthcoming years. According to the aims and targets of the next five year plan (1986–90) the most rapidly increasing area of our imports will be high technology, where the leading role and the delivery capability of American firms is indisputable. It is uncertain whether the United States companies will in reality be able to supply us due to policy constraints. There is a kind of uncertainty also in the area of trade policy as regards some Hungarian exports to the American market. That is so because 21 percent of our exports consist of products such as metals, shoes and ready-made apparel where the administration is already restricting the access to the market and the impact of these measures is already felt by us in steel and textiles. While Hungarian companies must obviously make efforts in order to lessen the vulnerability of our exports and to prevent the majority of the increment in our exports from being realized in "sensitive" products, obviously nobody would be pleased either in Hungary or in any other country if the traditionally liberal trade policy of the United States were to change.

We must remain realistic when forecasting the future. Size sets an objective limit to the development of economic relations; our country would surely buy ten times as much soy bean were it ten times larger. Geographic distance is a limiting factor, too. We cannot reckon with the United States ever becoming the most important Western trading partner for Hungary. We can foresee, however, quite realistically that the position of the United States will not deteriorate, but on the contrary, that the trade flows will increase at an above-average pace on the basis of mutual benefit.

NOTES

1. Department of Commerce, *Statistical Abstract of the United States,* 1937.
2. Department of Commerce, *Statistical Abstracts of the United States,* 1927.
3. Department of Commerce, *Statistical Abstracts of the United States,* 1937.

THE RESPONSIVENESS OF THE HUNGARIAN ECONOMY TO CHANGES IN ENERGY PRICES

István Dobozi

I. INTRODUCTION

In the past decade considerable research has been undertaken to understand the terms-of-trade and balance-of-payments effects of the dramatic increases in the prices of energy imports on the Hungarian economy. However, comparatively little attention has been devoted to the effects of the domestic energy price changes, although energy pricing has become an increasingly used instrument of energy policy in an attempt to reduce energy demand and to encourage energy conservation.

The aim of this paper is to estimate the responsiveness of users to these domestic changes in energy prices. Knowledge of the price elasticity of domestic energy demand is important on several grounds:

1. A high price elasticity of energy demand increases the ability of the economy to absorb the impact of higher energy prices in the long run. Thus, price shocks, after generating pronounced in-

flationary and recessionary effects over the short term, do not act as a constraint to economic growth over the longer term. By contrast, a low price elasticity implies weak reactions to increasing energy costs and a protracted adverse effect on output, inflation and other macroeconomic variables.[1]

2. The magnitude of price elasticity allows us to assess the feasibility of energy conservation through price-induced effects.
3. It may shed light on potential systemic or regulatory problems of a more general nature.

In this paper we estimate a series of energy demand models for various energy products and consuming sectors for which data were available. It is argued that simultaneous models are inappropriate and generally lead to biased estimates because the dynamic nature of energy demand, equipment depreciation and inter-factor substitution are not accounted for. Two types of dynamic models are used for estimating short-run and long-run price elasticities, namely the autoregressive Koyck scheme and the Almon polynomial lag scheme.

The variety and severity of estimation problems, partly discussed below, demonstrate that it is no simple matter to estimate price elasticities and that it is equally difficult to assess the reliability of the estimates that have been made. Comparisons of estimation procedures indicate that potentially large discrepancies may occur as a result of choices among competing models, estimators and data.[2] Uncertainty about the accuracy of a specific elasticity measurement can be somewhat mitigated if the results of alternative models are compared. Such a comparison reveals a range of elasticities about which one can feel more confident than about any one elasticity measurement.

Section I presents the dynamic models and discusses some estimation problems. The estimation results and their international comparison are provided in Section II. Section III deals with some of the factors that may be responsible for the relatively price-inelastic response in Hungarian productive sectors.

II. THE MODEL METHODOLOGY

It is assumed that the simple static version of the energy consumption function has the following general form

$$E_t = a + bY_t + cP_t + e_t \qquad \textbf{(Eq. 1)}$$

where E = energy consumption
       Y = real Gross Domestic Product
       P = real price of energy
       e = error term
       a = constant

The variables are expressed in logarithms, so that b is the income elasticity and c is the short-run price elasticity. Unless stated otherwise, we shall assume that the error term is normally distributed, independent of the explanatory variables, and neither serially correlated nor heteroscedastic.

The usual deficiency of static models such as Equation 1 is that they do not allow for any long-term reaction to price changes. Changes in the demand for energy sources is a dynamic process because reactions are not complete within a single time-period. Consumers are limited in their ability to respond immediately to a price change. Their immediate response is limited to more or less use of available energy-using devices. For example, firms are locked into existing capital structures and production processes, limiting their reaction to energy price changes to more or less intensive use of existing capital.[3] Until the capital stock is altered through depreciation, modification, and replacement, energy demand will be relatively little affected by price changes independent of income level changes, and thus relatively price-inelastic responses can be anticipated. An increase in the real price of energy generates conservation trends that will last for a longer period of time. A restructuring of the capital stock, inter-factor substitution, the gradual phasing out of energy intensive processes, etc., are the elements embedded in the long-term price elasticity. Thus it is anticipated that consumer responses to energy price changes will spread out over several years.

It is not unusual in the literature to assume a dynamic relationship between energy consumption and income changes, in addition to "dynamization" of the relationship between price and consumption. However, the same dynamic mechanism does not really apply in the case of income elasticity.[4] The income effect operates on energy demand through the utilization of energy-using equipment. High past incomes, unlike past prices, do not have a bearing on current energy demand. Past incomes may determine the capital stock in industry and appliances in the household, but there is no guarantee that these will be fully used at any given point in time. It is the movement in current income that, along with prices and other factors, by determining the utilization rates, establishes the level of energy demand. Thus income represents the capacity utilization variable and hence has only a short-term impact, while price changes have both a short- and a long-run impact on energy consumption. Energy demand is then assumed to be a function of income and prices according to the following double-logarithmic specification:

$$E_t = a + bY_t + c_0P_t + c_1P_{t-1} + c_2P_{t-2} + \ldots e_t$$

$$= a + bY_t + \sum_{j=0}^{\infty} c_jP_{t-j} + e_t \qquad \textbf{(Eq. 2)}$$

where a, b and c's are the parameters to be estimated. c_0 is the short-run price elasticity and $c_1, c_2 \ldots$ are the intermediate price elasticities because they measure the impact on mean E of a unit change in P in various time periods. $\sum_{j=0}^{\infty} c_j$ gives the long-run price elasticity.

Equation 2 represents an infinite lag distribution because the length of the lag is assumed to be infinite. In some cases it is reasonable to assume that

$$\lim_{j \to \infty} c_j = 0$$

The vanishing of the c_j in the limit means that following a change in the explanatory variable P, the dependent variable E eventually reaches, perhaps in asymptotic fashion, a new equilibrium. If all c_j after c_m vanish, the model reduces to a finite distributed lag of the following form:

$$E_t = a + bY_t + \sum_{j=0}^{m} c_jP_{t-j} + e_t \qquad \textbf{(Eq. 3)}$$

The infinite distribute lag model is clearly not suitable for direct estimation in its original form since it involves an infinite number of regressors. If the number of terms in the finite distributed lag is very small, then Equation 3 can be estimated using ordinary least-squares (OLS) regression. However, when there are many terms and little is known about the form of the lag, direct estimation becomes difficult for several reasons. First, the estimation of lengthy lag structure uses up a large number of degrees of freedom. Second, the estimation of an equation with a substantial number of lagged explanatory variables is likely to lead to imprecise parameter estimates because of the presence of multicollinearity. Both these difficulties can be resolved if one can specify a priori some restrictions on the form of the distributed lag.

There have been many suggestions in the econometric literature to put some "structure" on the lagged coefficients.[5] For this paper we use two of these structures, the Koyck distributed lag and the Almon distributed lag.

Suppose we start with the following infinite-lag distributed model

$$E_t = a + bY + \sum_{j=0}^{\infty} c_j P_{t-j} + e_t \qquad \textbf{(Eq. 4)}$$

Let us assign increasingly lower weight or importance to energy price in past time periods in the form of a series of geometrically declining weights:

$$c_j = c_o \lambda^j \qquad \begin{aligned} &j = 0,1 \ldots \\ &0 < \lambda < 1 \end{aligned} \qquad \textbf{(Eq. 5)}$$

where λ is the rate of decline of the distributed lag and $1 - \lambda$ gives the speed of adjustment. The Koyck scheme ensures that the sum of c's, which gives the long-run price elasticity of energy demand, has a finite value, namely,[6]

$$\sum_{j=0}^{\infty} c_j = c_0 \left(\frac{1}{1 - \lambda} \right) \qquad \textbf{(Eq. 6)}$$

As a result of Equation 5, the infinite-lag model of Equation 4 may be written as:

$$E_t = a + bY_t + c_o P_t + c_o \lambda P_{t-1} + c_o \lambda^2 P_{t-2} + \ldots e_t \qquad \textbf{(Eq. 7)}$$

$$= a + bY_t + c_o \sum_{j=0}^{\infty} \lambda^j P_{t-j} + e_t \qquad 0 < \lambda < 1$$

As it stands, the structural form Equation 7 is still not amenable to easy estimation since there remain a large number of parameters to be estimated and the parameter λ enters in highly nonlinear form.

Lagging all variables in (7) one time period and multiplying throughout by λ gives

$$\lambda E_{t-1} = \lambda a + \lambda b Y_{t-1} + \lambda c_o P_{t-1} + \lambda^2 c_o P_{t-2}$$
$$+ \ldots + \lambda e_{t-1}$$

Subtracting from Equation (7) and cancelling out yields

$$E_t - \lambda E_{t-1} = a(1 - \lambda) + b(Y_t - \lambda Y_{t-1}) + c_o P_t$$
$$+ e_t - \lambda e_{t-1} \qquad \textbf{(Eq. 8)}$$

$$E_t = a(1 - \lambda) + b(Y_t - \lambda Y_{t-1}) + c_o P_t$$
$$+ \lambda E_{t-1} + v_t \qquad \textbf{(Eq. 9)}$$

where $v_t = e_t - \lambda e_{t-1}$ $0 < \lambda < 1$

If the variables are measured in logarithms, the short-run price elasticity of demand is given by c_o and the long-run elasticity is given by $c_o/(1 - \lambda)$. Furthermore, the mean lag is given by $\lambda/(1 - \lambda)$, which may be taken as the average length of time it takes for a unit change in the explanatory variable P to be transferred to the dependent variable E.

The result of the Koyck transformation is an autregressive model which contains only three explanatory variables: the transformed value of income $(Y_t - \lambda Y_{t-1})$, the current value of price (P_t) and the previous value of energy consumption (E_{t-1}), which is of course the lagged dependent variable. The inclusion of a lagged dependent variable is equivalent to including a very large number of lagged explanatory variables with geometrically declining weights.

Two serious problems arise in the estimation of the Koyck model (9). First, if e_t in Equation 4 satisfies all the OLS assumptions, then $v_t = e_t - \lambda e_{t-1}$ in Equation 8 does not. Specifically, the v_t's are serially correlated because v_t and v_{t-1} are both defined with e_{t-1} in common (that is, $v_t = e_t - \lambda e_{t-1}$ and $v_{t-1} = e_{t-1} - \lambda e_{t-2}$).[7] In addition, a nonzero covariance is also created between the lagged value of the dependent variable used as an explanatory variable and the error term because from Equation 9 E_t directly depends on v_t and E_{t-1} will depend directly on v_{t-1}. Therefore E_{t-1} will obviously be related to v_t

since v_t and v_{t-1} are not independent. The second problem is that the Koyck model assumes geometrically declining weights. This may not be the case in the real world, thus requiring a more flexible lag scheme.

Violation of the OLS assumptions results in biased and inconsistent estimators for the Koyck lag model, requiring some correction procedure. The one used in this paper is the Durbin two-stage method.[8] In the first step we estimate Equation 9

$$E_t = a(1 - \lambda) + bY_t - b \lambda Y_{t-1} + c_o P_t + \lambda E_{t-1} + v_t \qquad \textbf{(Eq. 10)}$$

where the coefficient of E_{t-1} is an approximation of the true λ. The second step involves using this value of λ to transform the values of E and Y in the reduced form Equation (8)

$$E_t - \hat{\lambda} E_{t-1} = a(1 - \hat{\lambda}) + b(Y_t - \hat{\lambda} Y_{t-1}) + c_o P_t + v_t \qquad \textbf{(Eq. 11)}$$

and then estimating Equation 11 by OLS as the new error term, v_t, in Equation 11 is now free of serial correlation. The short-run income elasticity of energy demand is given by b and the short-run price elasticity is given by c_o. The long-run price elasticity is obtained by using Equation 6.

The Koyck lag structure considered so far involves infinite lags. An alternative is to assume that the influence of a change in P is complete after a finite number of periods, so that there is a finite maximum lag. Moreover, the assumption of the Koyck scheme that the lag weights follow a geometrically declining pattern may be too restrictive and not necessarily realistic in some situations. This difficulty can be circumvented through the use of the more flexible Almon polynomial distributed lag technique.[9] The Almon model assumes that the lag weights can be specified by a continuous function, which in turn can be approximated by evaluating a polynomial function at the appropriate discrete points in time.

Consider again the finite distributed lag model

$$E_t = a + bY_t + \sum_{j=0}^{m} c_j P_{t-j} + e_t.$$

where the error term e_t satisfies the usual OLS assumptions. Suppose that the lag pattern can be approximated by a polynomial of the following form

$$c_i = w_o + w_1 i + w_2 i^2 + \ldots + w_p i^p \qquad \textbf{(Eq. 12)}$$

where p is the degree of the polynomial. The length of the lag may be defined as the number of c's excluding c_o, and normally the degree of the polynomial is less than the length of the lag.

If we replace the c's in Equation 3 by their expressions in Equation 12, we have

$$
\begin{aligned}
E_t = a &+ bY_t + w_o P_t + (w_o + w_1 + w_2 + \ldots + w_p)P_{t-1} \\
&+ (w_o + 2w_1 + 4w_2 + \ldots + 2^p w_p)P_{t-2} + \ldots \\
&+ (w_o + mw_1 + m^2 w_2 + \ldots + m^p w_p)P_{t-m} + e_t \quad \textbf{(Eq. 13)}
\end{aligned}
$$

Rearranging terms gives us:

$$
E_t = a + bY_t w_o \left(\sum_{i=0}^{j} P_{t-i}\right) + w_1 \left(\sum_{i=1}^{j} iP_{t-1}\right)
$$

$$
+ w_2 \left(\sum_{i=1}^{j} i^2 P_{t-i}\right) + \ldots + w_p \left(\sum_{i=1}^{j} i^p P_{t-1}\right) = e_t \qquad \textbf{(Eq. 14)}
$$

Let us now simplify our notation by defining:

$$
Z_{it} = \sum_{i=0}^{j} P_{t-i}, \; Z_{2t} = \sum_{i=1}^{j} iP_{t-i}, \; Z_{3t} = \sum_{i=1}^{j} i^2 P_{t-i}, \; \ldots
$$

$$
\text{and } Z_{nt} = \sum_{i=1}^{j} i^p P_{t-1}
$$

Then, we can rewrite Equation 14 as

$$
\begin{aligned}
E_t = a &+ bY_t + w_o Z_{1t} + w_1 Z_{2t} + w_2 Z_{3t} \\
&+ \ldots + w_p Z_{nt} + e_t \qquad \textbf{(Eq. 15)}
\end{aligned}
$$

Equation 15 is an ordinary multiple-regression model and we can generate estimators of a, b and w's by the usual OLS procedure. Once the w's are estimated, the original c's or lag weights, can be calculated from Equation 12.

It is worth noting the advantages of the Almon scheme over the Koyck lag structure. First, it provides a flexible method of incorporating a variety of lag structures. Second, unlike the Koyck technique, in the Almon method we do not have to worry about the presence of the lagged dependent variable as an explanatory variable in the model and the problems it creates for estimation. Finally, if a sufficiently low-degree polynomial can be fitted, the number of coefficients to be estimated is considerably smaller than the original number of coefficients.

A major problem with the Almon approach is that the length of the lag must be specified. Unfortunately, there is no a priori way of knowing what the length is. Nor is there any a priori way of knowing the correct degree of the polynomial. The Almon procedure allows the data to determine the appropriate shape of the polynomial distributed lag. It is a matter of choosing the result that best fits the data, rather than using the data to test a hypothesis about the nature of the demand adjustment process.[10]

Before proceeding to the estimation results the potential problem of simultaneous equation bias must be dealt with. The OLS technique treats the independent variables as exogenous, reflecting the view that simultaneous equation bias is not considered serious. In a demand equation quantity and price are simultaneously determined if price affects quantity demanded and quantity demanded also affects the price. Price and quantity would not be interdependent if we could assume, for example, that energy supply were perfectly elastic. In this case price determines the point of consumption along the demand curve, but shifts in demand do not affect price.

The assumption of perfectly elastic supply is most frequently employed in the literature on energy demand in order to free the analysis from the complications of supply considerations.[11] In the Hungarian case, simultaneity is not likely to be serious. The use of single equation model can be justified on the grounds that rate structures are regulated centrally, so the price cannot be considered a truly endogenous variable, as in a competitive market situation. The central authorities are unable or unwilling to adjust price schedules immediately because costs are affected by volume. There is a time lag that, at least in the short run, breaks the connection between quantity and price. A second argument can be based on the fact that from 1980 for a given sector in the Hungarian economy the producer prices are essentially exogenous, being basically determined in world markets.[12]

III. ESTIMATION RESULTS

Time series data on direct energy consumption for the national economy and three sectors, industry, agriculture and households were collected. Direct consumption excludes consumption related to converting one source of energy into another. Data were obtained for aggregate energy and for several energy sources such as oil, natural gas, coal, electricity, heating oil and gasoline. When energy demand is analyzed at the aggregate level, many important shifts within the struc-

Table 1.   Aggregate Energy Consumption

	National Economy			Industry	Agriculture
Estimation period	1970–84	1970–84	1970–84	1970–84	1970–1984
Lag structure	Static	Koyck	Almon linear	Almon linear	Static
Total length/in years/ of lag distribution	0	∞	4	3	0
Parameter[1],[2]					
a	1.494	0.942	−0.985	−0.313	0.278
	(4.122)	(2.621)	(1.214)	(0.584)	(0.152)
b	0.767	0.987	1.610	1.255	1.068
	(7.197)	(4.670)	(7.075)	(9.002)	(1.974)
c_0	−0.092	−0.049	−0.096	−0.048	−0.065
	(1.911)	(2.247)	(3.271)	(1.803)	(0.337)
c_1			−0.085	−0.057	
			(4.480)	(4.411)	
c_2			−0.074	−0.057	
			(5.325)	(5.365)	
c_3			−0.063	−0.076	
			(3.330)	(2.979)	
c_4			−0.052		
			(1.786)		
Σc_j		−0.160	−0.318	−0.248	
d	−0.030	−0.156	−0.094		−0.011
	(1.963)	(2.576)	(1.431)		(0.289)
$\bar{R}^2$	0.972[3]	0.712	0.895	0.913	0.522
D.W.	1.702[4]	1.830[5]	2.231	2.668	0.741

Notes: 1. a = constant term; b = short-run income (activity) elasticity; c_0 = short-run price elasticity; c_1, c_2, c_3, c_4, c_5 = lagged price elasticities; Σc_j = long-run price elasticity/significant coefficients only/; d = weather elasticity;
   2. t-ratios in parentheses;
   3. Unadjusted for degrees of freedom;
   4. The estimates were corrected for serial correlation;
   5. The Durbin-Watson statistic is reported, although biased toward 2 in the presence of lagged dependent variable, for lack of any more relevant statistic.

Table 2. Oil Consumption of Industry

Estimation period	1960–84	1960–84	1960–84
Lag structure	Static	Koyck	Almon linear
Total length (in years) of lag distribution	0	∞	5
Parameter[1],[2]			
a	−1.649	−0.289	−2.506
	(5.851)	(1.689)	(8.347)
b	1.539	1.561	1.827
	(18.751)	(7.376)	(24.480)
c_0	−0.211	−0.052	−0.083
	(5.618)	(3.536)	(3.549)
c_1			−0.074
			(5.265)
c_2			−0.064
			(10.734)
c_3			−0.055
			(6.585)
c_4			−0.045
			(2.629)
c_5			−0.036
			(1.335)
Σc_j		−0.277	−0.321
$\bar{R}^2$	0.974	0.731	0.984
D.W.	0.920	1.723[3]	1.738

Notes: 1. a = constant term; b = short-run income (activity) elasticity; c_0 = short-run price elasticity; c_1, c_2, c_3, c_4, c_5 = lagged price elasticities; Σc_j = long-run price elasticity/significant coefficients only/;
2. t-ratios in parentheses;
3. The Durbin-Watson statistic is reported, although biased toward 2 in the presence of lagged dependent variable, for lack of any more relevant statistic.

ture of the economy are concealed. Energy demand behavior should also be modeled at the sectoral level, where the different pattern of adjustments can more properly be investigated.[13] The sectoral scope and the number of fuels investigated for the individual sectors were determined by the availability of data.

The income or activity variable represents real GDP for the national economy and real sectoral value added for industry and agriculture. Real values were obtained by using the industrial producer price index as deflator. In the case of the household sector the income variable was represented by real income using the general consumer price index as a deflator.

Energy prices are expressed in real terms using the industrial producer price index as a deflator for the national economy, industry and agriculture, and the general consumer price index for the household sector. Average energy prices used in the aggregate energy demand models, represent a Btu-weighted average of different fuel price categories. In several models to test the effects of winter temperature on demand, the average winter temperature is introduced.

All the models are specified in double-logarithmic form so that the estimated parameters of the explanatory variables can be interpreted as elasticities. Different degree polynomials with various lengths for the

Table 3. Natural Gas Consumption

	Industry		Households		
Estimation period	1963–84	1963–84	1963–84	1963–84	1963–84
Lag structure	Static	Almon quadratic	Static	Koyck	Almon linear
Total length (in years) of lag distribution	0	4	0	∞	5
Parameter[1],[2]					
a	−5.516	−1.489	−8.887	6.807	23.572
	(2.635)	(3.425)	(1.547)	(1.573)	(2.640)
b	2.123	1.441	4.251	2.531	2.156
	(4.774)	(16.041)	(10.023)	(3.880)	(2.996)
c_0	0.135	0.156	−1.378	−2.237	−0.767
	(1.024)	(3.052)	(1.596)	(3.311)	(2.009)
c_1		0.029			−0.874
		(0.986)			(3.175)
c_2		−0.041			−0.981
		(1.066)			(4.596)
c_3		−0.053			−1.088
		(1.913)			(4.634)
c_4		−0.007			−1.195
		(0.099)			(3.699)
c_5					−1.303
					(2.961)
Σc_j				−4.483	−5.334
d			−0.074		
			(0.487)		
$\bar{R}^2$	0.979	0.983	0.960	0.845	0.932
D.W.	1.245[3]	1.768	2.396	2.008[4]	1.741

Notes: 1. a = constant term; b = short-run income (activity) elasticity; c_0 = short-run price elasticity; c_1, c_2, c_3, c_4 = lagged price elasticities; Σc_j = long-run elasticity (significant coefficients only); d = weather elasticity;

   2. t-ratios in parentheses;

   3. The estimates were corrected for serial correlation;

   4. The Durbin-Watson statistic is reported, although biased toward 2 in the presence of lagged dependent variable, for lack of any more relevant statistic.

Table 4. Coal Consumption of Households

Estimation period	1960–84	1960–84
Lag structure	Static	Almon linear
Total length (in years) of lag distribution	0	4
Parameter[1],[2]		
a	4.421	14.848
	(3.783)	(3.686)
b	−0.363	−1.341
	(4.552)	(3.111)
c_0	0.482	0.028
	(2.186)	(0.176)
c_1		−0.060
		(0.555)
c_2		−0.148
		(1.713)
c_3		−0.236
		(2.179)
c_4		−0.324
		(2.067)
Σc_j		−0.560
d	−0.048	−0.012
	(2.165)	(0.807)
$\bar{R}^2$	0.730	0.885[3]
D.W.	1.008	(4)

Notes: 1. a = constant term; b = short-run income elasticity; c_0 = short-run price elasticity; c_1, c_2, c_3, c_4 = lagged price elasticities; Σc_j = long-run price elasticity (significant coefficients only); d = weather elasticity;
   2. t-ratios in parentheses;
   3. Unadjusted for degrees of freedom;
   4. The estimates were corrected for serial correlation, but the relevant SAS procedure did not generate the corrected D.W. statistic.

price lag were tried when using the Almon technique. That particular polynomial lag profile was chosen which provided the best statistical fit. Generally this was a linear structure. In those cases where only one dynamic model is reported the other model's overall explanatory power proved to be too low, as indicated by a low F-statistic.

Initially, cross-price elasticities were also estimated, but in all cases they proved to be statistically insignificant and frequently with the wrong negative sign. Since price-driven inter-fuel substitution was found to be negligible, only own-price elasticities are estimated.

The results of the estimation are given in Tables 1–7. The price elasticity estimates obtained with alternative models are summarized in Table 8. Generally speaking, as anticipated, the static formulation of

Table 5. Electricity Consumption

	Industry			Agriculture			Households	
Estimation period	1960–84	1960–84	1960–84	1960–84	1960–84	1960–84	1960–84	1960–84
Lag structure	Static	Koyck	Almon linear	Static	Almon linear	Static	Koyck	Almon linear
Total length (in years) of lag distribution	0	∞	3	0	4	0	∞	3
Parameter[1],[2]								
a	0.737 (3.545)	0.190 (1.240)	0.461 (1.689)	−3.568 (1.516)	0.615 (0.242)	−0.080 (0.035)	2.059 (6.244)	7.167 (2.600)
b	0.864 (62.584)	0.745 (10.330)	0.859 (43.931)	4.031 (16.956)	3.193 (11.926)	1.794 (7.553)	0.525 (2.496)	1.053 (3.561)
c_0	−0.017 (0.465)	0.006 (0.237)	−0.041 (1.425)	−2.117 (5.536)	−0.807 (3.896)	−0.763 (3.002)	−0.342 (9.616)	−0.380 (2.920)
c_1			−0.005 (0.421)		−0.614 (5.444)			−0.387 (4.690)
c_2			0.031 (1.794)		−0.420 (5.851)			−0.394 (4.805)
c_3			0.066 (1.874)		−0.227 (1.594)			−0.401 (3.108)
c_4					−0.033 (0.139)			
Σc_j					−1.841		−1.988	−1.562
$\bar{R}^2$	0.9095	0.858	0.997[3]	0.952	0.949	0.988	0.960	0.964[3]
D.W.	0.565	2.053[4]	(5)	1.709	2.169	0.804	2.353[4]	(5)

Notes: 1. a = constant term; b = short-run income (activity) elasticity; c_0 = short-run price elasticity; c_1, c_2, c_3, c_4 = lagged price elasticities; Σc_j = long-run price elasticity (significant coefficients only);
2. t-ratios in parentheses;
3. Unadjusted for degrees of freedom;
4. The Durbin-Watson statistic is reported, although biased toward 2 in the presence of lagged dependent variable, for lack of any more relevant statistic;
5. The estimates were corrected for serial correlation, but the relevant SAS procedure did not generate the corrected D.W. statistic.

Table 6. Heating Oil Consumption of Households

Estimation period	1970–84	1970–84
Lag structure	Static	Almon linear
Total length (in years) of lag distribution	0	2
Parameter[1],[2]		
a	−5.706	1.282
	(1.606)	(0.914)
b	3.251	1.941
	(4.895)	(3.920)
c_0	−1.101	−0.578
	(2.409)	(2.900)
c_1		−0.355
		(3.229)
c_2		−0.132
		(0.587)
Σc_j		−0.933
d	−0.206	
	(0.404)	
$\bar{R}^2$	0.801[3]	0.558
D.W.	1.733[4]	1.880

Notes: 1. a = constant term; b = short-run income (activity) elasticity; c_0 = short-run price elasticity; c_1, c_2 = lagged price elasticities; Σc_j = long-run price elasticity (significant coefficients only); d = weather elasticity;
2. t-ratios in parentheses;
3. Unadjusted for degrees of freedom;
4. The estimates were corrected for serial correlation.

the demand for energy is unsatisfactory. Although the static model generally gives an excellent fit to the data, the strong evidence of serial correlation indicated by the Durbin-Watson test suggests that this model is not well specified. Most of the computed yearly price elasticities are far too big mainly because they absorb part of the missing long-term price effect. Similarly, as a consequence of misspecification, the income variable tends to ''overexplain'' the effect of activity level on energy demand.

IV. AGGREGATE ENERGY

The elasticity estimates clearly depend on the choice of dynamic specification. The Koyck model produces significantly smaller elasticities than the Almon model. Of the two, the Almon model is to be preferred because of its greater precision. The Almon model has a fourth-order

Table 7.   Gasoline Consumption of Households

Estimation period	1960–84	1960–84	1970–84	1960–84
Lag structure	Static	Koyck	Koyck	Almon linear
Total length (in years) of lag distribution	0	∞	∞	3
Parameter[1],[2]				
a	−9.288	−2.910	−5.706	−9.341
	(16.909)	(10.980)	(5.302)	(11.909)
b	3.006	2.743	3.454	2.943
	(20.818)	(13.708)	(7.160)	(14.777)
c_0	−0.092	0.062	−0.005	−0.067
	(1.178)	(1.420)	(0.078)	(0.761)
c_1				0.002
				(0.046)
c_2				0.071
				(1.696)
c_3			0.139	
			(1.538)	
$\bar{R}^2$	0.995[3]	0.946	0.908	0.993
D.W.	1.233	1.308[4]	1.631[4]	(5)

Notes: 1. a = constant term; b = short-run income elasticity; c_1, c_2, c_3 = lagged price elasticities;
    2. t-ratios in parentheses;
    3. Unadjusted for degrees of freedom;
    4. The Durbin-Watson statistic is reported, although biased toward 2 in the presence of lagged dependent variable, for lack of any more relevant statistic;
    5. The estimates were corrected for serial correlation, but the relevant SAS procedure did not generate the corrected D.W. statistic.

linear lag structure. Only the first three lagged coefficients are statistically significant at the 5 percent level. This is not meant to imply unequivocally that the effects of a price change are exhausted after three years—only that the identifiable, measurable effect dissipates after that period. The effect of a change in price by 1 percent in the current period is to alter energy consumption in the opposite direction by 0.096 percent. This is clearly a rather inelastic response. As expected, the intensity of response becomes stronger, but remains inelastic, over the long-term when the total effect of a change in price by 1 percent alters the level of consumption by 0.318 percent. Observe that the lag structure results because the nature of the polynomial fit through the coefficients.

How do these elasticities compare with international experience? The statistical evidence suggests that both the short-run and long-run elasticity of demand for aggregate energy are smaller in absolute value than those generally obtained for Western economies. (See Table 9.)

Table 8. Short-run and Long-run Price Elasticities

	Short-run	Long-run
Aggregate energy		
National economy		
Static model	−0.092	
Koyck model	−0.049	−0.160
Almon model	−0.096	−0.318
Industry		
Almon	−0.048	−0.248
Agriculture		
Static	n.s.	
Oil		
Industry		
Static model	−0.211	
Koyck model	−0.052	−0.277
Almon Model	−0.083	−0.321
Natural gas		
Industry		
Static model	n.s.	
Almon model	i.e.	
Households		
Static model	n.s.	
Koyck model	−2.237	−4.483
Almon model	−0.767	−5.334
Coal		
Households		
Static model	i.e.	
Almon model	n.s.	n.s.
Electricity		
Industry		
Static model	n.s.	
Koyck model	n.s.	n.s.
Almon model	n.s.	n.s.
Agriculture		
Static model	−2.117	
Almon model	−0.807	−1.841
Households		
Static model	−0.763	
Koyck model	−0.342	−1.988
Almon model	−0.380	−1.562
Heating oil		
Households		
Static model	−1.101	
Almon model	−0.578	−0.933

(continued)

Table 8. (Continued)

	Short-run	Long-run
Gasoline		
Households		
Static model	n.s.	
Koyck model	n.s.	n.s.
Almon model	n.s.	n.s.

Notes: n.s. = statistically not significant at the 5 percent level (one-tail test).

i.e. = inconsistent estimate (it is statistically
significant, but the parameter has the
wrong sign).

Table 9.   Short-run and Long-run Price Elasticities of Demand for Aggregate Energy in the OECD Area and Selected Western Countries

	Short-run	Long-run
Author: Prosser (1985); Data: Final energy demand		
OECD countries (1960–82)[1]	−0.26	−0.41
OECD countries (1960–82)[2]	−0.22	−0.40
OECD countries (1960–82)[3]	−0.26	−0.37
Author: Kouris (1983); Data: Prmary energy		
OECD countries (1961–81)[2]	−0.147	−0.429
OECD countries (1969–81)[2]	−0.162	−0.450
Author: Kouris (1983a); Data: Final energy demand		
Canada (1960–78)[2]	−0.15	−0.41
United States (1960–78)[2]	−0.16	−0.47
Japan (1960–78)[2]	−1.13	−0.47
France (1960–78)[2]	−0.14	−0.39
West-Germany (1960–78)[2]	−0.18	−0.51
Italy (1960–78)[2]	−0.11	−0.34
United Kingdom (1960–78)[2]	−0.18	−0.41
Our estimate; Data: Direct energy demand		
Hungary (1970–1984)[2]	−0.049	−0.160
Hungary (1970–1984)[1]	−0.096	−0.318

Notes: 1. An Almon distributed lag hypothesis was assumed.

2. A Koyck distributed lag scheme was assumed to derive the long-term price reaction.

For the industrial sector the price elasticities were estimated by a three-order linear Almon scheme and they are rather small, -0.048 and -0.248, respectively. These are significantly smaller in absolute value than those generally obtained for the Western economies. For a comparison, see Table 10. For the agricultural sector no statistically significant price elasticities could be obtained either by the static or the dynamic specifications. This suggests an almost total lack of price responsiveness with respect to aggregate demand for energy.

Table 10. Short-run and Long-run Price Elasticities of Industrial Demand for Aggregate Energy in Selected Western Countries

	Short-run	*Long-run*
Author: IEA/OECD (1982); Period: 1960–79; Data: Final Energy Demand		
Canada	-0.15	-0.38
United States	-0.15	-0.36
Japan	-0.19	-0.48
France	-0.18	-0.39
West Germany	-0.19	-0.45
Italy	-0.14	-0.40
United Kingdom	-0.18	-0.40
Our Estimate; Data: Direct Energy Demand		
Hungary	-0.048	-0.248

Note: A Koyck distributed lag scheme was assumed for the Western countries to derive the long-term price reaction.

Oil

The dynamic models produce reasonably similar price elasticities. Clearly both the short-term and the long-term elasticity of industrial demand for oil is inelastic. Even if one accepts the higher estimate for the long-term elasticity, the aggregate effect of a change in price by 1 percent is to alter the quantity demanded in the opposite direction only by 0.321 percent over a period of four years. Again both the short-run and the long-run elasticities are considerably smaller in absolute value than those usually obtained for the industrial market economies.[14]

Natural Gas

For the industrial sector no significant price reaction could be estimated. In the United States short-run industrial demand has a short-run elasticity in the range of −0.07 to −0.21 and a long-run elasticity in the range of −0.45 to −1.5.[15] In sharp contrast to industry, the Hungarian household sector's gas demand seems to be fairly responsive to price changes both in the short run and in the long run. Both dynamic models produce reasonably similar long-term price elasticities, but they seem to be surprisingly high compared with estimates generally obtained for Western countries.[16]

Coal

No significant price reaction could be estimated for either sector. In the West short-run price elasticity of industrial demand for coal is in the range of −0.10 to −0.49 and the long-run price elasticity ranges from −0.49 to −2.07.[17]

Electricity

No significant price elasticities could be obtained for the industrial sector. Most of the Western studies reveal relatively low short-run price reaction in the range of −0.10 to −0.20 and a relatively stronger one, in the range of −0.50 and −1.00 in the long run.[18]

For the agricultural sector relatively high short-run and quite high long-term elasticity are derived by using a fourth-degree linear Almon lag structure. For the household sector the two dynamic models generate similar estimates. These elasticities are close to the upper end of the elasticity values for the Western countries.[19]

Heating Oil

A second-order Almon model, of poor overall explanatory power, yields a high elasticity value both for the short-run and the long-run. These values are quite comparable with estimates obtained for industrial market economies.

Gasoline

No significant short-term or long-term price reaction could be estimated. The consumer demand for gasoline seems to be strongly price-inelastic. The Western literature for gasoline demand is rather consistent in concluding that the price elasticity is near −0.2 in the short-run and is in the range of −0.4 to −0.8 in the longer term.[20]

V. THE STABILITY OF ELASTICITIES OVER TIME

Of major concern in the context of drawing meaningful inferences over the historical period as well as any forecast horizon is whether the observed relationship, and therefore, the price elasticities, are stable.

Stability is defined in the statistical sense of the estimated coefficients of the explanatory variables remaining constant over time. This implies that elasticities may vary depending on the period chosen for estimation. A way of investigating the time variation of a regression coefficient is to fit the regression on a short segment of n successive observations and to move this segment along the series.[21]

To estimate variability of elasticities over time the Almon model of the industrial demand for oil (Table 2) have been computed for ten over-lapping 13 year periods. The estimation results are shown in Figure 1. There is a clear evidence of upward trend in both the short-run and the long-run elasticity of industrial demand for oil. Before the mid 1970s no significant price reaction can be estimated which makes sense since during that period price variations were minimal.

Significant and increasing price elasticities are associated with a steeply rising trend in the real price of oil (see Figure 2). It is quite plausible that the increasing trend in the elasticities, reflecting a progressively higher speed of consumer reaction, is some non-linear function of both the level and the rate of change of oil prices. It is likely that consumer responses to real price increase may not occur until a threshold level of real price has been crossed.[22] As the level of real price becomes progressively higher a larger and larger percentage of the consumers' income will be spent on oil which will leave them less for other inputs with a dampening effect on output. Thus the strength of the incentive to reduce oil consumption is proportional to the level of real prices. It is also plausible that the observed time profile of oil

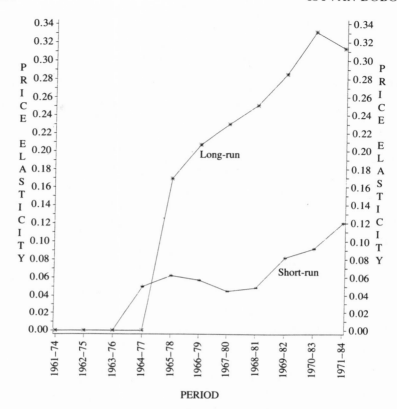

Figure 1. Price Elasticity of Industrial Oil Demand

elasticities is related to the intensity of the price shock in such a way that the disruptive effects of successive price shocks make oil conservation more imperative than under an alternative situation when price changes follow a more gradual pattern and their effects can be more easily absorbed. It is likely that consumer expectations regarding future price increases also tended to strengthen the response intensity.

We can conclude that there is no such thing as a ''true'' elasticity. The fact is that whatever elasticity value exists at one point in time would almost certainly be different, at least by a little, at another point in time.[23]

VI. SOME FACTORS BEHIND THE LOW PRICE RESPONSIVENESS IN THE PRODUCTIVE SECTOR

Our empirical results show that with the partial exception of the households the price elasticity of the demand for energy is very small. The

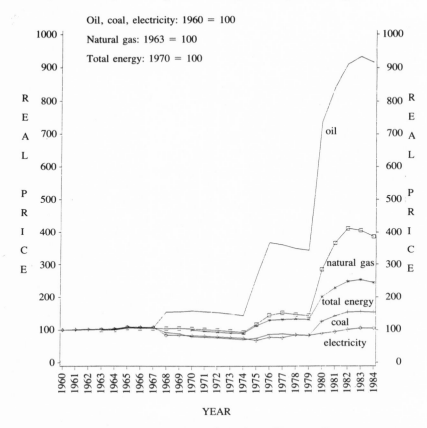

Oil, coal, electricity: 1960 = 100

Natural gas: 1963 = 100

Total energy: 1970 = 100

Figure 2. Real Price of Various Energy Sources

elasticity values tend to be unfavorable in international comparison. As suggested earlier, a low price elasticity implies weak reactions to rising energy costs and a protracted adverse effect on output and inflation. In these circumstances increases in energy prices are translated into an increase in the cost of output—an increase in cost nearly as large as the percentage increase in the price of energy times energy's share in the total cost of output.[24] The higher cost of energy will mean, ceteris paribus, a lower real national income, which in turn means lower real wages, profits, investment and consumption levels.

The particularly low short-run elasticity compared with the long-run elasticity implies that the Hungarian economy's short-run vulnerability with respect to the real price of energy is very high. To judge the direct effect on economic growth of a change in the real price of energy we estimated a variant of the Cobb-Douglas production function which explicitly includes the real price of energy.[25] It is found that in the period 1960–1984 the elasticity of industrial productivity with respect to the real price of energy is -0.142, meaning that, ceteris paribus, a one percent increase in the real price of energy reduces productivity by 0.142 percent.

Looking over a longer term, however, the reaction of the Hungarian economy to rising energy prices is somewhat better although substandard relative to the industrial market economies. Several factors might be responsible for this situation.

1.   Substitution difficulties between energy and other factors of production such as labor and capital. Generally, when energy is considered as a factor of production alongside capital and labor, the answer to whether or not energy availability can become a constraint on economic growth depends on the extent to which it is possible to substitute other factors of production for energy. The econometric evidence for the Western economies demonstrates strong long-run substitution possibilities between labor and energy. Although long-run energy-capital substitutability is a subject of controversy, most studies support the view that short-run energy-capital complementarity is replaced by substitutability over the long term.[26] Unfortunately, no empirical study is available for the Hungarian economy on energy-nonenergy factor substitution. Such work is planned by this author. Until we obtain reliable estimates on interfactor substitution it can only hypothesized that the relatively low Hungarian price elasticity values are probably related to difficulties to substitute nonenergy inputs for energy even over the long run. For example, some substitution between labor and energy is possible but this is difficult because labor in Hungary has become an increasingly scarce factor input.[27] Capital-energy substitution can be limited even when relative factor prices shift in favor of capital, or if energy conservation equipment are not available or are of low quality.[28] The general slowdown in investment activity in the recent period has probably impeded the substitution possibilities between capital and energy. It is likely that a better housekeeping approach rather than inter-factor substitution has been the dominant source of whatever amount of energy conservation has been realized.

2.   The empirical evidence suggests that the Hungarian enterprises do not yet have sufficient incentives to minimize cost. Even world parity scarcity prices may be insufficient to induce large scale conservation in the productive sector if other components of the economic mechanism such as subsidies, taxes, credits, etc. partly or totally neutralize or diminish the effects of prices. The general softness of enter-

prise budget constraints is a powerful factor behind the price-inelastic response. Kornai and Matits claim, on the basis of a large-scale empirical survey, that there are no visible signs of enterprise budget constraints becoming harder since the 1968 reform.[29]

VII.   SUMMARY AND CONCLUSIONS

In this paper we estimated a series of energy demand model is for various energy products and consuming sectors. We argue that static models are inappropriate and generally yield biased estimates because the dynamic nature of energy demand is not accounted for. This is confirmed by our empirical results. We applied two dynamic models, the autoregressive Koyck scheme and the Almon polynomial lag scheme, to estimate short-run and long-run price elasticities of energy demand. The elasticity estimates should be treated with caution since it is not appropriate to interpret price elasticity estimates without giving consideration to the type of estimation model employed, the other variables which bear upon energy consumption, the level of aggregation and the characteristics of the data. Uncertainty about the accuracy of a specific elasticity measurement can be somewhat mitigated if the results of alternative models are compared in order to generate a range of elasticities with which one can feel more confident than with any single elasticity measurement.

Our empirical estimation shows some evidence of responsiveness in the Hungarian economy to changes in the domestic prices of energy sources. However, with the partial exception of the residential sector, the demand response was found to be rather price-inelastic. In international comparison the Hungarian economy's price sensitivity is probably stronger than that of the traditional centrally planned economies, although no comparable data are available to prove this, but as revealed by our comparison, it is significantly weaker than that of the industrial market economies. This is in line with the position of Hungary as a system intermediate between centrally planned and market-oriented.

Significant differences exist between the short-run and long-run response intensity. It is found that the effect of a price change works through the demand over a period of time. This suggests that although in the short run there is very little flexibility to decrease the use of energy in the non-residential sectors, the flexibility becomes somewhat greater, though still inelastic, in the long run as a result of inter-factor substitution, capital stock turnover and other processes.

A stability test was run to estimate the variability of elasticities over time using industrial demand for oil as a case. It is found that there are important trends in the elasticities themselves; both the short-term and the long-term elasticities follow an upward trend over time. It is suggested that this trend may be some function of both the level and the rate of change of oil prices, as well as consumer price expectations.

The relatively low price elasticity of energy demand implies weak consumer responses to higher energy costs and a protracted adverse effect on output, inflation, balance of payments and other macroeconomic variables. Increases in energy prices are translated into an increase in the cost of industrial output and potentially into a reduction of cost competitiveness in the international markets. The low price elasticities also limit the feasibility of dampening energy demand through price-induced effects. This circumstance calls for an active supplementary use of non-price instruments to encourage conservation.

Two major factors are suggested to account for a good part of the relatively price-inelastic response: (1) substitution difficulties between energy and other factors of production such as labor and capital; and (2) the continual lack of strong managerial incentives to minimize cost.

ACKNOWLEDGMENTS

Data on direct energy consumption were obtained from Allami Energetikai es Energiabiztonsagtechnikai Felugyelet. Other data were derived from various issues of Statisztikai Evkonyv, Central Statistical Office Budapest, or through personal communication from the Central Statistical Office. Kalman Dezxeri provided valuable help in collecting the data.

NOTES

1. See Kouris (1983a), p. 73.
2. For a comprehensive discussion of the estimation problems of energy price elasticities, see, inter alia, Bohi (1981), pp. 1–53.
3. See Dobizi (1983), p. 205 and Bohi (1981), p. 15.
4. Kouris (1983a), p. 81.
5. See, inter alia, Johnston (1984), pp. 343–381 and Judge et al (1985), pp. 350–410.
6. This is because: $\sum_{j=0}^{\infty} c_j = c_0(1 + \lambda + \lambda^2 + \lambda^3 + \ldots) = c_0 \left(\frac{1}{1 - \lambda}\right)$

since the expression in parenthesis on the right side is an infinite geometric series whose sum is $1/(1 - \lambda)$ provided $0 < \lambda < 1$.

7.   In fact, only when e_t in Equation 4 follows a first-order autoregressive scheme with parameter $\alpha = \lambda$, will v_t in Equation (8) be non-autocorrelated. Then we have $e_t = \lambda e_{t-1} + u_t$ so that $v_t = u_t$ which is non-autocorrelated by assumption. Since there is no obvious reason why the values of λ and α should coincide we can normally rule this case out and expect v_t to be autocorrelated.

8.   Durbin (1970), pp. 410–421.

9.   Almon (1965), pp. 178–196.

10.   Bohi (1981), p. 21.

11.   Bohi (1981), p. 34.

12.   Dobozi (1983), p. 213.

13.   Pindyck (1979), p. 6. Bohi (1981, p. 149) suggests that price elasticities derived from data at finer levels of aggregation tend to be smaller than those obtained from greater aggregative levels. His observations support the argument that aggregation errors will tend to bias the elasticities upward because of the greater opportunities for variation in consumption that are correlated with, but unrelated to price responses.

14.   For various estimates on the Western countries, see the review by Pindyck (1979), pp. 222–224.

15.   See Bohi (1981), p. 159.

16.   It is not unusual to find long-term price elasticity of residential demand for natural gas in Western countries amounting to 2 or higher. See Bohi (1981), p. 94; Pindyck (1979), p. 160.

17.   Bohi (1981), p. 159.

18.   For a review of western estimates, see Bohi (1981), p. 159.

19.   For a comparison, see Bohi (1981), pp. 57–59; Pindyck (1979) pp. 162–163 and Nemetz and Hankey (1984), pp. 250–251.

20.   For a review of western estimates, see Bohi (1981), p. 130.

21.   Bohi (1981), p. 159.

22.   The psychological literature, mostly from laboratory studies but also from field studies of organizational behavior, supports the hypothesis that energy users often act as problem avoiders and the related hypothesis that responses to price may not occur until a threshold has been crossed. See Stern (1984), p. 38.

23.   For a similar conclusion in the context of the OECD countries, see Kouris (1981), p. 68.

24.   Pindyck (1979), p. 11.

25.   The reduced form equation of the industrial production function is the following:

$$\log (Y/L)_t = 1.320 + 0.869 \log (K/L)_t - 0.142 \log (P_e/P)_t$$
$$ (11.115)(15.942) (3.685)$$
$$R^2 = 0.988 \quad D.W. = 0.862$$

where Y = real gross industrial production;

   L = labor input (man-hours);

   K = real gross capital stock;

   P_e = nominal price of energy;

   P = industrial producer price.

Note the low D.W. value indicating positive serial correlation in the model. The

attempts to remove it were unsuccessful due to lack of convergence. A similar model
was estimated by Suzuki and Takenaka (1981, pp. 237–238) for the Japanese industry,
with a real energy price coefficient −0.1194 for the period 1965–1978, and for the
American industry with a real energy price coefficient −0.1062 for the period 1960–
1978.

26.   See, inter alia, Suzuki and Takenaka (1981), p. 235; Gregory and Griffin
(1976), pp. 845–857. For a review of elasticity of substitution estimates with respect
to energy and capital, see World Bank (1981), pp. 60–194.

27.   A similar conclusion is reached by Hewett (1984, p. 131) in the context of the
Soviet economy ''. . . Soviet conservation options are somewhat more limited than
they were in the West, where the increased relative price of energy induced enterprises
to substitute labor for energy. In the Soviet Union the price of labor will fall relative to
energy, but that will only increase the excess demand for labor.''

28.   The acute shortage of fuel efficient automobiles in Hungary is a good case for
illustration.

29.   Kornai and Matits (1983), p. 28.

REFERENCES

Almon, S., ''The Distributed Lag Between Capital and Expenditures,'' *Econometrica*, vol. 30, 1965, pp. 407–423.

Bohi, D. R., *Analyzing Demand Behavior. A Study of Energy Elasticities*, The Johns Hopkins University Press, Baltimore and London, 1981.

Dobozi, I., ''The 'Invisible' Source of 'Alternative' Energy: Comparing Energy Conservation Performance of the East and the West,'' *Natural Resources Forum*, vol. 7, No. 3, 1983, pp. 201–216.

Durbin, J., ''Testing for Serial Correlation in Least Squares Regression When Some of the Regressors are Lagged Dependent Variables,'' *Econometrica*, vol. 38, 1970, pp. 410–421.

Gregory, P. R. and J. M. Griffin, ''An Intercountry Translog Model of Energy Substitution Responses,'' *American Economic Review*, vol. 66, December 1976, pp. 845–857.

Hewett, Ed A., *Energy Economics and Foreign Policy in the Soviet Union*, The Brookings Institution, Washington, D.C., 1984.

International Energy Agency/OECD, *World Energy Outlook*, Paris, 1982.

Johnston, J., *Econometric Methods*, McGraw-Hill Book Company, New York, 1985.

Kornai, J. and A. Matits, ''A koltsegvetsi korlat puhasagarol vallalati adatok alapjan'' /On the Softness of Budget Constraint on the Basis of Enterprise Data/, *Gazdasaq*, No. 4, 1983, pp. 7–29.

Kouris, G., ''Elasticities—science or fiction?'', *Energy Economic* April 1982, pp. 66–69.

Kouris, G., ''Energy consumption and economic activity in industrialized economies—a not,'' *Energy Economics*, July 1983, pp. 207–212.

Kouris, G., ''Energy Demand Elasticities in Industrialized Countries: A Survey,'' *The Energy Journal*, vol. 4, No. 3, 1983a.

Nemetz, P. N. and M. Hankey, *Economic Incentives for Energy Conservation*, John Wiley and Sons, New York, 1984.

Pindyck, R. S., *The Structure of World Energy Demand,* The MIT Press, Cambridge, Mass., 1979.

Prosser, R. D., "Demand elasticities in OECD: dynamical aspects," *Energy Economics,* January 1985, pp. 9–12.

Stern, P. C. /ed./, *Improving Energy Demand Analysis,* National Academic Press, Washington, D.C., 1984.

Suzuki, K. and H. Takenaka, "The role of investment for energy conservation. Future Japanese economic growth," *Energy Economics,* October 1981, pp. 233–243.

World Bank, Energy Department, *Energy Pricing in Developing Countries,* Energy Department Paper No., 1, Washington, D.C., October 1981.

Author Index

Subject Index